S-57

CHINA'S QUEST FOR GLOBAL DOMINANCE:

REALITY OR MYTH

Edited By
Maj Gen P J S Sandhu (Retd)
Deputy Director and Editor, USI

BASED ON PROCEEDINGS OF
NATIONAL SECURITY SEMINAR 2010
HELD AT USI, NEW DELHI
ON 10-11 NOV 2010

(Established 1870)

United Service Institution of India
New Delhi

Vij Books India Pvt Ltd
New Delhi (India)

viii CHINA'S QUEST FOR GLOBAL DOMINANCE: REALITY OR MYTH

Editor's Note

Looking at the Globe, Napoleon Bonaparte once said of China, "Let her sleep, for when she wakes, she will shake the world". When the French Emperor uttered those words, few ever imagined the China of the 21 [st] Century.

Today, the whole world is watching China with great interest and that includes India. China has been termed – a threat, a challenge, an opportunity a concern, a competitor, the next superpower, a global player and many more things. It depends, who is looking at it and from where? In 2009, United Service Institution (USI) of India decided to commence a five years study programme on China. Towards that end, we held the National Security Seminar 2009 titled 'Rising China – Opportunity or Strategic Challenge' on 25-26 November 2009. Its proceedings have been published in the form of a book.

This seminar on 'China's Quest for Global Dominance : Reality or Myth' is a continuation of the above study . It focused on : China's grand strategy; economic future; military capability and PLAs modernisation; and, an assessment of China's strategic posture. The seminar was held on 10 and 11 Nov 2010 which co-incidentally happened to be between two important state visits to India by the US President Obama in Nov 2010 and the Chinese Premier Wen Jiabao in Dec 2010.

Apart from the Indian speakers, the panelists included soldier scholars, academicians and analysts from the USA, China, Japan, Taiwan, South Korea, Vietnam, Germany and Australia; all of them experts in their own right. It was a rich feast of ideas and views. The Keynote Address was delivered by Shri Brajesh Mishra, former National Security Adviser and the

Valedictory Address by Shri Kanwal Sibal, IFS (Retd), India's former Foreign Secretary.

At the end of the seminar , the subject and dates for the next year 's National Security Seminar were also announced. This will be held on 17 and 18 Nov 2011 and the theme would be 'Peace and Stability in theAsia-Pacific Region : Assessment of the Security Architecture'.

I also acknowledge the contribution made by Lieutenant Colonel B S Varma (Retd), Ms Archana Mishra, Ms Punam Pandey and Ms Archana Jain in compilation of these proceedings. I am thankful to Brig M S Chowdhury, VSM (Retd) for providing the photographs in the book.

- Editor

Welcome Remarks

Lieutenant General PK Singh, PVSM,AVSM (Retd), Director, USI

Good morning Ladies and Gentlemen. It is my privilege to welcome you to the USI National Security Seminar 2010. The theme of the Seminar this year is "China's Quest for Global Dominance: Reality or Myth".

I would like to take this opportunity to extend a very warm welcome to our Panelists who have travelled from across the globe to be here with us.

China's rise and the concomitant impact of this development on the global geo-strategic architecture is a matter of interest to all countries and particularly to scholars of international relations. Recent developments have indicated that as her economic power grows, China appears willing to play a larger role in global affairs. This seems to be accompanied by a growing assertiveness, specially in areas of her perceived core interests.

As India's biggest neighbour and also our largest trading partner , developments in China are a matter of great interest in our country This is natural because India too is a rising power . In order to ensure that both countries rise peacefully , it is vital that there is complete and clear understanding of each others intentions, capabilities and actions.

We at the USI have decided to undertake a five year study of China, with a Seminar being hosted every November Many of you will recall that in November 2009 we hosted an international seminar with the theme being "Rising China: Opportunity or Strategic Challenge".

Ever since last year's seminar, we have been studying various facets of China's rise globally. Some of the issues which keep cropping up and need answers are :-

(a) Has China's rise been peaceful? Or is that a mere slogan to hide her use of force both internally and externally?

(b) What is China's grand strategy? What is her doctrine of "core issues" – are these core issues predictable and durable or can the list keep expanding? Which of China's strategic decisions have fuelled suspicion amongst her neighbours?

(c) What drives China's assertiveness? Will some assertive action lead to confrontation and what shape can this confrontation take?

(d) There is perceptible volatility in the Asia – Pacific Region and we see countries jostling for power Will we see a balance of power or a concert of powers, or hegemony or some other arrangement for which no term has been coined as yet?

(e) As regards economy, the Chinese seem to have got it right. We need to examine if there are any distortions in fundamentals of the Chinese economy. Also, will there be any rebalancing of the Chinese economy and what challenges will it pose?

(f) What will be the impact of China's economic and military might, not just on the simmering territorial disputes but also on the global commons? Will China's anti-satellite test of 2007 and anti-ballistic missile test of 2010 coupled with its cyber capabilities lead to a balance of power in space? Will all this lead to a more competitive security environment and expansion of military capabilities?

(g) Is world domination a long term goal of China and will the present system permit China to assume global leadership?

To answer these and many more complex questions we have with us a very distinguished international panel who over the next two days will not only enlighten us with their frank and learned views but also take questions from the house. I would like to place on record our sincere appreciation for all our chairpersons and speakers from the USA, Japan, South Korea, Australia, Taiwan, Germany, the UK and India who are participating in our seminar.

Out of the 27 confirmed speakers, three are unable to join us for reasons beyond their control. Shri Brajesh Mishra, former National SecurityAdviser (NSA) was suddenly taken ill and has conveyed his regrets – however, he was kind enough to send his KeynoteAddress which will be read out shortly Professor Mike Pillsbury of the Department of Defence, USA, due to a death in his family and Professor Lei Zhao of International Institute of Strategic Studies, Beijing due to some travel documentation problem are unable to attend but have sent their best wishes for the success of the Seminar.

Before I have the Keynote Address read out, I would once again like to thank each one of you for participating in this Seminar

Now I will request Commander Sandeep Dewan, Research Fellow at USI to please read out the Keynote   Address on behalf of Shri Brajesh Mishra, former NSA.

Keynote Address

Shri Brajesh Mishra, IAS (Retd) Former National Security Adviser

This is a timely conference especially because we are meeting between two important state visits to India: President Obamas' visit that just finished and Premier Wen Jiabao's visit in a few weeks' time, in December 2010. That the American President and the Chinese Premier (as well as the leaders of the other three members of the P-5) are visiting India the same year does say a lot about India, about our position in global affairs

But before we congratulate ourselves too much, we also have to examine carefully the condition of global affairs today, for it is traversing through a period of instability . We cannot say for sure for how long this period of instability will last. The reasons for this instability are not far to seek. It lies in the transition of global power that is currently underway   . There are two aspects to this transition. One reason is the relative decline of the United States but the more important reason is the rise of China.

The US economy was roughly half the world's economy in 1945 and has gradually declined from that position to roughly 20 per cent today So, the USA's relative decline has been a long and slow process.Added to that decline is the misadventure in Iraq and now the, decision to withdraw from Afghanistan without fulfilling the tasks of decisively defeating theTaliban and AI-Qaida.

What is clearly much more dramatic has been the rise of China over the last two decades. China' s rise clearly is going to impact not just its neighbours in Asia but the entire world. But to ask whether China is seeking global dominance or not is, I think, somewhat unfair . It is akin to asking 'when did you stop beating your wife?' carrying a presumption of guilt in the question itself.

Great powers will always seek to dominate their neighbourhoods and as much of the rest of the world as they can. There is nothing peculiarly Chinese about it. But the obverse is equally true. China's rise is likely to be as problematic, tense and destabilising as that of any other power. Normally, this would not have to be said in so many words. But over the last decade, there have been a number of scholars who have asserted that China's rise will be unlike that of other powers, that it will be peaceful and so on. Much of this is frankly bunkum as China's behaviour in the region over the last year provides sufficient proof.

My sense is that China's rise will be much like that of other great powers in the past, no more destabilising but certainly no less so. But clearly there is a great deal of concern about China's rise and the driving ambition to be Number One in the world. I think there are five dangers that accompany China's rise. Some of these are general issues that result from any power transition. But some are specific to China. Similarly, some are dangers we cannot do very much about. But some are dangers that can be managed better, especially if China is careful.

The first danger lies in the process of transition itself. When new great powers rise and display the ambition to be Number One, it does create some chaos in the international order. The new power will want a seat at the high table, a say in how the world is run. Usually such new powers are also impatient ones. They want to assert their role soon, sometimes even before they have the capacity and wealth to back up that role. Think of Germany or Italy in the late 19 th and early 20 th century. Such impatience can create tensions and crisis.

There are also questions about what such a transition might do to existing international institutions. When new great powers rise, they will want global institutions and regimes to reflect the new balance of power . Will China accept the current institutions and regimes? What modifications will be needed? How will we decide? Will the liberal trading regime that the USA set-up continue? Will the nuclear non-proliferation regime completely collapse? These are important questions that could lead to turbulence in the global order.

The second danger is, what kind of global system we end up with. Will it be a bipolar system? Or will it be a multipolar system, one with many powers? Each has its dangers as well as opportunities for us.   A bipolar system has its own dangers. Think of the bipolar Cold War. The chances of a war between the two superpowers were remote because of nuclear weapons, but that did not prevent them from competing with great vigour in various parts of the world, especially the third world. Such vigorous competition visited devastation upon many parts of the world. If the current power transition should lead to a bipolar world, then we could expect somewhat similar outcomes.

We are already seeing competition in various parts of the world, in Central Asia, in Africa. So far this has been over resources. But this could quickly become political conflicts as both sides realise that political control is needed even for resource extraction.   We can assume then that these conflicts will begin to resemble the Cold War competition soon.

For us in India, this bipolar competition will be a lot more troublesome than the Cold War. During the Cold War, neither superpower was our neighbour. They both had interests in the region, but these were sporadic and episodic. So we were able to balance the two sides. W e may not be able to achieve such fine balance if the two superpowers are the USA and China. China is our neighbour, and a country with which we have an active territorial and other problems; I will speak more about this in a few minutes. This means that we might become more active participants than we were during the last Cold War, even if that is not our choice.

Of course, things could become a lot more problematic if the power transition leads to a multipolar order. Imagine five or six powers competing for the same resources instead of two, and you will have some sense of the troubles we will face. When one of those great powers is our neighbour, life could become somewhat complicated. The two dangers that I have so far talked about are not particular to China, but something that are more general. But the next three dangers are specific to China.

The third danger that I see is in China' hyper-realist view of the world.

This is what one prominent China expert Alastair Iain Johnston called the 'parabellum paradigm'. China tends to see the world as an arena of power competition. There is power competition, but sometimes, a hyper-realist view of the world can create the very competition and fear that you are trying to avoid. China has made such miscalculations already

Over the last one year, China's miscalculations with its neighbours as well as other great powers demonstrate that China is prone to making even more wrong decisions than other powers are. There has been a tendency to see China as ten feet tall because of the secrecy and opacity in Chinese decision-making, to see China's behaviour as being very strategic and far-sighted, especially in comparison with democracies such as India and the USA which always seem to shoot themselves on the foot and which always seem incapable of making policies that are long-term and strategic.

But China is also subjected to pulls and pressures, between different bureaucracies, between different arms of the government. There are violent protests in some parts of China, even if these are less visible to the outside world. It is these pulls and pressures that lead to contradictions and incoherence in national policies of all countries. The opacity of China's decision making masks these internal pulls and pressures but we can see at least some of the manifestations in Chinese behaviour. The short point is this: China, like all other great powers, is bound to make both strategic and tactical errors, both of which generate dangers for the rest of the world, as well as, opportunities.

I will give just two examples of China's strategic errors. One is its transfer of nuclear technology to Pakistan. It is quite possible that if China had not encouraged Pakistan in the manner it did to acquire nuclear weapons, then India would not have built nuclear weapons. But China was so convinced that India was building nuclear weapons that it helped Pakistan build nuclear weapons forcing India to start its nuclear weapons programme. So, Chinese hyper-realism led to a result that China could not have wanted and could have avoided a nuclear armed India. They are now repeating that mistake with North Korea.

Similarly, China's relations with Japan show signs of strategic short sightedness, if not foolishness. Japan has invested heavily in China. Its historically pacifist attitudes since the end of the SecondWorld War as well as its guilt about its imperialist role in the region would in all likelihood have prevented Japan from playing an active role in balancing China. But China' own behaviour appears to be convincing more and more Japanese that China is a country that they must worry about. The situation is still recoupable and so far, no lasting damage has been done. It might still be possible for China, by better behaviour, to reduce Japanese concerns and prevent Japan from considering the need to balance against China. However   , if China does not take heed, it is very likely that over the next decade, Japan will take active measures to balance China, potentially including building of nuclear weapons.

This brings me to the next point - the role of Chinese nationalism. All powers that play important roles in global affairs have to have a sense of 'great powerness', the idea that they are important and that they have justified and legitimate larger role in world affairs than others. This is especially true of the PLA which seems to be playing a prominent role in the process. Such ideas are almost always dangerous for others. Whether it was the European idea of bringing civilization to the rest of the world, or the American idea of promoting democracy or the Soviet idea of spreading socialism, the consequences to those subject to these drives is never pleasant. China appears to be basing its great powerness on its own nationalism. Now   , nationalism is no stranger to India or other powers, but in China nationalism seems to be playing the role of the default ideology. With Maoism and socialism on the back-burner, the Chinese leadership appears to be using nationalism deliberately as an ideological glue.

This is very dangerous. We have seen nationalist demonstrations against the USA as well as against Japan. Stoking such populist ideology can force crises between China and other powers. It is clear that even the Chinese government is aware of the problem. For example, China has been trying to tamp down anti-Japanese protests. But this kind of balancing act might not always succeed. Encouraging hyper-nationalism and then trying to manage it from getting out of control is a dangerous game.

The fifth and final element of danger that I want to talk about is the secrecy and opacity that surrounds Chinese national security policies. This is not a new issue.   A number of experts as well as governments have expressed concerns about this issue. Now all countries do keep some aspects of their national security plans and projects secret.That is nothing new But in China's case, the rapid rise in its military expenditure is leading to concerns among its neighbours and others.A part of this rise in military expenditure is the result of China's increasing wealth.As it becomes wealthier, its military expenditure also rises proportionately But China's understating of its defence budget and the opacity of its military plans can only lead to concerns. China can easily ameliorate such concerns by being somewhat more transparent.

So, in sum, there are many dangers that accompany China's rise. While some of these dangers are unavoidable, there are others that China can control.

At the same time, we should also not ignore that there are some elements of stability. The most important element of stability is that most great powers today have nuclear weapons. Nuclear weapons introduce an element of caution in great power politics, such as, that we can no longer think in terms of a war between these powers.

So, we can be reasonably certain that irrespective of however many serious crises we may have, we can rule out the possibility of a direct war between the great powers. This is a major and radical change in how international politics works. However this does not mean that the world will be completely stable.As during the last ColdWar, competition could lead to suffering in parts of the world where these powers compete, such aAfrica.

Another element of stability is the fact that we have well established global institutions that help to ameliorate conflicts even if they cannot fully resolve them. These institutions, as well as our experience in working with these institutions, will be a force for stability in the future.

A final source of stability is the interdependent nature of our economies. The global economy is interlocked in a manner that it never was before. Hence, any disruption will afect everybody equally. This should prove to be a deterrent also to leaders to prevent their disagreements from getting to be too loud. But in relations with India there are clear signs that China will not allow India to play a greater role in Asia and global affairs. It is for this reason that all weather relationship between China and Pakistan has evolved into a virtual military alliance. This is clear from the changed attitude in regard to Jammu and Kashmir , the proposal to have a reliable road and railway system leading to the Gwadar port, the projects being executed in Pakistan Occupied Kashmir (POK), the new nuclear deal and the supply of defence equipment, including fighter aircraft. All this is meant to keep India embroiled with Pakistan, so that India is unable to play a significant role outside South Asia.

The irony is that the American policy in Af-Pak region, which includes largesse of billions of dollars and military equipment including F-16 aircraft, has the same adverse impact on our national security as China's assistance to Pakistan. Even after President Obama's great speeches during his recent visit to India, the content of the strategic partnership benefits the United States more than India. All the business deals done, the lifting of the sanctions on the Entities List, giving us some defence equipment we require urgently, like the other business deals, benefits the USA in a commercial way.

Participants

Lieutenant General PK Singh, PVSM, AVSM (Retd) was commissioned as a 2/Lt in the Indian Army in 1967. During a military career spanning 41 years he has seen active service in the Western, Northern and North Eastern Theatres and participated in the 1971 Indo-Pak War. A graduate of the Defence Services Staff, Wellington and the National Defence College, New Delhi, he has held several important command and staff appointments. After commanding a Corps he was appointed Director General Operational Logistics and Strategic Moves at the Army Headquarters. He was appointed C-in-C (Army Commander) in August 2006 and retired from active service in September 2008. His academic qualifications include M.Sc and M.Phil from the University of Madras and a Post Graduate Diploma in Business Management. He took over as Director of United Service Institution of India (USI), New Delhi on 1st January 2009.

Dr C Raja Mohan is an Indian academic, journalist and foreign policy analyst. He is currently Strategic Affairs Editor of the Indian Express, New Delhi. He was a member of India's National Security Advisory Board during 1998-2000 and 2004-06. His recent books include *Crossing the Rubicon: The Shaping of India's Foreign Policy* (New York: Palgrave, 2004) and *Impossible Allies: Nuclear India, United S tates and the Global Or der* (New Delhi: India Research press, 2006).

Dr Ashley Tellis is a Senior Associate at the Carnegie Endowment for International Peace, specialising in international security defence, and Asian strategic issues. He is an expert in non-proliferation, US foreign policy, US national security, South Asia, India, Pakistan, and China. While on assignment to the US Department of State as senior adviser to the Under Secretary of State for Political Affairs, Dr. Tellis was intimately involved in negotiating the civil nuclear agreement with India. He was commissioned into the Foreign Service and served as Senior Adviser to the Ambassador at the US Embassy in New Delhi. He also served on the National Security Council staff as special assistant to the President and senior director for Strategic Planning and Southwest Asia. Prior to his government service, Dr. Tellis was senior policy analyst at the RAND Corporation and professor of Policy Analysis at the RAND Graduate School.

Professor Richard Rigby is the Executive Director of the ANU China Institute. He joinedAustralia's Department of ForeignAffairs in 1975, where he worked until the end of 2001: postings includedTokyo, Beijing (twice), Shanghai (Consul-General 1994-1998), London, and Israel (Ambassador, 2000-2001). He then joined the Ofice of NationalAssessments as Assistant Director-General, responsible for North and South Asia, where he worked until taking up his current position with the ANU China Institute in April 2008. While engaged in government work, Richard continued to pursue his academic interests with a series of translations, book reviews and articles on China-related topics. His personal interests in Chinese studies are primarily literary and historical, but his profession has ensured a thorough immersion in all aspects of contemporary China and other majorAsian cultures.

Professor Jaeho Hwang received his PhD in International Relations from the London School of Economics (LSE), and is a research fellow at the Centre for Security and Strategy within the Korea Institute for Defence Analyses (KIDA). He is now aVisiting Research Fellow atYonei University and Kyungnam University, and was earlier a Visiting Research Fellow at University of Leeds, China Foreign Affairs and University of Melbourne. He is a member of editorial board for Korean Journal for DefencAnalysis. His major research interests are Chinese security and foreign policy , as well as political and security issues in NortheastAsia.

Professor Swaran Singhteaches Diplomacy & Disarmament at the Centre for International Politics, Organisation and Disarmament (CIPOD), School of International Studies, Jawaharlal Nehru University, New Delhi. He is President of Association of Asia Scholars (an Asia-Wide Network with Secretariat in Delhi), General Secretary of Indian Association of Asian & Pacific Studies (Varanasi) and Member of Bangkok-basedAsian Scholarship Foundation's Regional Review Committee for SouthAsia. He is a Visiting

Professor at University of Peace (Costa Rica) and Lady Sri Ram College (New Delhi).

Shri Brajesh Chandra Mishra IAS (Retd) was the first National Security Adviser (November 1998 to 23 May 2004) and Principal Secretary to the former Prime Minster of India, Atal Bihari Vajpayee. He was India' s permanent representative in Geneva and ambassador to Indonesia. He was also India's permanent representative to the United Nations (After 1979 to April 1981). He continued with the UN on deputation till June 1987. He was the key motivator of foreign policy and principal spokesman on all major issues. After demitting office, he had initially expressed reservations against the Indo-US civilian nuclear deal; however, later he publicly endorsed the deal.

Dr Rajiv Kumar is the Director General of the Federation of Indian Chamber of Commerce and Industry (FICCI). He is the former Director and Chief Executive of the Indian Council for Research on International Economic Relations (ICRIER). He is a member of the G-20 Advisory Group, Ministry of Finance, Government of India, Member of India Brand Equity Foundation (IBEF) Board of Trustees, and also on the Board of Directors for the United States-India Educational Foundation (USIEF). He worked at the Asian Development Bank, Manila for nearly ten years (1995-2005) and was the Chief Economist at the Confederation of Indian Industries, New Delhi during 2004-06.

Mr Prem Shankar Jha is widely acclaimed as an eminent journalist in India who has made an intensive study of the Indian Economy He worked in the USA as Special Assistant to Mr Paul G Hoffman, Managing Director UN Special Fund. Mr Jha was a Member of the Indian National Commission for UNESCO in 1975-1977 and a Delegate to the 63rd Session of the Indian Science Congress Association, Waltaire, 1976.

Shri Mohan Guruswamy has wide ranging professional experience of 30 years. It includes teaching at the John F. Kennedy, School of Government, Harvard University; North-Eastern University Business School, Boston and the Administrative Staff College of India, Hyderabad. He was adviser to the Finance Minister, Government of India (1998-99) holding the rank of

Secretary on economic and financial issues. Presently, he is the Chairman of Policy Alternatives, New Delhi, an independent think tank focussed on policy analyses.

Lieutenant General Vinay Shankar, PVSM, AVSM, VSM (Retd) is one of the Council members of United Service Institution of India. He was commissioned in the Regiment of Artillery in June 1960 and took part in 1962, 1965, 1971 operations. He is an accomplished army aviator and served in counter-insurgency affected area of Nagaland.

Vice Admiral Hideaki Kaneda (Retd)is Director for the Okazaki Institute and a Trustee of Research Institute of Peace and Security. He was a Senior Fellow at Asia Centre and John F Kennedy, School of Government, Harvard University, and a Guest Professor of Faculty of Policy Management at Keio University. He served in the Japan Marine Self Defence Force from 1968 to 1999.

Brigadier Gurmeet Kanwal (Retd) is the Director of Centre for Land Warfare Studies (CLAWS), New Delhi. He has authored several books including *Nuclear Defence: Shaping the Arsenal; Indian Army: Vision 2020; Pakistan's Proxy War; Heroes of Kargil; Kargil '99: Blood, Guts and Firepower and Artillery: Honour and Glor y.*

Vice Admiral (Retd) Arun Kumar Singh retired as Flag Of ficer Commander-in-Chief (FOC-in-C) of the Eastern Naval Command in 2007, after over four decades in uniform. On promotion to two star ranks in 1996, he was appointed to the first dual hatted post of 'Flag Officer Submarines' and 'Assistant Chief of Naval S taff (Submarines)'. As Flag Of ficer Commanding Eastern Fleet (FOCEF), he conducted exercises in 2000-2001, with the Navies of China, Japan, South Korea,Vietnam, Singapore, Thailand, and Indonesia. In 2003, he was promoted to three star rank and was Director General, Indian Coast Guard (DGICG) during the 26 December 2004 Tsunami. He was later promoted as Commander -in-Chief and served as CINCAN (Port Blair) of the tri-service Andaman & Nicobar Command. His last appointment, prior to retirement was FOC-in-C of the Eastern Naval Command, Vishakapatnam. Post retirement, he writes and speaks on various issues related to national security, defence forces, Indian Navy and Coastal

Security.

Dr Ming-Hua Tang is currently the Director of Defense Research Division for Integrated Assessment Office at Ministry of National Defence. DrTang received his PhD in International relations at University of Nottingham in UK in 2007. In addition, he was the staff of Department of Strategic Planning (2000-03) and Deputy Director of Policy and Planning Division for Office of Deputy Chief of General Staff for Intelligence (2007-09) at Ministry of National Defence.

Air Commodore Jasjit Singh,AVSM, VrC, VM (Retd) joined the Indian Air Force in 1954 and retired in 1988. He served as the Director of Operations of the Indian Air Force, before being deputed to the Institute for Defence Studies and Analyses, New Delhi, where he was Director from 1987 to 2001. Founder Director of the Centre for Strategic and International Studies, he currently heads Centre for Air Power Studies (CAPS), New Delhi.

Professor Chengkun Ma is the Director of Institute of PLA Study, NDU, ROC (Taiwan). He has received his PhD in China's war behaviour study at National Taiwan University, and has specialised in PLA affairs. His representative articles are "China' s Security S trategy and Military Development" and "China's Three Warfare against Taiwan". He published a monthly paragraph on China's military affairs, "PLA News Analysis, PNA". His analysis of China issues from Chinese perspectives is welcomed by foreigners.

Commander Sandeep Dewan is presently a Research Fellow at the CS3-USI. He was commissioned into the Indian Navy on 01 Jan 1987. He has had instructional tenures at the National Defence Academy, Defence Services Staff College, Wellington, India and Defence Services Command and S taff College, Sri Lanka. A graduate of the Defence Services S taff College, Wellington he has a Master of Philosophy and a post graduate degree in Defence and S trategic Studies from the Madras University. He has published articles and papers on Maritime Domain Awareness, PLA Navy and Asia Pacific security issues. He has presented papers on 'India and the Asia Pacific Sea Lanes' at the 3rd Xiangshan Forum at Beijing and on 'China's Quest for Seas Beyond its Shores' at the National Security

Seminar at USI, in Oct and Nov 2010 respectively.

Professor Changhee Par k is Associate Professor of Military S trategy Department at Korean National Defence University in Seoul. He is also Chief of Military Affairs Research Division, RINSA (Research Institute of National Security Affairs), KNDU. He received his MAin National Security Affairs from the Naval Post-graduate School in Monterey , CA and Ph.D. from Korea University in Seoul. He was a member of Executive Course at the Asia-Pacific Centre for Security S tudies at Honolulu, Hawaii. His research area encompasses China's military affairs, war strategy and national security affairs.

Professor Srikanth Kondapalli, JNU is an Associate Professor in Chinese Studies at Jawaharlal Nehru University (JNU). He is also an Honorary Fellow at Institute of Chinese Studies, Delhi and Research Associate at the Centre for Chinese Studies, University of Stellenbosch, South Africa. He served at the Institute for Defence S tudies and Analyses (IDSA), New Delhi for 12 years. He learnt Chinese language at Beijing language and Culture University and was a post-Doctoral V isiting Fellow at People' s University, Beijing from 1996-98. He was also a Visiting Professor at National Chengchi University, Taipei in 2004 and a V isiting Fellow at China Contemporary International Relations, Beijing in May 2007.

Shri Shyam Saran belongs to the 1970 batch of the Indian Foreign Service. He was posted to Embassy of India, Beijing, from 1974 to 1977. He served at the Headquarters of the Ministry of External   Affairs, New Delhi, as Under Secretary and Deputy Secretary from 1977 to 1979. He served as First Secretary in the Permanent Mission of India, Geneva, as   Alternate Representative to the Conference on Disarmament. Subsequently   , till September 1986, he was Counsellor and later Charge d'   Affaires of the Embassy of India, Beijing. Thereafter, he served as Deputy Chief of Mission in the Embassy of India,Tokyo, till August 1989. Mr. Saran served again at Headquarters, New Delhi, as Joint Secretary heading the Economic Division, the Multi-Economic Relations Division, and the East Asia Division of the Ministry of External Affairs. Thereafter, he served as Joint Secretary in the Prime Minister 's Office, New Delhi, till December 1992, looking after

External Affairs, Defence and Atomic Energy. In 1992, Mr . Saran was appointed as High Commissioner of India to Mauritius where he worked till April 1997. After Mauritius, he served asAmbassador of India to Myanmar from April 1997 to July 2001. He has served as Ambassador of India to Indonesia from August 2001 to October 2002 and Nepal from November 2002 to July 2004. Mr . Saran served as Foreign Secretary from August 2004 to September 2006. In October 2006, he was appointed as Special Envoy of Prime Minister on Nuclear issues. He was also appointed as Special Envoy of the Prime Minister for Climate Change Issues in April, 2008.

Professor Klaus Langestudied at the Universities of Munich and Prishtina (1965-70) and completed his Doctorate in Philosophy . He researched on behalf of DFG and VW Foundation (1971-76) and was a Lecturer in Political Science at the University of Munich (1972-78) and Senior Lecturer as political science and philosophy at the University of Durban-Westville, SouthAfrica. He was Head, Department of German and foreign politics at Hanns Seidel Foundation Munich (1983-92) and Head, Department of International Security Politics, HSS- Foundation Munich (1992). He wasVice President and Director of Research, Institute for African and International S tudies, Vagen Munich (1985-95). Thereafter, he has held numerous assignments as a Visiting Professor, Director and Academic Consultant at various international institutes in SouthAfrica (1992-93), Moscow (1997), University of Peshawar, Pakistan and University of Belgrade. He is a member of GKNDC (German Intelligence Forum); RUSI, London and MCC (Military Commentators Circle), London.

Shri Jayadev Ranade (Retd) is a former Additional Secretary, Cabinet Secretariat; Government of India. He is a seasoned China analyst with over 25 years experience in the field. His foreign assignments have included Beijing, Hong Kong. His last foreignposting, prior to retirement in late 2008, was as Minister in the Indian Embassy inWashington. Mr Ranade is presently a Distinguished Fellow with the Centre forAir Power Studies. He contributes to many leading publications, mostly on strategic and security issues relating to China.

Dr Yi-hua Kan is currently an Associate Research Fellow at the Institute of International Relations, and an adjunct   Associate Professor at the Department of Diplomacy at National Chengchi University. He is also the Executive Director for the EU Centre inTaiwan, established by the European Commission in January 2009. Dr Kan received his PhD in International Studies from the University of Cambridge, the United Kingdom. He has broad academic interests covering security studies (both conventional and new), Asia's regional security, European integration, international conflicts and resolutions, globalisation and trans-Atlantic relations.

Shri Kanwal Sibal, IFS (Retd) is India's former Foreign Secretary . He served as India's Ambassador in Russia, France, Egypt andTurkey. He has also served as India's Deputy Chief of Mission inWashington, apart from a range of other critical assignments. As Foreign Secretary, he successfully guided the then NDA government through some of the most turbulent foreign policy issues, including the second Iraq war. As ambassador to Russia, he was instrumental in reshaping the Indo-Russian ties at a critical juncture when Russia's relationship with India needed fresh momentum. He is considered one of India's finest diplomat. He is now a regular columnist for several publications apart from pursuing his interests in a global education system.

First Session
China's Grand Strategy

Opening Remarks	Lt Gen PK Singh, PVSM, AVSM (Retd), Director, USI
Chairman's Introductory Remarks	Dr C Raja Mohan, Strategic Affairs Editor, Indian Express
First Paper	Dr Ashley Tellis, Carnegie Endowment, the USA
Second Paper	Prof Richard Rigby, ANU, Australia
Third Paper	Prof Jaeho Hwang, South Korea
Fourth Paper	Prof Swaran Singh, JNU, New Delhi
Discussion	
Chairman's Concluding Remarks	Dr C Raja Mohan, Strategic Affairs Editor, Indian Express

Session 1: Opening Remarks

Lieutenant General PK Singh, PVSM, AVSM (Retd)

We begin the first session of the Seminar, the sub-theme of which is China's Grand Strategy. What is China's grand strategy, how has China's perceived threats and opportunities shaped this grand strategy? In furtherance of its grand strategy, how will China develop, manage and utilise its comprehensive national power to secure its national aims? Have China's strategic decisions fuelled suspicion of her neighbours? How will countries of the region hedge their bets? Will they be forced to choose sides? These are some of the questions I think most of us, are looking for in answers.

To examine these and many other interesting facets we have an eminent panel chaired by Dr C Raja Mohan, Strategic Affairs Editor of the Indian Express. The speakers are Dr Ashley Tellis from the USA, Professor Richard Rigby from Australia, Professor Jaeho Hwang from South Korea and Professor Swaran Singh from JNU, New Delhi. Without taking any more time I will hand over the session to Dr Raja Mohan.

Session1:Chairman's Introductory Remarks

Dr C Raja Mohan

Ladies and gentlemen, welcome to this Session on China's Grand Strategy. Before I handover to the speakers let me begin by congratulating the USI for taking this five year project of studying China. While the interest and the impact of China has grown on India significantly in the last few years; China has begun to loom lage in most of our debates whether it is economy social sector or the national security. Our capacity to actually study China dispassionately, developing the capacity to objectively study China, the impact of China and the meaning of what China is going to do to the world is very important. I hope this project will actually contribute to creation of those capacities in India (at all levels), to be able to understand and study China. After all, the 'Rise of China' is the single-most important geopolitical fact of our time. Whether we like it or not, China is going to rise and it is going to impact almost every single aspect of our lives in the coming years.   As somebody said China has just had a couple of bad centuries and that it is back, to be the Number One power eventually in the international system.

China is also different from other powers, in the sense that China is going to be 'powerful before it is rich'. It does not matter what the per capita income of the Chinese is, (today it is around $4000), but the aggregate size of China's economy has already crossed close to $5 trillion—$2 trillion of trade plus—$2 trillion of current account surplus. The aggregate terms of the Chinese capacities today are dramatic, and all this has been achieved in less than two generations. Therefore, China is going to be powerful before it is rich. So long as China does not stumble internally; China, being a strong purposeful State, can extract even a significant portion of its aggregate revenues towards military and national security capabilities, which is going to have a decisive, definitive impact on every single aspect of international security.

When we talk about grand strategy then it is about, how China will use its expanding resources that are at its command today that can be applied to grand strategic purposes? If the grand strategy is about finding a credible relationship between means and ends, China is inevitably going to redefine its goals and objectives from the international system and how it looks at the world around it. This is going to have an ef fect on how the Asia, the international system and the international economic order are going to be organised. In all of these aspects, China today is in a position to influence and shape, if not lead at some point of time, the order in the international system.

To discuss these issues of Chinas grand strategy, we have an excellent panel. It is regrettable we dont have a Chinese on this panel todayI suppose even if the Chinese are not there, the spirit of the Chinese and the dragon is there in the room because there is no way of ignoring China' s presence today. Even though the Chinese are not here, what is important today is that the debate on China is universal, everyone is debating China. It is important for us to look at very consequential, very interesting debates within China about its grand strategyThere is an extraordinary level of sophistication today how China is debating internally; and unlike in the past, quite a bit of it is available today, how China is debating its own future. We need to pay attention to see both the external debate about China and the internal debate in China and China's place in the world.

Let us begin with DrAshley Tellis.

Session 1: First Paper

Dr Ashley Tellis

Let me start by thanking Lieutenant General PK Singh and USI for hosting the seminar and also for inviting me to participate in it. The subject of course could not be more important, it is the central question that affects the international system. The timing could not have been more appropriate as well because the thrust of my presentation is going to be that, what we are witnessing at the moment is the evolution of Chinese Grand Strategy in (new) directions that it has not gone to before — at least since the time Deng began the great opening that resulted in the rise of China as a new great power. In other words, the present moment represents a profound crossroads, where we might be witnessing the beginning of the end of the kindlier, gentler China, which Deng was insistent that China be, until such time it had reached a certain threshold of power accumulation. Obviously this is going to be a big process. In the lives of nations these transformations are never singular events; they are processes. Yet, what we have begun to see, since the end of the financial crisis, is a China that is much more confident; and of course as Prime Minister Manmohan Singh pointed out, a China that is somewhat more assertive than it has been in the past. I want to illustrate this by basically trying to reflect on what China' goals are and how the means to achieve those goals have been changing even as we speak before our eyes.

The goals that China has set for itself, ever since it began the process of current reforms, still remain the same. Those are three goals fundamentally. The first and most important is to protect domestic order and social well-being. It is very important for China, particularly because of the nature of the political system that the country has, and also because the Communist Party considers preservation of its own rule as obviously being the central objective to which all activities that China undertakes are directed to. So, clearly maintenance of domestic order and social well-being remains central. It remained so before Deng, it still continues. Second is to protect China against a variety of external threats either to its sovereignty or to its territory. That objective too has remained constant. The third is to attain, and to maintain geopolitical influence, as a major if not the singularly most important player, in theAsia-Pacific region and eventually the globe.These three objectives have been at the core of Chinas' modernisation experiment for at least 40 years.

However, the means that have been used to secure these goals are in the midst of very dramatic transformation. Deng's famous aphorism "hide brightness, cherish obscurity" or translated in various ways as, 'lying low, don't make waves,' etc., etc., is now either dying, or is at least on the way to being eclipsed by an alternative mode of doing businessAs often happens in Chinese diplomatic style, the great aphorism will still obtain even though its meaning will be entirely emptied. So, China will still insist that it is pursuing a policy of lying low when it continues to do in fact exactly the opposite.

About 20 years ago, Michel Swaine and I wrote a book called 'Interpreting China's Grand S trategy' where we ar gued that as long as China continues to undergo this strategy of comprehensive modernisation, it would maintain what we called a 'calculative strategy'. That calculative strategy had three components. When we see China today, the calculative strategy that served China well is now slowly being transformed into a strategy where China is becoming increasingly assertive. By being assertive, I don't necessarily mean violent, what I do mean is that China is no longer content to have the international system or the geopolitical environment leave its impress on China; instead, China now wants to shape the geopolitical environment that affects its national strategy and its choices. So, from the calculative strategy where China was content to focus internally and leave all else alone, China has now moved to a point where in order to ensure the success of its internal strategies, it wants to shape the environment within which it operates, and that of course, has very profound consequences.

So, let me just flag three elements that I see as being characteristic of this transition.When we wrote the book we argued that the notion of a calculative strategy, in China's political practice, has three dimensions.The first dimension was characterised by a focus on very pragmatic economic policies centred on expanding economic growth at home, (through market institutions) but embedding these market institutions essentially in a liberal economic order. In other words, doing what you need to reform your economy internally in order to get all the benefits of market society but enjoying those benefits while being embedded in the liberal economic order that was maintained essentially by the US power throughout the post-war period. In order to do that China needed amicable political relations with all the major states in the international system, including those on its periphery I see this component as having undergone very subtle changes in the last few years, in two ways. China still continues to maintain what is a quasi-market system within its own country Despite the reforms that Deng brought about since 1978, the internal Chinese economic system is not a genuinely free market. It is rather a free market that is embedded in an overarching system of State control. There is no fundamental change in this overarching system of State control as yet. But China has become increasingly uncomfortable with simply accepting the fact that it will have to survive and prosper in the liberal international order that is maintained by others. So, in the last two years it has moved in different ways to try and shape this liberal international order to protect what are essentially State power and its own core interests. There are two examples which serve as good pieces of evidence to illustrate this fact.

First, what China has done in recent months with respect to the managing of rare earths exports clearly indicates that, it is not simply going to acquiesce to the rules of the game which require that trade be conducted purely on the basis of commercial considerations. Rather its international relations will be driven as much by commercial considerations while continuing to protect, what are seen as absolutely uncompromisable State interests. The continued Chinese effort to protect what is clearly an undervalued currency again remains evident of the fact that the liberal international order is something that China can continue to partake off, so long as that liberal international order is not seen to fundamentally undermine what are core economic and political interests of the State. So, you see a transition that although there is still an emphasis on pragmatism, there is a great emphasis on market society there are subtle changes taking place in how these are reflected in practical policies that affect both ordinary Chinese and of course the rest of the international system.

The second dimension that characterised the calculative strategy was generally a restraint in the use of force towards the periphery and efforts to modernise the Chinese military but at a very modest pace. In both these dimensions you can see very interesting differences. First, an increased willingness on the part of China to use force for diplomatic purposes in a way that was simply ahistorical for the Chinese.   Today China feels no difficulty about thinking of using its emerging naval capabilities to either show the flag in the Persian Gulf or to show the flag in the larger arenas of East Asia. It has no difficulty today of engaging in a public debate that talks about the acquisition of new power projection capabilities built around carrier battle groups. The Chinese national security debate increasingly talks about the need to be able to sanitise vast areas of 'geographic periphery'. It is increasingly reflected in what is a very energetic Chinese military modernisation that has been underway for at least one decade, if not longer After 1995, it has resulted in the acquisition of very impressive anti-access and denial capabilities that make for the first time the real prospect that the USA will be unable to service the extended deterrence obligations that it has to key countries which exist on China's periphery. So, again you see a transformation from what was a 'de-emphasis on military capabilities', (a certain passivity with respect to managing military matters) to now an 'activist effort' to provide and develop the capabilities that China sees as being essential for its long term interests.

The third dimension of the old calculative strategy was 'expanded involvement' in regional and global regimes, primarily in order to secure asymmetric gains. So, China was a very active member of the WTO. China was very actively involved in the whole range of international political and economic institutions with the objective of essentially exploiting, what existed outside, to enhance China's own interests in accumulating comprehensive national power. This objective too, has very subtly transformed in the last two years and we are beginning to see only the first stage of what will be a process that lasts for a long time to come. What is that transformation? The transformation is that today China's participation in international regimes is no longer aimed simply at securing asymmetric gains. But it is fundamentally focused on remaking the rules to advance China's own interests. China is, no longer, willing to be simply a passive entity which looks for ways to protect its interests in a world that is dominated and made by others. But rather, China seeks to be an active entity that enters this world in order to change it, to reflect its own preferences and its own interests.

If I were to summarise quickly , what the changes in China' s grand strategy have been, I would have to look at the earliest incarnation of this strategy when Deng began the reform programme in 1978. In comparison to that strategy , today you can see changes in three ways: a shift from strategic passivity to strategic activism; a shift from a willingness to emphasise the need to keep disputes dormant to now an assertion of claims (even if China is not ready to enforce those claims through military action), clearly there is a belief that these claims must be asserted in order to draw some mental lines that warn people about limits that should not be crossed; and third, an emphasis that previously focused primarily on the protection of territory and sovereignty to now the active defence of a larger set of interests. The beauty, of course, of defining your objectives in terms of interests is that they never have to be specified because interests will always expand relative to the power you have in the international system. So, the emphasis now is on defending interests, as opposed to tangibles like territory coupled with the desire to engage now in rule making as opposed to simply rule following. This constitutes just the beginning of what will be another transformation that will probably last for at least the next two to three decades.

Why has this change come about and what is the future of this change? I would speculate that this change is now manifesting itself for three basic reasons, all of which end up being mutually interactive and reinforcing. The first is that China has succeeded in accumulating some minimum quantum of Comprehensive National Power (CNP). Everything we knew about the China in 1978, and the China that we know in 2008, are entirely two different Chinas. When you reach this point, where you have maintained or accumulated this quantum of CNP, you begin to think of your interests in very different ways. The financial crisis, or the global economic crisis, has only reinforced this point because it has convinced the Chinese that the relative balance of power is now finally shifting in its favour I have to mark this proposition with a very large asterisk because 'the USA is down but not out' and there have been numerous instances in the past when nations have assumed that 'the USA is out' when it has just been down. But at least for the moment let me just say that China's accumulation of sufficient power coupled with the perception that the USA is simply not what it used to be has enabled China to now reach a point where it can begin to now shape the international system in far more activist ways than was possible before. The second element which has moved the process along is the rising tide of 'nationalism' in China. You don't have to be a Sinologist to look at internal Chinese discussions and find an enormous upsurge of national confidence, sometimes bordering on belligerence that again is part of the internal transformations that are taking place in Chinese society.

The third is possibly a factor that is transient but may not be so, and that is the peculiar demands made by elite political competition, particularly in the context of transitions to a new Chinese regime associated with the 2012 Congress. When we did the book on China' s grand strategy it was fascinating to watch how the most acute periods of Chinese geopolitical activism were always when there were regime transitions within China. The rise of a new regime and the decaying of an old regime always turned out to be the moments when you had great and very frenetic change. So, we may be at a moment where we are seeing some of these factors come together.

I want to end my presentation by making just one point. While we see a rise in Chinese assertiveness in the way that I described, we must not presume that this period of assertiveness is permanent or will last forever because it is intrinsically tied to China's geopolitical and economic successes and the geopolitical and economic successes of others. So to the degree that China does better than others, this trend will be sustained. But to the degree that others can make a comeback or to the degree that others too rise, there will be objective constraints in how this assertiveness is manifested. So, we are at the beginning of a process where in terms of the old Chinese curse, 'we live in very interesting times'.

Session 1: Second Paper

Dr Richard Rigby

Abstract

*Does China have a grand strategy? Scholars tend to talk and write
about such things more than practitioners, and foreign scholars began
to ask this question before their Chinese counterp arts. The latter,
though are now increasingly active, and although Chinese policy makers
tend to deny the existence of a grand strategy, this does not mean
that at least the elements of such a strategy are not present. Indeed
one could argue that at least since the formulation 'wealthy country
powerful army' was created in the 19th Centurythis has provided the
broad framework and goal pursued by all Chinese governments, the
present-albeit more successfully than any previous - included. It also
appears clear that there is broad agreement on how to achieve this
goal, at least up to a point. But the issue is also debated, with some
vigour, and China's success in coming through the global financial
crisis has brought more relevant issues to the fore, more quickly   ,
than China's policy makers — or their foreign counterparts -probably
expected. This is further complicated by the growing multiplicity of
players and the increasing complexity of foreign/security policy making.
It is important to note, though, that for China's leaders, despite the
growing international challenges resulting from China's rise, domestic
issues continue to be paramount, although these increasingly impinge
on external policy, and vice versa. In framing policies to deal with
China's rise, other countries need to be aware of both aspects.*

There are almost as many definitions of grand strategy as there are grand
strategies, but the following covers well what I have in mind in the remarks
I am going to make today: Grand strategy deals with the causal links between
a nation's strategic objectives and the means to achieve themAccording to
Barry Posen, grand strategy is a theory about how a state can best 'cause'

security in light of national resources and international constraints. The making of a state's grand strategy, therefore, is contingent upon the judgment of its leaders about how the world works, which in general parallels the theories of international relations. To formulate a sound grand strategy leaders must be able to accomplish two tasks: first, (a) they must select a strategy that is appropriate for the power of their country and the shape of the international system; and second, they must be able to cope with the inevitable and unexpected challenges to that strategy emerging along the way[1].

It seems true to *say* that external observers began to speculate and write about China's grand strategy well before the Chinese themselves. A significant marker was the seminal work of Swaine and Tellis at the very beginning of this century.[2] Since that time, there have been plenty more articles, speeches and books, prominent amongst which we should mention the work of Avery Goldstein.[3] This was picked up quite soon in India not least by Subhash kapila.[4] The Chinese themselves, at least in openly available work, seem to have joined the game relatively late in the day . This is not necessarily surprising. I can recall a time *back* in the 1980s when Australian diplomats, of whom I was one, were very keen to discover the secrets of Japan's grand strategy. We had the devil of a job finding one, and the Japanese were no help to the point where we eventually concluded that there wasn't one, and I believe this to have been a correct conclusion.

Where China is concerned, however, in more recent times a growing number of Chinese scholars have themselves been writing about China' s grand strategy, to the point now where a Chinese writer can refer to the 'flourishing development' of such studies in China.[5] One might mention by way of example one of the first to enter the fray, Men Honghua, a scholar at the Institute of International Strategy of the CCP Central Party School.[6] Men argues that China should base its rise towards global power on a firm base of regional primacy, and in this regard it should use its attraction as a force for regional economic integration as the means for taking regional leadership the economic benefits for regional states ensuring that they would be unlikely to oppose China.[7]

Other prominent PRC scholars writing about grand strategy include

Shi Yinhong from Renmin University and Ye Sicheng from Peking University (his '*Inside china's Grand S trategy: The Perspective fr om the People's Republic* has been published in English). Shi's works include a number of significant articles, books and lectures.[8] Shi argues that the core of grand strategy lies in comprehensively using all available national resources, or of a multinational alliance, in order to pursue the nations' fundamental political objectives.[9] Ye Sicheng, in his "Grand Strategy of China: Main Problems and Strategic Choices of China as a World Power" [2003] takes a historical approach, and looks at the PRC government's choices and grand strategic plans from 1949 on, while studying the relationship between the international aspects of China's rise and its domestic development.[10]

One lapidary but quite useful statement which seeks to encapsulate Chinese thinking about these matters comes from Cicir 's Lin Limin who *says* simply, "In the 21st Century China's -grand strategy is to safeguard its peaceful rise."[11] We should also bear in mind those formulations other than 'grand strategy' can also cover similar ground or at the least be closely related, e.g. core problem, central task, or even the increasingly used 'core interests'. For instance, we have two recent articles from Cicir 's *Contemporary International Relations* referring to the core problem of Chinese diplomacy as 'finding balance between integrating China into the modern World order and maintaining its autonomy';[12] One may note that this is at least as old as the self-strengthening movement of the 19th century; and describing China's central diplomatic task in the current period as boiling down to 'building a peaceful external environment for the domestic modernisation drive'.[13]

Much of this thinking differs little from that of non-Chinese writers. For instance, we have Avery Goldstein writing in 2001 that as a consequence of international constraints and China's experience in the early post-cold war years, a de facto grand strategy has emerged - one that seeks to maintain the conditions conducive to China's continued growth and to reduce the likelihood others would unite to oppose China.[14]

Goldstein's reference to a 'de facto' grand strategy is relevant to this discussion. Admittedly he was writing before the emegence of the Chinese discussion that we are referring to, but it seems to me that much of this discussion is a reflection of what has happened, or is currently happening, rather than some sort of *a priori* plan for action. As such, it fits in well with Deng Xiaoping's analogy of "Feeling the stones while crossing the river"

In a recent discussion, Vice-Foreign Minister Cui Tiankai told me that, while International Relations scholars in China as elsewhere needed to make a living, they therefore, put forward various ideas and themes. China's real grand strategy was not to have a grand strategy. Of course this was in part a dialectical joke of the sort Chinese interlocutors like to engage in, but it was more than that, and does reflect what I take to be the truth, that China's foreign policy does not reflect some pre-existing grand plan. Equally , importantly, however, Cui did go on to acknowledge that in the light of China's rapid growth and transformation, there was indeed a real need to think about grand strategy, or whatever one wished to call it. What would China do with its growing power? This was a question not only foreigners, but also the Chinese themselves, were asking. But he also added that the biggest issues were all at home not abroad. The main emphasis of government policy was still domestic, and any foreign policy grand strategy would have to serve this goal.[15] I believe this is absolutely correct, but would add that with China's increasing involvement in the global economy and in regional and global affairs generally, there is no longer any neat dividing line between the domestic and the international - they are interconnected more than ever before.

This interconnection brings us back to what has arguably been China's grand strategy. Regardless of the type of government - King, Republican or Communist - since the mid-19th Century , *'Wealthy Country, Powerful Army'* in its essence has scarcely changed. See, for example, the following declaration by Hu Angang and Men Honghua "W e like to hold that the objectives of China's grand strategy should be to make the people rich and the country strong, that is, constantly raising the percentage of its CNP in the world's total so as to become a big world power in the middle of this Century. The basic objectives of China' s grand strategy in the future 20 years should be including six goals: "high growth, great national power , affluent people, national security , improvement of international competitiveness and sustainable development".[16]

Now the reference to 20 years raises another question. In both the West and in China, this assumption about a window of some 20 years or so has been widely made. On the part of the   West, particularly the United States, the thought has been that we would have about this much time to bring a growing China into the global system. By which is meant that the post-War system with which the USA and the West are generally comfortable, in ways that certainly do seek to accommodate China, but not to alter the system fundamentally nor challenge the leading position of the USA. For China's part, the idea was that China needed the West, especially the USA, for a variety of reasons. It did not make sense, during the period while China was still a rising rather than an actual great power to challenge the USA or Western interests more generally in a frontal fashion. This did not mean, of course, that China should not seek to defend its own national interests, or to pick up any low-lying fruit that the USA might offer (and there was enough of that during the GW Bush administrations; but China would not seek to provoke fights or clashes, and would continue to present a peaceful face to the world because this was what served China's interests best. Such an approach was well characterised by another of Deng Xiaoping' formulations, that of *'keeping a low pr ofile, while taking appr opriate action as the occasion pr esented itself '*.

In the aftermath of the Global Financial Crisis (GFC), however , it is apparent that the situation is not as it *was*. It is clear now that China has come through, and come through better, than most. If it were not so, we in Australia - and not just in Australia - would be in trouble. But now there are new considerations to be taken into account. As we have noted, since the 19th Century successive Chinese governments have sought 'wealth and power'. Throughout the period of opening and reform this has been exemplified most by the USA; hence the calculation that China needed at least 20 years of peace and cooperation with the USA while it catches up (and we in the West have calculated we have this amount of time in which to bring China into the sort of global community that suits us). Now Iraq (and Afghanistan) have shown the limitations of the US power , and the GFC, (with its origin in the sub-prime loans crisis) has done the same for the US wealth. So there are those in China, looking at its continued growth and the success with which it came through both the GFC and the Asian financial crisis of 1997, which are beginning to question the basis of China's relatively compliant behaviour vis-a-vis the West, and particularly the USA. This is not yet, and may not become, mainstream thinking in China. But it's definitely a factor, and helps to explain China' s more forthright, if not aggressive, positions on a number of issues over the past year or so. The window we thought we had may not be open for as long as originally predicted.

Another complicating issue in seeking to define China's grand strategy, and even more in trying to understand how it is practised, is that Chinese foreign policy making is becoming more complicated by which I mean there are more players, and the various lines of decision making and authority are increasingly unpredictable, not that it was ever all that clear. But it's less so now, as Chinese society becomes less monolithic, different interest groups emerge and the power of the Central government to impose a clear and consistent policy line is not what it was. I'm talking here about such groups as powerful Central ministries (e.g. the Ministry of Commerce vs the MOF and the PRC Yuan re-evaluation), for instance the Nuclear industry (e.g. a new reactor for Pakistan), the PLA (a series of statements over the past year that are clearly out of sync at least with the MFA), local governments, Chinese netizens and so on![17] This also has its impact on China's International Relations community. The well-known scholar Yan Xuetong has indeed lamented the negative impact, an increasingly noisy and populist commentariate, which tends to view international politics as a hostile bipolar **zero-sum** struggle, is having on the more balanced security-studies establishment[18] (there are, of course, Western equivalents, particularly in the USA).

It is clear, then, that in order to understand China' s grand strategy - whether under this name, another , or no name at all we need more than ever to be aware of the debates being thrashed out in China, both at the official and unofficial level. Of course, grand strategies in the end matter more as a reality demonstrated by the practice of States rather than what particular scholars, Chinese or foreign, might write or advocate; but the ideas advanced in the course of these debates and discussions do influence, and become part of the reality. At the current juncture, the debate over the continuing validity or otherwise of Deng's "Bide our time..." formula is of particular importance, and I strongly recommend a close reading of a recent article on the subject by Wang Saibang, of CICIR.

Wang describes a situation in which at least some people feel the time has come to move on from this, and as I have noted, we have already seen the evidence of this in practice. Wang, however, does not agree. He argues that changes in the international situation mean that China is now in a very complicated and contradictory foreign policy environment. 'China Threat' and 'China Responsibility' theories are running simultaneously . China's confidence has been greatly increased by its success in coming through the GFC. There is a popular expectation that China will be given greater international respect, tolerance levels of the more negative aspects of the USA's China policy have gone down, and as China' s own concerns are diminished there is a growing feeling of impatience and desire for quick results.

However, Wang argues the real reason for China's success in improving its international position is all the hard work done over the previous 30 years. China needs to pay more attention to neighbouring countries. Being an influential regional Great power is the prerequisite for seeking to become a global power. If China keeps on with its nose to the grindstone for another 30 years, the position of global great power will come about naturally and many apparently intractable issues will be solved automaticallyThe world can't do without China and China can't do without the world. China needs to promote its own development through contributing to global development. China should make full use of external resources and markets, and should avoid mercantilist policies.

Wang goes on to say that while upholding the nation' s major core interests, it will be important to pay more attention to how this is done, to avoid being more strategic, avoid blindly wandering into clashes, do more quiet diplomacy etc. the position should be firm but the attitude more sincere and friendly. The outside world (especially the USA and other Western powers), has to be givensome time to adjust more negative policies towards China.

I believe this *sets* out the situation as clearly as I have seendone in the relevant Chinese literature. But I would also observe that actions taken in recent months, not least in the South China and Yellow Seas (and you in India will doubtless be able to think of some examples closer to home), seem hardly to accord with the sensible approach being advocated byWang.

The thought that I would wish to conclude with is this. In general terms, China does indeed have a grand strategy but, it is a work in progress and we should notexpect always to observe consistency in its applicationWe should follow China's own foreign policy and security debates closelybut always with theunderstanding that for China's leadership the issues with the greatest resonance will continue to be domestic for years to comeYet given China's growing engagement with the rest of the world, thedomestic and international are ever more closely interconnected.

Endnotes

1   Dr Y uan-Kang W ang, 'China's Gr and Str ategy and U .S. Primacy: I s China Balancing American Power?, The Brookings Institution, Centre for Northeast Asian Policy Studies, July 2006.

2   Michael S waine, Ashley T ellis, *Interpreting China's Grand Str ategy: Past, Present and Future,* RAND, Santa Monica, 2000.

3   Av ery Goldstein, 'The Diplomatic F ace of China' s Gr and Strategy: A Rising Power's Emerging Choice', *The China Quarterly* [month?] 2001; *Rising to the Challe nge: China's Grand Strategy and International'Security,* Studies on Asian Security, sponsored by East- West Center, Stanford Univ ersity Press, 2005.

4   Dr Subhash Kapila, 'China's Grand Strategy and Military Modernisation', South Asia Analysis Group, Paper no.642, originally presented in March 2003.

5 Chen Y ue, Pr ofessor and Ex ecutive Dean of the School of I nternational Relations, Renmin University of China, 'Political Science in China: the Domestic Scene and a World Vision', Contemporary International Relations, Marchi April 2010.

6   Chinese n_$, ftJJt_ OOA_III_Hflm_, . 2005 _t*A_t/jWX*i

7 Shang Baohui (2010) 'Chinese F oreign Policy in T ransition: Trends and *Implications',Journal of Current Chinese Aff airs,* [Germany], 39, 2, pp 49-50. Coming December].

8   For example, "International Politics: Theoretical Exploration, Historical Survey and Strategic Thinking" (2002), "From Napoleon to the Vietnam War: Eleven Lectures on Modern Strategy" (2003), "History of Contemporary International Relations: From the End of the 16th Century to the 20th Century" (2006), "National Politics and National Strategy" (2006) and "Basic Character of World Politics in the 21st Century and China's Proper Strategies" (2006) - Chen Yue, *op.cit.,* p.71.

9 Chen Y ue, *ibid,* p.71.

10 Chen Y ue, *ibid,* p.71.

11 World Geopolitics and China's Choices', *Contemporary International Relations,* MayjJune 2010, p.16

12 Li Shiy ong, 'The Cor e Pr oblem of Chinese Diplomacy ', *Contemporary International Relations,* JanjFeb 2010, p. 109.

13 Cui Liru, 'Thirty Years of China's Diplomacy: T_ajectory and Challenges Ahead,' *Contemporary International Relations,* Nov-Dec 2009, p.1.

14 Hav ery Goldstein, 'The Diplomatic F ace of China's Grand Strategy: A Rising Power's Emerging Choice', *The China Quarterly* [month?] 2001, p.838.

15 Conversation at the ANU, Canberra, August 10 2010.

16 Hu Angang, Men Honghua, The Rising of Modern China: Comprehensive National Power and Grand Strategy') originally published in Chinese in *Strategy and Management* No.3, 2002} presented to 'Rising China and the East Asian Economy, KIEP confe rence Seoul March 19-20 2004.

17 Linda Jacobsen and Dean Knox, 'New F oreign Policy Actors in China'. SIPRI Policy Paper 26,September 2010; John Pomfret, 'In China, officials in tug of war to shape foreign policy ', *Washington Post,* September 24, 2010.

18 Wi lliam A Cal lahan, 'China's gr and str ategy in a post -western world', *openDemocracy,* www.opendemocracy.net. accessed 23/08/2010.

Session 1 : Third Paper

Professor Jaeho Hwang

Thank you Chairman. It is my great honour to participate in the prestigious USI National Security Seminar. Today, focus of my presentation will be on China's grand strategy. As indicated in the contents, I will address seven questions and make one suggestion. The first six or seven questions are related to grand strategy and the final question relates to diplomatic strategy Then, I would like to provide some suggestions for China's grand strategy.

First question, is there a grand strategy? It is not easy to find whether the Chinese government has an of ficial document as a grand strategy . Whether Chinese leaders or related government sectors i.e. Ministry of Foreign Affairs, has such documents or had meetings regarding the matter as of late is not clear. Chinese government officially never mentions about the grand strategy. However, putting together the Chinese behaviour and foreign policy, remarks by policy authorities, statements and papers of security experts help understanding China's grand strategy. So, like most of the other countries the Chinese seem to have been affected by the historical experience, political events, economy and geostrategic environment.

Second question, what is the objective of the grand strategy? The long term goal of China's grand strategy is being Number One. However , it is very hard to interpret that desire for being number One points to world domination. That desire can be interpreted as a quest for pride and glory . Based on these questions, China's national security interests can be said to be composed of 'defending sovereignty securing territorial unity, stabilising political system and sustaining economic development'.

The third question refers to 'China' s 'perspective of its own grand strategy'. According to the Chinese book, ' *Vision for China's National Security Strategy*' written in 2009, China sees the rise as an improvement of the State's capacity which is a process of becoming a super power; and then influence global order very greatly. According to this book the USA went through three different periods to become a Super Power: 1865 to 1922 being the follow-up period, 1923 to 1945 reciprocal balance period, since 1945 it was the superiority period. However , China's rise is yet a hardware side development. China is expected to go through follow-up period until 2020, i.e only the economy sector China will still have limited global influence for several decades to come. China is facing two major challenges. First is how to overcome tangible and intangible checks and balances from international alliances against the late comer? Second is whether China has the ability to sustain its growth? For these reasons, China is 'working on substances' instead of seeking shortcuts.

The next question is about the timetable of the grand strategyRecently, there are 'grand strategy' related reports in China; however, China rather prefers these as international strategyWhile global strategy means managing global affairs, international strategy report means actively participating in the global society. So, the first five years of Xi Jinping' term as the Head of the China PRC from 2012, will be classified as international strategy. The second half of his term will be 'transition periodòf becoming a global strategy Then the Sixth generation leaders, from the year 2022 to 2032, may be the testing period of global diplomacyAfter 2032 will be the 'adopting period' of global strategy on full scale but such prospects can occur faster than expected or delayed when there is a change of speed in China' s rise and ruling international order depending on the rate of change in the US-China national power.

So, what factors make a grand strategy possible? First, of course is competitiveness based on economic power and second is internal stability It is not easy to ensure this in the long term. One party system will continue in the short term. First ten years of the 5th generation leaders will be on the one party system. There could be a change in the composition of the Standing Committee as the 6th generation come in. This means ethnic minorities and women could come out to be represented in the standing committee. Inner party democracy serves as a de facto multiparty system—numerous factions within the CCP serve as a multiparty system. Third, there is the consensus among leaders and people that if anyone breaks the stability he becomes public enemy. Then the fourth is diplomatic power China's influence in the international community comes from diplomatic power and not from military economic and cultural power . Hardware diplomacy during the Bush Administration let the enemies to adopt wait and watch policy and friendly states to turn their backs on China. But China' s diplomacy succeeded to some extent by tolerating differences and pursuing co-existence.

So, what are the challenges for China' s grand strategy? First, inconsistent economic growth; second, domestic societal problems, such as the gap between the poor and the rich and also the regional gaps, environmental issues, etc; third, self-purification i.e, inability of the ruling mechanisms within the CCP; fourth, pluralist challenges to the authority of leadership; fifth, leaders without authority may succumb to populism i.e. nationalism or patriotism etc; sixth, large scale disorder caused by democratization of the public and urges for diversification; and seventh is mishandling Taiwan issue; and finally external factors mobilising the coming together of anti-China camp for encircling China.

So, what is China's diplomatic strategy? By looking at China's past diplomatic strategies, the basics were, 'hiding ones capabilities and biding one's time.' Later on, Hu Jintao added active participation, if necessary . Now, internally and externally , observers of China' security are fiercely debating whether Chinese diplomacy has completely shifted to achieve 'active participation'. Recently we have witnessed China' s very aggressive behaviour over its disputes with its neighbours on certain islands in the South China Sea; for instance, Senkaku Island incident with Japan. So, I would like to define Chinese strategy as fighting without completely destroying situation i.e. keeping doors open for negotiations. So, it is like Microsoft Word upgrading its software every three years. Therefore, may be this year, China's foreign policy behaviour seems to be another version of 'active participation'. I am not sure whether you agree with me or not—China' s diplomatic strategy would specify, how it will achieve the ultimate goal of their grand strategy.

Now, I come back to Chinas diplomatic strategy again. Diplomacy of

Deng Xiaoping's and Jiang Zemins' s time was basically 'hiding one' s capability and biding time', Hu Jintao diplomacy is a combination of 'active participation' and 'hiding one's capabilities and biding time' at the same time. My prediction is that Xi Jinping's i.e 5th generation leaders' foreign policy will be more and more 'active participation'. At this time, how can we predict the 6th generation's diplomacy? Using the concept of 'hiding one's capabilities and biding time'again; if we translate directly we can say 'hiding of sharp knife in the sheath', then there would be three options for the 6th generation leaders to choose from. First wielding a knife 'whichever way' they want to or force others to do so. Second, 'the knife could be rusty' since it stayed in the sheath for too long. Third, the knife could be used to 'give proof' periodically to everyone and protect other people from threats. So, China's grand strategy will gradually 'crystalise', and diplomatic strategy will be utilized to facilitate this.

Personal Suggestions on China's Grand Strategy

First, China calls itself a developing country However, if we do not accept this notion, it would be only in the sense of 'psychologically' developing country not from economic aspect. China still has a strong historical victim mentality which needs to be overcome mentallySecond, China must become a soft power; although its hard power aspect must be strengthened, it must strengthen its soft power such as culture, social system, institutions and norms etc. Third, China's *toi bhoi* means fighting, but without completely breaking the overall situation, will be seen frequently depending on the situation and also as well as its needsIn a relationship, conflict is inevitable and happens all the time. However the important thing is how to get through this conflict and solve problems. Number four, China threatens itself. The threats have evolved through military and economic threats. If China really wants to be a super power it should not give other rivals a chance to threaten them. From the idea of *toi bhoi*, 'fighting means not physical but oral fight'. China's diplomacy should emphasize, 'not breaking, not fighting, i. e., to keep the negotiations going without resorting to fighting. From showing hard negotiations over certain disputes to showing military muscle will demonstrate China threat theory . Finally China needs to ask itself several questions.

What kind of country is China and what kind of leadership does it want to be. So, I would like to conclude with one question and that is, "W e don't know who you are, do you know who you are?"

Session 1 : Fourth Paper

Professor Swaran Singh

Contemporary debates on China' s grand strategy remain premised on assumptions that China's rise has global and systemic ramifications and that Beijing remains all set to lead the post-W estern global order .[1] These assumptions were triggered specifically by the fact that, following the collapse of Soviet Union in 1990, ColdWar-driven discourses in international relations had hoisted People's Republic of China as the new second pole thus unleashing a hype of 'China threat' theories across western countries. The propensity of the sole surviving super power, the US, to use force and coercion in conduct of its foreign policy was to further reinforce this line of thinking. Rising China, as a result, was bound to see this US dominance in world affairs as exposing (even threatening) to their core national interests.

The exponential growth in China' s own foreign trade, its enormous foreign direct investment (FDI) inflows, and consequent insatiable demand for markets and resources (especially energy) from early 1990s was to further drive China's power elite into thinking about China's place in the 21st world. As a consequence, debates on rising-China and its implications, both inside and outside China, have since become the staple diet of sinologists, foreign policy and strategic communities across the world. It is interesting to note that this trend since then has become both the cause as well as consequence of gradual unfolding of Beijing's official articulations on China's grand strategy for the 21st century world. And now, as China approaches its historic transition of power to its 'fifth' generation leadership – which is expected to take place in 2012 – the shrill of these increasingly dichotomous debate is expected to become only sharper, even intimidating.

As if in anticipation, world has already begun witnessing Beijing becoming far more assertive on its territorial claims against neighbouring

countries, namely, Russia, Japan and India; and its naval forays in the Gulf
of Aden during 2010 have more than demonstrated China's political resolve
and military reach that provides a solid backbone to its future vision.[3] For
instance, in spite of being the largest emitter of carbon gases, China has
turned the tables, and emerged as the torch-bearer for mitigation of climate
change, leading the most efective group of countries, namely the BRICS –
or Brazil, Russia, India China, SouthAfrica – while other major players like
the US, European Union,   Australia, Japan, all stand mar ginalized. Such
examples can be exhaustive and even confusing for a reader.

But the pertinent question to ask at this stage is the following: Do all
these visible episodes and indicators reflect unfolding of any coherent and
subtle new design that alludes to China's grand strategy in-the-making? It is
in the context of this rapidly changing backdrop that this paper seeks to
examine these emerging contours of China's grand strategy and to underline
its implications for regional and international security paradigm.

Dichotomous Debates

At the very outset, one most fundamental question in these debates has
been as to whether this recent unfolding of China's grand strategy outline
represents a revisionist or a status quo character. On this broad conclusion
depends China's acceptability amongst world's major powers as also the
efficacy of China's grand strategy outline obtaining it any footprint on the
emerging new world order of the 21 st century. Conversely, this level of
global acceptance of rising China also has a direct co-relation with the rise
of China itself as also with these varied interpretations about China's growing
capabilities, its intentions and its larger future vision for humankind. This is
from where the connotations of this evolving outline of China's grand strategy
will be elicited and formalized in due course of time. Opinions on this as yet
remain inconclusive, at best tentative.

Alastair Johnston, amongst others, stands out as the pioneering scholar
in the English speaking world who has worked on China's grand strategies
from early 1990s. In his celebrated first work, *Cultural Realism: Strategic
Culture and Grand S trategy in Chinese Histor y,*' published by the

Princeton University press in 1995, author believes that "to the extent that grand strategy addresses timeless and universal problem in the management of threats to political hegemony and territorial control, one should expect little cross-cultural variations." But his conclusions seem to have evolved since then. In his more recent work '*Social States: China in International Institutions, 1980-2000,*' published by the Princeton University press in 2008, author confesses that there has been "considerable, if subtle, evidence of the socialization of Chinese diplomats, strategists, and analysts in certain counter-realpolitik norms and practices" and that this "casts doubts on a materialist explanation for realpolitik norms and practices rooted in the effects of international anarchy." Granting credence to constructivists'propagation of centrality of ideas, identities, institutions, he now prescribes serious engagement of China as it does seem to open opportunities to evolve China' realpolitik grand strategy.

Similarly, Michael Swaine and Ashley Tellis in their ' *Interpreting China's Grand Strategy: Past, Present and Future*', published by RAND Corporation in 2000 had been another celebrated team on the subject and both of them have also continued to expand their China analysis. However given their mandate in their original Air Force project in 2000, they had confined their study to post-reform geo-strategic analysis on China' s rise and restricted it further to examining its implications for the US security . They had then concluded that China, at best, had only a "calculative" strategy with limited and restricted repercussions for   American security. Their aforesaid report, therefore, did not expect China' s grand strategy to be much different than that of other great powers, including the US. Therefore, they also broadly fall in the group of scholars that believed that China is all set to become a status quo power and fall in line to conventional wisdom of western historians like Robert Gilpin. Gilpin had written his famous book titled ' *Hegemonic War and International Change* ' in 1983. This book talks about war being inevitable as a rising power will get into contestation with the power in control of international orderOf course Swaine andTellis stop short of saying that it will lead to a war but they do seem to allude to these possibilities. Rising power, they believe, would repeatedly precipitate situations in economic, political, social, cultural context with the rising power and this will be kind of a continuous irritation rather than one big bang crisis. It presented an innovative approach to underline how US sought to deal with the China's military might.

But later works of Swaine and Tellis seem to have evolved beyond this restricted paradigm. Ashley Tellis and Michael Wills produced a study titled '*Strategic Asia 2005-2006: Military Modernization in an Era of Uncertainty*', published by National Bureau of Asian Research in 2005. Here, they allude instead to China "gradually accumulating sophisticated military capabilities" which are now seen as "potentially posing a credible threat to modern militaries operating in the region" that is across Asia where US had been increasingly engaged since 9/11 crisis. Likewise, Michael Swaine et al, in their later volume titled, *Assessing the Threat: The Chinese Military and Taiwan's Security*', published by Carnegie Endowment for International Peace (Washington DC) in 2007, prescribe serious engagement of Beijing given that "If deftly managed, Beijing relations with Asia could not only further constrain Taiwan's strategic support in the region, but also perhaps limit US options in an escalating crisis or conflict with China over the island." Broadly speaking, each successive work seems to take China far more seriously. This is not just a result of China's continuous rise but also reflects growing complex nature of China analysis by western scholarship.

One positive spin-off effect of this increasingly nuanced approach in China analysis around the world has been the increasing variety of opinions that can now be seen inside China's own strategic community. And lately, successive debates on China's grand strategy inside China have become especially intense and interesting. These Chinese debates now make a seminal contribution on China's grand strategy as they remain sharply different from what has been seen in China analysis in the English speaking world as also in highlighting a variety of thinking inside China's own strategic discourses.

Chinese Interpretations

To begin with, most Chinese scholars remain convinced about China's uniqueness and destiny. Even from narrower strategic perspectives they see China's grand strategy as driven by geopolitical competition amongst civilizations and not mere countries. Historically , therefore, successive generations have engaged in evolving a discourse on China' s grand strategies.[4] Increasingly, most of them consider China's victory in this linear progression as guaranteed, if not imminent. While there have been older studies that examine China's grand strategy during SunYat-sen, Mao Zedong, Deng Xiaoping and Jiang Zemin years yet most consider President Hu Jinato' articulation of "rising peacefully" (heping jueqi) and "building harmonium world" (hexie shijie) speech at the United Nations during September 2005 as first formal and contemporary outline by Beijing.[5] At its core, this was nothing but externalization of President Hu's similar notions about China's domestic life where 'Three Represents' and 'Spiritual Civilization' thesis of Jiang Zemin had since evolved into Hu' s 'peaceful development' and 'harmonious society' paradigm. There are, of course, questions raised as to whether China's external outline would also assume a strong state driven 'harmonization' but these questions have remained, so far , unanswered thereby strengthening western skepticism.

It is important to underline that amongst China's more recent academic writings in general and its strategic analysis in last two decades in particular have witnessed an evolution of a whole range of opinions being articulated and debated in pubic though there yet remain some broad uniformities. For instance, most scholars on China's grand strategy have been aguing that if 21st-century has to become 'the Chinese century' then these debates need to be understood using distinctively Chinese concepts and semantics. In terms of their broad dichotomy within China, two major traditions of China' domestic debates are described as (a) those who endorse the 'catch up mentality' and see China's rise within current international system of laws, norms, institutions and structures and (b) those with a 'new era mentality' that stresses China's uniqueness and highlights a geopolitical competition unfolding gradually, but inevitably. Though most of these commentaries remain subdued and modest yet some of these have occasionally reflected an ambitious streak. The radical Wen Wei Po, for instance, had once described Beijing to be the "formulator, participant and defender of world order"

The first major book to raise debates on China's grand strategy inside China had come soon after President Hu's formal articulation at the United Nations in 2005. This is a book by ZhaoTingyan titled *'Tianxia Tixi: Shijie Zhidu Zhexue Daolun'* [The Tianxia System: The Philosophy for the World Institutions] published by Jiangsu Jiaoyu Chubanshe in 2005. Zhao has been a prolific author and is an expert with China's Academy of Social Sciences in Beijing. Following China's going global in its economic policy Zhao argued in his Tianxia System, the Chinese culture must also go global This is because for China to become a world power, it must "create new concepts and new world structures" that exploit its own "resources of traditional thought." But conforming to official *hexie shijie* thesis of President Hu Jintao, Zhao's Tianxia System seeks to revive verbatim an ancient Chinese paradigm that implies selfless global unity that is geographical, psychological and institutional which is described as peaceful, orderly and generous with an intent that puts it in contrast to western hegemony violence and oppression paradigm. This has triggered serious criticism from western scholars William Callahan, for example, calls Zhao's Tianxia System outline as China's new hegemonic order.[6]

Zhao Tingyan's 2005 book triggered this open debate which has since witnessed several regular writings and discussions that broadly supported his Tianxia System paradigm. But the tenor of debate had been evolving over time and year 2010 was to witness publication of an entirely different and far more assertive work by none other than by Senior Colonel Liu Mingfu from China's National Defense University in Beijing. This book, titled '*The China Dr eam: The Gr eat Power Thinking and S trategic Positioning of China in the Post-American Age'* , carries the message for a need of China today to give up its traditional modesty and clearly outline and begin working for its goals. This book has not only revived this debate but especially presented grand strategy outline distinct from that of the official China. Liu propounds "military rise" as a must to support China's "economic rise." He portrays international system as quasi-Olympian competition amongst great powers representing major civilizations and sees this as "period of strategic opportunity" for China to surpass the US. He does not see conflict with the US as inevitable for he believes that China's military rise will deter the USA.

Most experts see this book by Liu Mingfu as natural progression from earlier book of Zhao Tingyan as it reflects increasingly assertive China. Others see Liu Mingfu's book as continuation of an earlier famous book that had come out of China's National Defence University in late 1990s. Written by Qiao Liang and Wang Xiangsui and titled UnrestrictedWarfare, this book was published by Beijing's PLA Literature and Arts Publishing House in February 1999. This was seriously debated both inside and outside China and was seen as China military's response to the US demonstration of its technological superiority during the first Persian Gulf Wr. The broad thesis of this 1999 book had been that in order to compete and defeat the unrivalled American military machine, China must deal withAmerica on all fronts i.e. economic, legal, social, and in international relations. It sought to blunt American edge by using all means including corporate espionage and stealing technologies to ensure parity with and then victory over the US.

Now it seems that this kind of radical thinking is gaining ground inside China. And here, the coming two years of power transition are expected to further add weight to such kind of radical arguments. Such analysis have already triggered speculations about divisions between and radicalization of China's power elite. For instance, on 1 1 January 2011, China's test of its stealth fight aircraft J-20 while US Defence Secretary was visiting was seen as unprecedented and PLA's attempt to influence China's foreign policy. What is especially intriguing is that when Secretary Gates reportedly asked President Hu about this J-20 test, President Hu and his team were found having no knowledge of this event which showed that the civilian leadership was not even kept in loop on this historic test flight of China's first stealth fighter aircraft.[7] Such insinuations have been repeatedly made by western media including the long peace that Newsweek had carried in 2010 about factionalism in China's Communist Party between what article had called 'populists' and 'elitists' of China's politics. It is this increasing frequency of such insinuations that have got China's neighbours interested in exploring into China's grand strategy.

Asian Interpretations

Avery Goldstein's work titled Rising to the Challenge: China's Grand Strategy and International Security, published by the National University of Singapore press in 2008 remains one useful addition from Asian perspectives. It alludes to how China has been trying to reassure the world about its peaceful rise in what China considers to be in reality a unipolar world Author assumes that rising China does not seek to disrupt this unipolar world order in which US dominates. Prima facie, this does seem a kind of a contradiction in terms. According to Goldstein, China seeks to tackle this contradiction in two ways. Firstly, China seeks to make itself indispensable and ensure that the rest of the world begins to see China as indispensable in more than one ways. As a result, the major key players in international order not only become increasingly dependent on China but also become reluctant to trample upon China's core national interests. Secondly, another important component of China's grand strategy is an activists' approach to establish China as a responsible stakeholder, a term increasingly popularized by the US official discourses on China. This stakeholder profile of China in international system makes it appear benign and therefore acceptable to major powers as also to its peers and neighbouring countries.

But of course Avery Goldstein sees repeated tests that China will have to continuously face and deal with as it moves ahead as a major player in international relations. Also, with increasingly assertive China during last few years, these analysis of Goldstein begin to appear bit dated as Asian neighbours of China seem to become far more paranoid and concerned with China's new assertiveness which is bound to increase further in coming two years as it completes its transition of power to 'fifth generation' leaders. In a book published by Routledge in 2010 titled, 'Rise of China: Beijing's Strategies and Implications for the Asia-Pacific', edited by Hsin-Huang, Michael Hsiao and Cheng-yi Lin, put together work of seventeen, largely Asian, authors who provide the local understanding on China's rise with a strong regional focus. These authors present this situation as one of serious concern for China's neighbours. For instance, Japanese scholar , Masako Ikegami (p.22) believes that "China's grand strategy to mitigate and challenge the U S hegemony could eventually lead to a new Cold War" and that makes China's grand strategy about its "peaceful rise" nothing but "a mere rhetoric or a strategic propaganda." Vikram Sood from India accuses (p. 237) China of a "long history of deceit and duplicity" that makes China's rise full of "potential for future conflict," while Chien-peng Chung of Taiwan believes (p. 181) that China's involvement in Asia's regional organisations remains guided by its fear of "containment by the US." Put together the debates on China's grand strategy are becoming far shrill and dichotomous as also increasingly complex and uncertain about their premises and propagation.

Indian analyses of China's grand strategy seem to feel in tune with these rising tenor of China analysis of radicalisation of China. This is partly so because most experts working on China's grand strategy have been from India's military or strategy community that is oriented to focus on worst case scenarios. Some studies by senior journalists have also been subject of simplifications in debating China's rise in either/or binaries. A typical conclusion often talks of China's grand strategy "reflects a sinister design" of reinforcing China-Pakistan axis and perceiving South and Southeast Asia as regions that "fall within its sphere of influence" where it sees "India as the main obstacle to achieve its strategic objective of supremacy in mainland Asia."[8] Some of them have, for long, been talking of China's military planning for subjugating India to psychological warfare in future and recommending urgent need for an Indian grand strategy towards China.[9] In one of the recent balanced analysis by Harsh Pant in his book titled ' *The China Syndr ome: Grappling with Uneasy Relationship* ', published by Harper Collins India in 2010, author exorcises India's foreign policy makers to stop demonising China and to evolve their own coherent long term strategy to deal with rising China. This seems to be the answer and a confident India will perhaps have a more balanced assessment of China's rise and its grand strategy and its implications.

Innovations is the Key

China's 2008 White Paper on China's National Defence published in January 2009 states: "the future and destiny of China have been increasingly closely connected with the international community China cannot develop in isolation from the rest of the world nor can the world enjoy prosperity and stability without China." So as international security moves from coercive and competitive to common and cooperative paradigm it is innovation and partnership that are emerging as the buzzwords in international relations discourses. In the era of smart and soft power , countries like China will have to frontload, not military prowess but their economic, political and cultural influence as the core component of their grand strategies. They need to see themselves as benign 'stakeholders' in international drive for prosperity and peace-building. Even armed forces here will be more involved in reconstruction and relief and joint military exercise will be the only way to demonstrate one's military prowess if a rising power has to stay on course and become world power.

The debate on the 'China model' and 'Beijing consensus' is already indicating that some of it is already happening. The strategy of acquiring innovation, illustrated by the Lenovo acquisition of the personal computer division of IBM, has clear benefits for the mid-term. The strategy of attracting Chinese graduates back from abroad is also very likely to pay off. But government spending per student in China has not risen, and this points to difficulty in fostering indigenous innovation.[10] The US industrial firms, on the other hand, are increasingly adopting much the same strategy of building new research partnerships and setting up R&D facilities outside the country Although this was initially driven by the lower cost of operation abroad, it now is often motivated by the relative availability of talent. The National Science Foundation reports that the US based companies now have 23 per cent of their R&D employment located abroad.[11] According to the Global Innovation Barometer report released by General Electric Co (GE) on 27th January 2010, China is ranked the fourth-most innovative country in the world after the US, Germany and Japan and this speaks volumes for our debates missing the wood for trees.

To conclude, it is this limited focus on bean-counting of China' s stockpiles that seem to make assessments of China' s grand strategy a bit too narrow and a bit too paranoid. Chinas own debates on the subject seem to allude to the larger canvas and subtle paradigms. What some of these contemporary debates seem to be missing is a focus on China's efforts in transforming the very fundamentals of discourse on world affairs and changing the rules of the game and undermining the components of national power that privilege the US as world power. The real strength of China, as they say, lies in the fact that it continues to challenge the conventional wisdom and yet continue to flourish.The debates on China's grand strategy, therefore, need to cast their net wide and deep, and keep a tab on China's initiatives and discourses in light of Chinese characteristics where innovations in analytical toolkits remain critical to crystal gaze the Chinese mind.

Endnotes

1   Martin Jacques, *When China Rules the World: The Rise of the Middle Kingdom and the End of the W estern World*, (New Y ork: Penguin Pr ess, 2009), p . 365. Also, in purchasing power parit y, for instance, China has alr eady been declared world's largest economy with $14.8 trillion followed by US at $14.6 trillion for 2010. See Arvind Subramanian, "Is China Already Number One? New GDP Estimates", 13 January 2011, *Peterson Institute for International Economics*, at http://www.iie.com/realtime/?p=1935

2   Denny Roy, "The "China Threat" issue: Major Arguments" , in *Asian Survey*, Vol. 36, no. 8 (August 1996), p. 758; Bi ll Gertz, *The China Threaet: How the People's Republic Targets America*, (Washington DC: An Eagle Publ ishing Company, 2000), p. 5; Khalid R. Al-R odhan, "A Critique of the China Threat Theory: A S ystematic Analysis", *Asian Perspective*, Vol. 31, no . 3 (2007), p. 44-45.

3   V aishnavi Tanvir, "Growing Chinese Assertiveness: Love Thy Neighbour?", *Mainstream* (New Delhi), V ol.xlviii, no. 4 4, (October 23, 2010); El izabeth C Economy et al, "Checking China' s Territorial Mov es", at *Expert Roundup* 21 October 2010, (Council on Foreign Relations), http://www.cfr.org/publication/23196/checking_chinas_territorial_moves.html

4   See for example, Brantly Womack (ed.), *China's Rise in Historical Perspective*, (New York: Rowman & Li ttlefield, 2010); Peter Kein-hong Yu, *The Crab and Frog Motion P aradigm Shift: Decoding and Deciphering T aipei and Beijing's Dialectical Policies*, (Lanham, MD: University Press of Ameica, 2002), p. 7; Brigadier Subrata Saha, China's Grand Strategy: From Confucius to Contemporary, (US Arm y War College, Carlisle Barracks, PA, 2010) at ht tp:/ /www.dtic.mil/cgi-bin/GetTRDoc?Location=U2&doc=GetTRDoc.pdf&AD= ADA518303

5   Sujian Guo and Baogang Guo (ed.), *China in Search of a Harmonious Society*,

(New York: Lexington Books, 2008), p . 33; Suisheng Zhao (ed.), *China and the US: Cooperation and Competition in Northeast Asia* , (New York: Palgrave Macmillan, 2008), p. 81; "Hexie Shijie yu Quanqiu Zhil i", [Harmonious World and Global Governance], *Tianjin Shiwei Dangxiao Xuebao* [Journal of the Party School of Tianjin Committee of CPC], No. 2, (2007), pp. 5-10.

6 William A. Callahan, "Chinese visions of world order: post-hegemonic or a new hegemony?", *International Studies Review*, Vol. 10 (2008), pp . 467-468.

7 John P omfret, "China tests steal th air craft before Gates, Hu meet ", *The Washington Post*, 12 January 2010.

8 S . D. Pradhan, "Denial of visa part of China' s grand strategy", *The Times of India*, (New Delhi), 30 August 2010; also J. Mohan Malik, "Indai and China: Bound to Coll ide?", in P . R. K umaraswamy (ed.), *Security Be yond Survival: Essays for K. Subrahmanyam* , (New Delhi: Sage, 2004), p. 129.

9 Subhash K apila, "India needs a grand strategy towards China" , South Asian Analysis Group, Paper No. 841, 19 November 2003 available at http://www.southasiaanalysis.org/%5Cpapers9%5Cpaper841.html

10 Stephen Merrill, David Taylor, and Robert Poole, *The Dragon and the Elephant: Understanding the Development of Innovation Capacity in China and India: Summary of a Conference* , (Washington DC: The National Academies Press, 2010), p. 19.

11 National Academy of Sciences et al, *Rising Above the Gathering Storm, Revisited*, (Washington DC: The National Academies Press, 2010), p. 46.

Comments by Panelists on Other Presentations

Professor Richard Rigby. I have already expressed my agreement with Ashley, so I will leave it there. The final remarks from Professor Hwang were actually quite important. His statement: "W e don't know who you are. Do you know who you are?" That is a very real question, where China is concerned. It is a question that many Chinese are actually aware of. A few weeks ago I attended a small seminar with a group of scholars from the Australian National University and some middle aged and younger Shanghai based scholars. We met in Sujo for a couple of days to talk specifically about this question: What do you do when you have wealth and power? For 150 years China has been regarding wealth and power as a goal, now it is beginning to think differently. Somebody said, "Actually it is not a goal at all, it is only a means to an end but what is the end? Somewhere along the way perhaps we have rather lost the plot because we don't actually know what we stand for anymore. We don't stand for traditional Chinese values." Let me come back to that because some people are saying, " *In fact that is what we ar e standing for now . W e certainly don't stand for traditional Maoist, Marxist, Leninist values, we know what the United States stands for , we know what a number of other countries stand for but what pr ecisely is this China that we belong to?* " So, this furious search for values and for meaning takes some people back into the Chinese tradition and ethics.

Let us look at some other directions i.e. religious, philosophical, pursuit of money, sex, etc.They also open up the question:When we talk about the rise of China, when we contemplate a risen China, i.e. say in 10, 15, 20 years from now, what sort of China is it going to be? Frankly we don' t know, they don't know and Hu Jintao does not knowHe presumably thinks, he would like it to be the way it is now and only more so; but that is really not going to happen. I don't know any Chinese I talked to in the PRC, who do not think things are going to be very different.

If you ask most of the people in ChinaWill China be democratic in 50 years? Almost everybody says yes. If you say 30 years, then they say well, we don't know. If you say 10 years almost everyone will say , 'no'. The question then is, whether in 50 years' time if you ask the same question you might get exactly the same answer as well. It is this lack of clarity, about precisely 'what sort of China a risen China would be,' that leads us to think at a greater degree of uncertainty and insecurityOn the part of other people looking at a rising China, that is not the case where India is concerned.We have pretty good idea about what India is going to be like. But with China we don't know. This is an important issue.

Professor Jaeho Hwang. The G2 concept has become very popular since President Obama's Asia tour in November 2010. It has raised several questions. Why is the USA bringing this concept and what are the motivations behind it? I also observed that some amongst the rivalling nations such as India and Japan, (if you pronounce G2 in Chinese with a very strong accent it means i.e. ' *Jeetu*'), it arouses jealousy . So, we have to consider the rivalling nations stance also. The third point is that in countries, which are geographically neighbouring China such as Korea, may be a G2 concept may not be real; it is still an ongoing debate. But G2 is already reality in the Korean peninsula.

Last year's Copenhagen Climate Summit and 'climate change' is an important agenda in the international community but climate around Korean peninsula has already changed. So, everybody thinks of the USA and China as G2 but to Korea sometimes, China and Japan are the G2. So, whatever new concepts arise or the way security situation keeps changing, we always have to see them from all different angles.

Professor Swaran Singh. This is a unique opportunity to question the co-panelists. I have a question from the book that Ashley and Mike Swaine wrote. You had prefixed that 'territory' and 'territorial' integrity were the first drivers of China's grand strategy; I have noticed that in your presentation you did not mention that. Maybe you would want to expand on that.

I also have one question/comment for Professor Hwang. It was mentioned that China's rise and grand strategy are visible only in terms of hardware and that software will take decades to evolve. I thought Chinese actually were stronger on the software. Perhaps their capacity to communicate and articulate, and make others understand their software was where the lacuna was. Would you like to say something on that?

Professor Ashley Tellis. Let me make a general point which came out of the presentation that Richard had made. The central issue really is: What will China be as it acquires greater 'maturation' in its capabilities? To my mind the debate really ends up between those who believe that there is something 'uniquely Chinese' which will allow it to escape from the competitive pressures of international politics and redesign a global system which is harmonious both inside and outside versus those who believe that no matter what China's intentions may be, ultimately they will be submerged by the pressures of competitive politics and will therefore push it in the direction of behaving like any other great power. That is really the central question. It is interesting in this context that the differences between the Chinese and Western conceptions are odd. If you look at the 'Tributary Period' of China and use that as a template, for China, the preference always was for formal hierarchies, even when the distribution of power was actually quite equal. In fact it is very odd, but if you look at the Tributary System there were periods in the Tributary System where the Chinese Emperor would actually bribe powerful regional States simply to come and offer tribute because the act of offering tribute was far more important than any material differences in power . So you had this peculiar State where nominally hegemonic State was actually offering these barbarians in the periphery incentives to come and kowtow before the EmperorThe Western conception of order was actually remarkably the opposite. We believe in formal equality among States. In fact there is no great defender of State sovereignty than the USA and India. In China, we all believe that the sovereignty of States etc., i.e., equality of formal sovereignty means nothing, because at the end of the day it is material differences of power that produce certain outcomes. Which of these two worlds would be the world that is likely to be reproduced as a result of Chinese power? I think it is going to be a very interesting thing to watch.

Just a brief answer to Professor Swaran's question. In the book we have emphasised three things. First, the overwhelming Chinese obsession is with the 'protection of order' and there are philosophical questions to this because it has something to do with the 'mandate of heaven'; second, the 'deep rooted fear of chaos in the Chinese psyche'; and third, protection of order invariably has both political and spatial kind of components. So, protection of territory becomes the spatial component but not to the exclusion of the other elements as well.

Session 1: Discussion

Issues Raised (By the Chairman)

Whether it is Eastern or Western power, some features are common for all powers. All great powers use force for many purposes other than (merely) territorial defence. As China rises to become a great power, what would be the implications in respect of the following three criteria :-

(a) When they decide to use 'force', would it be limited only to territorial defence? What is the likelihood of their using force on issues other than protecting their territorial interests?

(b) If the interests of a great power are larger and global, they always have 'forward presence' i.e. deploy forces not inside their territory , but on other people's territories far away from their shores. What is the debate internally in China in terms of 'forward presence' bases i.e. deployment away from own shores?

(c) All great powers provide security for other people through alliances. What is the notion of alliances in the Chinese mind as they debate their future?

Response

Three benchmarks that merit consideration for identifying great powers are: (a) they provide security to others (b) they have forward power projections and (c) they have an overall purpose. In this context it is pertinent to analyse the ongoing 'connotations of power change' in China. There is a definite slant away from military power to other components of power. An example of that view is that the greatest culprit in terms of 'mitigation' (the USA) is today leading the world debate on, how to deal with climate change mitigation? That is the way of influencing decisions around the world, without using military or it could be through G 20 talks. Some of the above issues have been dealt with in the subsequent responses as well.

Issues Raised

In my view no rise can be peaceful particularly in the context of China because they have no political reforms; the rise is entirely economy oriented and an assertive PLA calls the shots. In the context of 2012 change in leadership (fifth generation) two names have been mentioned; Xi Jinping and Mr. Li, who are weak and perhaps incompetent.   Would these developments: firstly, lead to diminishing of the Chinese goal of dominating the world as Number One Power? Secondly, as far as India is concerned, with the PLA getting more assertive because of change in leadership, would the situation become more volatile on our borders?

Responses

(a) Whether fifth generation leadership would gradually make China weaker and whether that weakness would increase the propensity of China being more aggressive towards India, along with other implications is an important point. In the last 60 or 70 years there is a definite trend of 'increasing self-confidence' in China. From Mao onwards, the level of engagement through Deng, through Ziang, through Hu Jintao and now Li Qiching and Xi Jinping is definitely increasing China's global engagement. Both these leaders today are said to be more comfortable in dealing with international engagements than even Hu Jintao. So, in some ways if transparency shot up after Hu Jintao took over, the transparency would definitely increase. Therefore, our capacity to understand China would definitely improve.

(b)   As regards the Chinese assertiveness, it is likely to continue inevitably because China's stability is dependent upon constant 'very high growth rates' which require raw materials, energy from outside world and markets. Therefore, access and safety of SLOCs will gradually push China to 'go on expanding influence' from the Pacific Ocean to the Gulf of Aden. In terms of its increasing assertiveness, if we read access as assertiveness, it will continue.

Issues Raised

The concept of assertiveness in the Chinese context is a little bit enigmatic. What is the reason behind their assertiveness? Is it just because of enhanced confidence on account of growing military muscle or does it have something to do with the 'possibility of the ruling elite losing its legitimacy' due to increasing difficulties in 'management of the social fabric'? Can we call it an anticipated 'quest for conflict' in order to 'conjure up national unity?

Responses

The big distinction about assertiveness today vis-à-vis previous Chinese approaches is really the distinction between 'coping' and 'shaping'. The traditional Chinese leadership strategy attempted 'to cope with' the world as it affected itself; the current Chinese leadership is attempting to shape the world as it affects Beijing. Great fleet appearing in different parts of the world is one dimension of it, but the theoretical difference is: 'do you simply lie low and do the best you can because you live in a world that is, defined by somebody else's rules?' or 'have you now researched a point where you say, I do not need to lie low as I did before, because I can now assert by making rules?' There is an element of assertiveness in that thinking but that is not the principal driver. The principal drivers are structural.

China has now reached a point where it recognizes that its economic success is intimately linked with being able to shape world order to its advantage. So, it will continue to go out and do that because that is what continued economic success requires. It can be seen to be manifesting in a variety of areas— international institutions, military areas, diplomacy etc. The diverging element may be something transient but in the long term it is structural.

Issue Raised

Is the 'over confidence' and 'assertiveness' displayed by the Chinese in the second half of last year (2009) indicative of their desire to become a dominant power in the world?

Response

China prefers the policy of 'participating in the global society')(*o so chow*) which suggests it is trying to 'reshape the international order'. This is more typical of the Chinese. Keeping the geographical surroundings of China in view, we have to recognize that the Chinese mentality is not really 'offensive or to expand' but is rather indicative of 'protecting themselves' from their geographical vulnerabilities. Six Party talks, SCO, India-Pakistan-Chinese relations, ARF or ASEAN+1 and the Sub-Mekong Area Economic Zone were organised for 'defensive' rather than 'offensive' purpose, keeping Chinese geographical necessities in mind.

Issue Raised

While China continues to rise, theWest and particularly the USA, perceive, the 'Rise of China' in a different way. What are the Chinese perceptions on their own rise and how has the rest of the world perceived this phenomenal rise of China'?

Response

The United States response to China will shape the Chinese perceptions and the decisions they make in the future. This is bad news for rest of the world, because the USA as a 'power in decline' would not look kindly at the process of China's rise and will have great dificulty accommodating itself to their 'decline of relative power'. That would evoke worst possible choices in the Chinese perceptions and that could take the world on a course that neither side would prefer to go.

Issue Raised

Is there a notion of alliances in the Chinese mind as they debate the future?

Response

In China, nobody is talking about entering into alliances. They continue to say that they would rather prefer that other people also do not enter into alliances (against them), although there is not very much they can do about that.

Issue Raised

What efforts are being made by China to project their power across the world, especially in terms of creating bases to safeguard their interests?

Response

The Chinese efforts to project their power are clearly visible in the Indian Ocean. This is also to safeguard its own SLOC and because of its growing requirement of energy.

Issue Raised

What role will the emerging fifth generation leadership play in China?

Responses

The perception that the next leadership is going to be 'particularly weak', is not correct. Since Mao, each new leadership with absolute authority of one single person has diminished. That is not a bad thing, when you consider the disasters which took place under Mao. Where Xi Jinping is concerned, those who have met him and other political leaders generally regard him as an extremely competent person and there might not be any particular problem under his leadership. However, there are some doubts about Li Qichiang. But, weak leadership would not be a problem.

The PLA is certainly a powerful voice - it was never completely irrelevant. Under the 'four modernizations', 'PLA modernisation' was the last. Things have gone completely according to plan and now it is PLA 's turn to assert themselves. This is not causing any great concern to the politburo. This may cause angst in the Foreign Ministry but it is not of much consequence. If the Standing Committee of the Politburo wanted any of the senior Generals or Colonels to 'shut up' they could make them to do so. Allowing the PLA to voice their opinions serves its purpose. In this context appointment of Xi Jinping to the Central Military Commission (CMC) gives a further evidence of the fact that things are going according to plan and that PLA is still very much the Party' s Army. However, if there was a 'major collapse' i.e. either the economy falling completely or if China was involved in some external shock which could threaten the Central government,

PLA obviously is the only other organization which could move in. It would be only under extreme circumstances that it could actually emerge as an independent player.

Issue Raised

How successfully has the Chinese leadership dealt with the 'economy' related issues?

Responses

Decline of China's economy may be really bad for everybody because it is clearly interconnected with international community. Therefore, it will not only endanger Chinese leaders, it will also have an immense impact on the international community. However, danger to the Chinese leaders comes, not from the economy related issues; but, social issues in China would be more dangerous.

Issue Raised

What kind of Global order China seeks to dominate?

Response

The Chinese did not raise the issue of China model. It was invented in the West and Beijing Consensus is something mentioned by Joseph Cuperamos— quite a few years ago, which had a negative impact on the Chinese. However they did not invent it. One of the big differences between China and erstwhile Soviet Union is that China does not have to actually impose its model on other people. Other countries, particularly in Africa have found it attractive. An authoritarian government doing well is a really unpleasant model for demonstration. This is a phenomenon we have to deal with rather than something which China is actually pushing as an instrument of state policy

Issue Raised

At the beginning of this 21 st century the Chinese Parliament passed a resolution to observe a National Humiliation Day . Later, wiser counsels prevailed and they stopped from designating a particular day for this. Are we going to see history dominate the Chinese vision of New Global order?

Response

'National Humiliation' is certainly going to continue to be an important part of education within China. It is something which should be considered quite 'unfortunate'. It is, however, understandable in the light of China's history from the First Opium War, through upto 1949 anyway, but not later. After 1949, most of the injuries were self-inflicted. It is also quite understandable that China would never again wish to find itself in a situation which it was in 1840s and the mid-20[h] century. We should hope that they would get over it, but it is going to take some time for them to do so.

Chairman's Concluding Remarks

Dr C Raja Mohan

I think much has been said, so I will just share a few concluding thoughts. One issue that has come up: are we looking at China through the western eyes? That has always been part of our debates and the reason why we read only western books, I hope the Indians write more books about China that are good and credible. That is our problem, we don't have the capacity to write good books on China because we don't have enough people studying the Chinese language. Today in every small college in the United S tates Mandarin is being taught, Mandarin has just replaced French as the most popular foreign language in the United States. In India you can count on your fingertips how many places Chinese is being taught. So, I think if you don't build your capacities to study China we are going to go constantly wrong. Therefore, it is not that the expertise will automatically produce the right solutions. America has lot of expertise, it does not, however, produce the right solutions always, but the question of having the capacity is very important. So, I would say 'capacity building' is fundamental in terms of our understanding of China.

The second thing, there is a danger when we debate Chinese strategy We have so many immediate grievances, the immediate slides that you have with the Chinese because the Chinese are under our skin in some sense. But when we study grand strategy of China we must differentiate and we must put aside those immediate grievances. Therefore, when we study China it must be China qua China. W e must be able to distance ourselves from the immediate and the contentious to say where China is going. Do we know China enough, that is the question and I think irrespective of whether they know where they are going or not we should know where the Chinese are going and therefore, 'we need to put in more effort to understand what the Chinese are saying'.

A third set of issues is:Are we romanticizing China through non-western eyes? If there is one problem, it is of looking through the western eyes, the other problem is constructing that there is a non-western way of thinking about China or China is going to be an eastern power as opposed to the western power. I don't know if this is actually a worthwhile debate, but it is very popular and expresses itself in many forms,Washington Consensus or Beijing Consensus, the East wind is prevailing over the West— there is a long tradition to this. However , the problem is that; let me give you an example of Rabindranath Tagore. When he went there in the 1920s, and spoke at Beijing University, a Chinese Communist Party cadre stood up and attacked his speech because Tagore was saying, "look we must not blindly imitate the West, East must follow its own spiritual civilization"The young Chinese communist cadre said "this is rubbish, this spiritual nonsense, we don't want, we want westernization, we want modernization, we want industrialization". Today of course spiritual civilization is part of the Chinese Communist vocabulary. So, to get carried away with this East versus West has limits.

We have got to see power in its fundamental terms; China has all the classical characteristics of a great power of the past.The big Navy, forward presence, impact on international institutions etc. and not look at their changes in clothes or style etc. the Chinese jackets and style are getting very popular and there will be more Confucius institutes. But we should not mistake a great power with the Chinese characteristics. Probably that would be a better way of describing, where China is going?And not that it is some kind of an eastern power. Still Communism is a western concept. In May 1999, the Chinese National Movement said that 'Science' and 'Democracy' are very western concepts. We should not get trapped by this East versusWest. My own sense is that the real question is whether China is going to be a classical great power? Our challenge is going to be far more consequential because the central question is why we are not discussing Indian strategy. My sense is, if we understand the Chinese strategy a lot of things will sort themselves out for constructing an Indian strategyA debate on Indian strategy is required, because both China and India will have to grow on the basis of resources from other people. The welfare of these two billion people is not being constructed on self-reliance and socialism. It is being constructed by having to acquire your energy resources from somewhere else. So, it is automatic. China and India will be like other powers. They might be neo-colonial powers and that they could be using force. These are issues we need to debate. This whole project of studying China' s grand strategy hopefully will contribute to understanding the terms under which we must define our own grand strategy over the longer term.

Just one last thought. What we did in this session was to paint with those broad brush strokes, like a Chinese painting. The big broad brush strokes that we did, have been a good beginning for the rest of the Seminar The project as a whole hopefully will flush out the finer strokes on economy on military strategy and then the painting will be complete and hopefully it will give us some insights into China.

Second Session

China's Economic Future

Session2:Introductory Remarks

Lieutenant General PK Singh, PVSM,AVSM (Retd)

After having deliberated on 'China's Grand Strategy' we now take on yet another fascinating facet of China's rise, which is their remarkable economic growth. We have a distinguished panel of experts and an eminent chairperson for this session.The implications of China's rapid economic progress on the rest of Asia and globally will be highlighted by these eminent panelists.To chair the session we have Dr Rajiv Kumar . He has an illustrious career . Presently, he is the Director General of the Federation of Indian Chambers of Commerce and Industry (FICCI).

Session 2: Chairman's Opening Remarks

Dr Rajiv Kumar

China's economic 'growth' and economic 'future' are actually the most important issues of our times. Whatever has already happened and what they have achieved is quite historical. It shows that it has awakened the 'sleeping dragon'. After its awakening in 1980, China has achieved one of the greatest economic miracles in human history . It has awakened more than 500 million people out of poverty . The magnitude of the economic progress they have made over these years can be assessed from the following anecdote.

During my first visit to Beijing in 1995, I stayed in a posh hotel, known as 'The ChinaWorld'. There, I met a person from UnileverHe had reached there for the first time in 1984 and at that time had stayed in the only hotel there, The Beijing Hotel. He had noticed that those days a bell would ring at 7.30 o'clock in the evening to announce dinnerInitially, he did not understand why they should ring a bell for that. As soon as the bell rang, there was a huge rush to the dining room. Howeverhe would stay back wondering why should there be a rush like that in a 'five star ' hotel. Later he learnt to his great dismay, that by 8 o'clock, all the meat had finished and nothing except just the bread was left behind. Between 1984 and 1995, to the time now in 2010 (when I went back again earlier this year) the China World Hotel had grown into one of the plushest hotels. It is much better than anything that we have in our Country. I could see that China of the old days has already been left behind; and now there were much bigger things there. For example, the 6th and 7th Ring Roads had come around. Earlier in 1995, where there were only bicycles, now, there were none.

Recently, I met the same person again when I went to ShanghaiThese days he has become a very strong advocate of the Chinese financial sectors, whereas earlier, he had written a couple of articles predicting the collapse of the Chinese banking system in the next two or three years. This was because the Non Performing Assets(NPA) were high; the Chinese banking sector was not following any of the prescriptions of the   Western anglo-saxon financial sector development; it was all dominated by the public sector banks; they were very large and controlled by the government etc. Nicholas Dadi had also said the same thing, " *Give it just two or thr ee years and this is not going to last any longer because the NP   As are just far too high and China cannot sustain this sort of model of financial sector growth.*"

In the next few years i.e. after around 2000 or so, the Chinese government using growth as their saviour made sure that the non performing loans became a smaller part of the total assets because the 'denominator ' kept rising. Then they used their own fiscal resources to recapitalise all their major banks; starting with the Bank of China, the Industrial and Commercial Development Corporation (ICDC) and the People' s Construction Bank, and even the   Agricultural Bank of China, which is supposed to be in a worse state than the three of them. This is when they floated 10 per cent of their equity into the market. That has made the four major Chinese banks to be counted amongst the largest ten banks in the world. The ICDC capitalisation, at about a trillion dollars, is perhaps bigger than any of the Western banks and they did not melt down when the Lehman happened.

Recently, when I met some of the bankers, they told us that, because of the failure of one bank (the Guangdong Savings Bank), they cleaned up another 50 smaller banks and the Non-Banking Financial Companies (NBFCs) and also cleaned up the financial sector The point to take note is that they have decided to go 'the way they wanted to go'. Now reluctantly people say that the Chinese have got it all right and they cannot put a wrong foot forward. They have now rightly decided to move economic development westwards and inwards. One question that still remains to be answered is: In the future is it possible for the Chinese to maintain this almost breathless rate of growth? Can they continue to do it? What are the structural factors that may allow them to do so or prevent them from doing so? These are the issues we should focus on in this session.

I will request the panelists to leave the past behind, unless of course it is leading into the future. The Chinese past achievements are very well known. They have been recounted in Mohan Guruswamy's book, 'Chasing the Dragon'—describing China's achievements in the field of education, technology, industry and services. Their service sector exports are more than ours. We can use it for steering into the future. China has made the transition from a poor low income country to the lower rungs of the middle income economies. It is there now . Their per capita income in nominal terms is more than $3000 per capita; in Purchasing Power Parity (PPP) terms it would be probably about $6500-7000.

What are the impediments or favourable structural drivers for China, to make the transition to a middle income economy that is comparable to those of the Latin American economies which are having above $5000 per capita income? Can they get to the $5000-8000 per capita? How would they achieve it, given the demographic structure and the fact that the Japanese faced a 'push back' from the world community in the 1980s when they had reached $20000 per capita income? China is facing that push back against their export driven growth already when they are about $3000-4000 per capita.

The second question is: How can they make the switchover in their economy? Are they willing or capable of making this switchover from an 'external demand' driven economy to a 'domestic demand' economy? What are they trying for and how are they achieving it? The third question is: What is China's strategy for raising the 'productivity levels'in their industry because sooner than later, Chinese wages will have to rise? The Chinese will face pressure from their working population and the wages would have to rise. What is the Chinese government strategy for raising the productivity levels in agriculture and in industry and what are the prospects for that?

Finally, China has already ensured that 20 per cent of their young people reach the higher education level. The challenge they are now facing is: Can they make the transition to the knowledge and high tech economy?

Can they make the transition to products and services which are much more high technology intensive than they have been so far? Since the answer is yes: What is their strategy for taking the education sector , R&D and technology further ahead? These are the important questions which need to be looked into. In the end, of course, we know that the switch from 'external' to 'domestic' demand must come with the greater movement towards the western and central provinces. Whether they would be able to achieve a lowering of 'inequity' that they have seen between the southern coastal regions and the interior provinces? China has faced a huge and rising inequality/ within the society since 1980s. This is documented and reflected in Wen Jiabao's slogan of achieving 'a harmonious world'. Can all that happen? Of course, the question of political transition would also arise. However, I do not want to raise that because I want to remain focussed on economic issues related to Chinese rise.

With those opening remarks I request the panelists to 'peer into the future'. I have great pleasure in inviting Mr Mohan Guruswamy to make his presentation.

Mr Mohan Guruswamy has to leave soon after making his presentation. Therefore, after he has spoken, the panelists and the participants may ask him questions about the issues covered by him. That would form Part I of the 'discussion' in this session.

Session 2: First Paper

Mr Mohan Guruswamy

Thank you for inviting me this afternoon. Predicting the economic future of China? Perhaps, parrots could do a better job. On the roadside, you see these parrot boxes from which a parrot pops out and picks up a card that tells you your future. In the 'World Cup Football' matches, the octopus got its predictions right and all the experts got them wrong. As an economics graduate student I had asked Professor Samuelson whether he predicted the Great Depression right. Samuelson had replied that on the last weekend before the banks closed at the faculty at Harvard; as usual the Janitor came to them enquiring whether anyone wanted to encash their cheques. Those days the Professors got paid weekly , so the Janitor would collect all the cheques, and go to the bank at Harvard Square to collect the money on their behalf. He said "Most of the Harvard Economics Faculty confirmed to him that they neither wanted the cheques nor cash, saying that they had got enough money. Despite his nudging, they said, "Dont worry about it we are alright". So, when Monday came only the Janitor had money and all the economics professors had to borrow money from him. So, predicting the economic future is pretty much like that.

I would also share a conversation I had with Professor Scalepeno in 1990 in Vladivostok. At that time, Scalepeno was at the University of California in Berkeley. He was considered the world's foremost expert on China. I asked him, "Professor, what do you think is going to happen to China?" He looked at me and said, "In the year 2000, China would collapse. It will break up into warlordism. There would be warlords all over the place and this China as we know will not exist." When the year 2000 came, I waited upto the 31st December 2000, hoping that something of that prediction would come true. So, we economists never get this 'future' thing right.

In 1980s, when I was doing a term paper , Lotus software had just come. It was great fun spreading the software sheets and analysing the data. You had to put a number in, and then you added a percentage looking for figures say 50 years down the line. The numbers would then start moving around. At that time, both India and China were growing. China's growth had already touched around 10 per cent. When I fed data about India at 8 per cent to 10 per cent in the year 2000 we were getting really astounding figures. The world was going to look quite different at the beginning of the 21th century. So, I went to my Professor and told him that this is what I want to write my dissertation on. He said, "Don't waste time, do something more practical. Do you think that India is going to come out of the hole they were in, and is China going to rise to eminence? Be reasonable?" He went on to make a big name for himself as a great economist proffering advice to many countries. But at that time, he could not believe that India would make such an astounding progress in economic terms.

The question that we need to ask now is: Is GDP everything? One thing is very clear that GDPs are going to grow . We also know that dire predictions have mostly been wrong, that theories get discarded and we also now know that 'people' matter. There was a time in India when we were all growing up, when everybody said "India' s problem was its population- it had too many people." Books by Paul Earlick and people like that wrote doomsday scenarios. Paul Earlick actually wrote in his book "Imagine the year 2000, and you are walking around Connaught Place, you will see 2000 people falling down dead, of starvation." I grew up in the 1960s with a morbid fear of being around in New Delhi in the year 2000 and seeing dead bodies all around me.This did not happen. Now we are being told that 'people' are the basic drivers for economic growth. When Chairman Mao was told by his advisors that America is thinking of attacking China with nuclear weapons, Mao very cryptically looked at him and said, "Don't worry, because in the end the bomb won't destroy the people, the people will destroy the bomb". What he basically meant was that if you have a larger number of people, you will triumph.

All that the economists can see is just around the next corner . They don't really know what is beyond that. After that they are like the parrots.

According to a Chinese quotation, "They regard history as a mirror" and they say that they can understand and see, "What will be rising and what will be falling". Hu Jintao quoted this, when he met King Abdullah in Saudi Arabia. What he implied by this was that Saudi Arabia's old ally America is not going to be there indefinitely . But history still offers you methods of looking at the future. I will draw your attention to the famous chart from Angus Maderson, the historian who looked back at the world. In 1748, Britain took over Fort St George in Madras at the beginning of the British Empire. At that time Indian economy was quite high up and was perhaps world' s No.1 economy. There was no Britain, no France, there was no Russia and only a little bit of Western Europe economy existed. That is how it was, in the past. China and India were right on top in the 18th century. If you look at the past 'as a mirror' you will see some indication as to what is going to happen in the future.

If you look at from 1979 onwards, when reforms began in China; India had also started moving upto 4 to 6 per cent growth and was still moving upwards. If you project it up to 2010; you get a slightly steeper curve for India and an even steeper curve for China. When people look at this and make projections, they get absolutely scary figures. Robert Fogel, Director of Centre for Population Economics at the University of Chicago, the Graduate School of Business, said "Here is a monster economy in the making and by 2040 in PPP terms China's GDP would be US $123 trillion." That would be 40 per cent of global GDP in that year—nearly three times the total output of the entire world in 2000. Forty years from now i.e. in 2050, he is projecting all these massive changes in China. Of course, Chicago economists never get it right, as whatever economic prescriptions they have given to the world for curing themselves, very few have worked out. The saving grace here is that Fogel is at Chicago, so we need not take him too seriously. But Fogel is predicting that China's per capita income in 2040 will be US $85000 per head and that is a twenty threefold increase in 40 years. That would get us into a situation where people would start saying that this kind of futuristic projections cannot last, and China would stumble and fall. On the other hand, you also have guys who have created these huge Chinese monsters, and made them to look like, as if they are 20 feet tall.

However, may be he is right in projecting the 'decline of Europe' because that seems to be on the cards. The important reason for this is 'the people'. Europe's population is not growing. Most parts of Western Europe would go into a population decline. Russia will lose 45 million people. Russian population today is 150 million and it would get reduced to a little more than a 100 million people in 2050. France, Scandinavia and Italy's population will also be small. In fact, most of Central Europe would have relatively smaller population; Eastern Europe's population would then start declining, and the UK's would start declining too. Only one major power which would still be growing is the USA. InAsia, Japan is not growing and we all know what is happening in Japan.

Now, let us look at a new study by Price Waterhouse Coopers. They seem to be branching out into economic prediction. They have got a new line now and, like Goldman Sachs, they are predicting the future. In 2030, they say that the world's 'top ten' economies would be: China followed by the USA, India, Japan, Brazil, Russia, Germany , Mexico, France and Britain—that is a fair prediction.According to current figures the line-up as we know today is: USA, Japan, China (China and Japan have switched places last month), Germany, France, Britain, Italy, Russia, Spain and Brazil, India is still at 11. But if you use PPP terms, India comes upto No 4.

The important point here is that both India and China are growing faster than forecasted by Goldman Sachs, (that famous BRICs report), faster than forecasted by the IMF , faster than forecasted by the World Bank and faster than forecasted by the CIA also. These forecasts predict that China will actually surpass the USAin 2027.According to Jim O'Neil (who made the acronym BRICs famous in the world and is the economist for Goldman Sachs), China would overtake the US economy by 2027 instead of 2041. Actually there are many people who are now saying that by 2020 China will surpass the USA. So by 2030, according to this report the USA will account for 16 per cent of the world GDP, China 19 per cent and 9 per cent for India.

But, something different is also happening. In the famous fable the hare goes to sleep; but that is not happening and the hare is bounding along, but it is actually the tortoise that is turning into a hare. So, it is kind of a two hare race in which the tortoise (India), is going to mutate into a hare in 2020 according to this report. India is likely to give China a run for its money , mainly because of its people. In theory, India in 2020 will have a younger and more productive population profile. Whether Mr Sibal can make 'universal literacy' possible in the next 5-10 years is a debatable point. However, hoping that we get our literacy and all the vocational training programmes in place, India would be poised to give China a run for its money after 2020.

In my estimate, the period up to 2020 or up to 2025, is a period of high vulnerability for India—should anything go wrong in the country or should the Chinese decide to do something to push India back from its development course. These are high risk periods for India.   A few years ago when I presented a paper on the subject, 'W ill India Catch Up with China?' in Shanghai, a leading Chinese economist told me, "Don't feel bad China is like an elder brother. I was born ahead of you, I got educated ahead of you, went to school ahead of you and went to college ahead of you, started working ahead of you, then I got my first car ahead of you, then I got married, so you are my younger brother and you follow me, you are following 10 years to 15 years behind me, but you will also catch up." However   , thereafter, he added a caveat, "But on the other hand you could pick up bad habits; you could start drinking, you could start gambling, you could do all kinds of things. So, I don't know what is going to happen to you; but since we have passed that phase, maybe you can learn from us.

Steering around the corner, one thing is very clear that by the end of the decade in GDP terms, China at $28 trillion is going to be bigger than the USA at $22 trillion; and India's GDP would be $10 trillion and still growing very rapidly. India's growth rate around that time will outstrip China' that is also pretty clear now.

According to old GDP projections: China in 2050 will be $ 44 trillion, EU $ 35 trillion, the USA $ 35 trillion and India $ 27 trillion. The thing to take note is that if India does one or two per cent more per year in this period, actually those numbers will all get reversed. India will actually jump into

No.1 place. The good news is that India is doing two per cent more than projected but nobody knows for how long that will last. This is the stuff our dreams are made of. Most Indian leaders hold the view that with China at No.1, India should be amongst the top three—the rest of the countries would be pygmies in the world then.

Now, let us discuss China' s 'population projection'. It has already stabilised at 1.3 billion, which means that it is growing. When a country's population stabilises, it starts getting older and greyerIndia's population in 2050 would be merrily chugging along at 1.6 billion and not be slowing down. Though the Government of India has told the UN that India' s population will stabilise by 2047, it is not going to happen. India is going to reach stable population growth around the year 2090. That is good news because the number of people is going to increase. The bad news is that India's BIMARU states are going to grow and the rest of India will stop growing.

India's 'prime working age group'numbers are increasing, which means that India's 16-34 large group crosses China in 2014 and will really be on top in 2050; whereas, in respect of everybody else, it is going down. When we look at the dependency ratio: India's meets China's on the way down. As our dependency ratio keeps decreasing, China's is rising; and then the two meet again around 2015, thereafter we cross them.The result is that in 2050 India would have more working hands; the working age population of India is going to be more than 60 per cent of what it is nowand in the case of China and the USA, it will start coming down.

Let us now look back at Japan in 1950, 2005 and 2050. Japan was a 'perfect pyramid' in 1950; in 2006, it started looking like a 'pagoda'; in 2050, it would start looking like a 'beer glass', small bottom, big mouth, not growing at all. Japanese economy will find it extremely difficult to grow because they would not have enough people to 'consume' its produce. They will also not have enough people for producing things;, but they will have 'lots of savings'. In case of India and China, China' economy looks like a 'pagoda', and India's looks like a pyramid; China' s becomes more of a 'pagoda', India's becomes less of a 'pyramid' more of a 'dome', I call this a war between the 'pagoda' and the 'pyramid'. People like to see this as the 'dragon' and the 'tiger'. It is not like that. It is the pagoda and the pyramid which are going to determine our future. Our dependency ratio hits astride in 2025. After 2025, if things go well for India and Mr Sibal gets everybody educated and trained, nobody can stop India after 2025. But is that going to happen? I don't know the answer. Although we would have more hands to plough and on the keyboards; but, the important thing would be to have them on machines which means industrial growth. India is going through a process of growing without really industrialising. Our service sector is 50 per cent of our GDP , industry is 22 per cent. Overall growth cannot be maintained by going that way alone. India has to create jobs in the factory sector to achieve balanced growth in future.

The late surge being predicted is that: India's middle class will keep growing to reach its peak around 2030. At that time it will be the world's largest middle class. But China is also changing because their pattern of international trade is undergoing change. It is moving more towards North America in terms of Chinese exports. For them,   Asia is becoming less important, Europe is getting more important and SouthAsia is also getting more important. The important thing to take note about China's pattern of international trade is that, it is addicted to the USA. Presently China has a trade surplus of almost $ 220 billion with the USA. If that stops, or if it decreases, that would hit China. Last year   , when the US economy 'contracted' China lost 22 million jobs.

What is China selling to the world? China sells electrical machinery and equipment, most of them low technology stuff; toasters, fans, stuff like that; power generation equipment which is middle technologyapparel which also is low technology based on labour; iron and steel production which is also low technology based on labour; optics and medical equipment, also low technology stuff and footwear, $26 billion worth of footwear . With trading partners like the USA, Japan, Hong Kong, South Korea, Taiwan, Germany, Australia and India; do they really need any more enemies?

China's export market's dependence on the USA, Japan, South Korea, and Germany is pretty obvious. The question really is: Can the USA do without China? My prediction is that the USA can substantially decrease its imports from China, transfer its imports elsewhere, and still get along quite well. Wal-Mart imports US $ 30 billion worth of goods, out of which 10 billion dollars are shirts and shoes. The USA can easily shift that destination somewhere else and China would be in trouble.

To conclude, let us see, what would happen to China in future? It has transited from a 'totalitarian' State to being an 'authoritarian' State. It is now heading towards becoming a 'One-Party' Democracy—not a 'Multi-party' democracy. They don't really want to know anything much about it. There is, however, more discussion and more debate within the Party and that is becoming apparent. Nobody knows, what would happen when China becomes a 'Multi Party' Democracy with a free press, independent judiciary and assured individual liberties? What would happen when China's GDP growth rates slow down because they have not brought 'everybody into the tent?' What would happen when rest of the world also turns protectionist? The 'Tea Party' is already talking of protectionism in the USA. There is also looming crises in Tibet and Xinxiang. If China democratises, then some of these crises would also manifest themselves. Therefore, now it is really up to the Chinese leaders to think about their future course.

The important thing is that four years ago, none of the present leaders were there in the picture. Xi Jinping was not even in the Standing Committee of the CCP. The tussle between the militarists, who talk of threats and military challenges from the USA, demands for more money for the military might pull China the Soviet Union way . On the other hand, the civilian leadership (Xi Jinping is a Shanghai man), would want to move towards business? We do not have answers, for what direction the Chinese leadership or the people may decide to take in the future. But one thing I can predict with surety is that *China is not going to collapse, it is her e to stay and we have to learn to live with it* .

Session 2: Discussion- Part 1

Issue Raised

You gave us a nice projection of comparative growth figures between India and China. In the Indian figures, has the 'parallel economy' been taken into consideration at all by any of our economists? Does it not have any adverse effect on the growth at all?

Response

(a) Parallel economies are constant, so the growth does not matter unless you consider that the parallel economy will grow faster It raises the total GDP but it does not change the rate of growth.

(b) The Chinese did exactly the same thing in 2005. They added 17 per cent to the GDP by bringing in, after a consensus, what had till then been an 'informal' economy.

Issue Raised

Presently, the Chinese economy is basically centrally driven which means it is controlled by the Government. Later, whenever it comes into the private hands; what changes do you expect and what impact it will have on China' future growth?

Response

That impression or deduction is not really correct. The big companies are State owned enterprises but, unlike our State owned enterprises where the joint secretaries rule the roost, in China the State owned enterprises are pretty independent. They are run as autonomous units. That is one aspect. The second is that, it has been empirically evidenced that the FDI companies i.e. the companies with foreign direct investment, actually account for 70 per cent of China's exports. So, the private sector in China is pretty strong and pretty vibrant. Most of the small units are all privately owned. To say that the State controls everything in China is a big mistake. China is pretty much loosely governed now. The State does set guidelines, and the S tate has the ability to jawbone events and also inflation. But let there be no doubt that the industries pretty much do what they want to and they will grow on their own autonomously.

Issue Raised

You began your presentation by saying that China's rise is purely economy dominated and not by politics. But we have these views expressed repeatedly that unless China changes its political system, its economy would go down and the country might break up. May we have your comments on this aspect?

Response

Well, the Chinese political system need not change. If China comes to encounter difficulties, the US economic system would have to change and the world financial system would also have to change. The old Brettonwoods compact predicted a situation, where people do not build up huge trade surpluses. But in the last 20 years, we have seen a situation where people have got huge deficits. The USA now accounts for 70 per cent of the world's reserve currency and can print any amount of it. So, if the USA wants to balance its budget, as Barack Obama has promised in next five years, the US will have to double its exports, which means balancing its trade mostly. If the USA does that, for China it means a declaration of war because that will signal an end of China' high growth period. If that happens, you would not see this astounding growth of China. India' s growth that way is more uniform, it is more driven by internal consumption and internal investments and is less internationalised.

In Chinese economy 'exports' and 'imports' are equal to about 75 per cent of its GDP; and in India it is half of that. So, the Chinese could get hit by that. Last year when the American slowdown took place, the Chinese lost 22 million jobs in the first three months, people were asked to go home and they were worried about disorders. The Procurator General, who had reported 80000 disorders the previous year, reported 120000 disorders in the following year. So, China also is sitting on this tinder keg. If the USA settles down to straighten its economy and its financial system, this 10 per cent growth rate in China would not continue to happen for very long.

Issues Raised

(a) It is said that China is the biggest polluter , biggest exporter and biggest manufacturer. Can all these things be allowed to go on simultaneously and how long will it take them to mend these aberrations?

(b) When people are getting rich in China and would also have more individual liberties (to whatever extent they are granted), why would the Chinese people want to change their system of governance? What is the use of doing that? Why should they change their system of governance to democracy, when the present system is serving them well?

Response

There is no doubt that China is a major polluter but whether it is the only big polluter is a debatable thing. Even we pollute as much; the Americans also pollute, and many other countries also pollute. It however becomes another issue when somebody else wants to impose norms on other countries, where the pollutions are now 'on the rise' like India or China. They stipulate that you will not produce more rice, because that results in methane; and you will not have so many cows because the dung creates methane. The response to such impractical stipulations will be in the 'negative'. They would challenge that and say , what happened when you were burning hydrocarbons for building highways?

So, whether China is going to be democratic we don't know. But one thing is very clear at this moment in China: China is undergoing a period of intense 'nationalism'. It is not just the leaders who are being assertive; even in day to day discourse, the Chinese people are becoming assertive and confident of themselves. They start their talk by asserting: 'We the Chinese', repeatedly when they talk about anything Chinese, especially when they cite the Beijing Olympics. Although the Chinese are going through a phase of intense nationalism, I do not say that they are very happy with the present system that they have. There would be discontented people but mostly people go along with the kind of government they have. It is the elite or the well-educated who are unsatisfied and discontented with the way things are. But people don't really challenge governments and presently people in China think that they are 'going on to good things'.

Chairman's Remarks

On the pollution bit I can say with some confidence that the efforts now being made by the Chinese, to move to cleaner energy and to reduce the carbon emissions, are actually quite incredible and amazing. They are far ahead of us and you will probably find (this is one thing I can predict with some certainty), that is the use of hybrid cars and automobiles, Maglite trains etc., catching up in China much faster than in any other part of the world. They are taking the pollution issue seriously but they of course will not take instructions from anybody. They are a very proud Nation as they should be; and that is also true of their rising middle class. However, I am not so sure about the 'rising middle class' accepting a curb on political freedoms as it seems to be to Mr Mohan Guruswamy. I think expecting a greater freedom is a part of the human development process. It is in the human DNA that you do start expecting greater freedom, and there will be a political transition in China. Whether they can manage it, as the Koreans did, is something which we have to see. I suspect that they will, because they are a very focussed set of people.

Issue Raised

One of the key elements in the 'Five year Plan' in China is structural reforms. What is wrong with their structure now? Will structural reforms in China have anything to do with political reforms? What will be the future consequences of the ongoing structural reforms in China?

Response

They are struggling right now to make China's growth and development more equitable between the regions. That is one problem which they are working hard to overcome. The second structural reform, we are talking about, is 'decentralising the government'even further. The process of doing it has really done extremely well. I have been looking at how China spends money on public servants. In the 1950s, it was 75 per cent of the total salary bill for the 'central government' and only 30 per cent at 'local government' level. Presently, it is the other way round.Whereas in India, it has been that the 'central government' level gets 45 per cent of the wages, the 'state governments' account for 42 per cent of the wages, 'local governments only get 1 1-12 per cent of the wages. So, there is no decentralised government area.

Secondly, when you talk about Chinese democracyI am very fascinated by the debate that takes place within the Party. It is far more vibrant than debates in any of our parties. There are no consequential debates within our political parties in India. I always joke that China has a democratic 'oligarchy' whereas we have a 'multi oligarchic' democracy. Every party has sons, daughters and daughters in law who step in; Lalu has got his sons, Karunanidhi has got his son and daughters. They are all like feuding oligarchies, which come to the people once in five years wanting their votes; there is no debate. Is there any discussion on Five Year Plans and things like that in India? It does not really take place. From that point of viewthe Chinese experiment is quite fascinating. W e are however satisfied with having elections every five years and assuming that we are a democracy.

Since there is a transition period in which the changes take place and Hu Jintao has started talking of 'An Advanced Democracy in 2030', let us see how they experiment with that?

Session 2: Second Paper

Dr Yu-Ning Hwang

It is my honour and pleasure to give a talk at USI about 'China' Economic Future'. In the past few decades China has experienced a very successful economic growth. China's rapid economic growth, at an average growth rate of approximately 10 per cent is one of the most debatable issues. However, it has also widened regional and economic inequalities amongst the Chinese people. In the past 10 years, the per capita GDP has risen more than three fold. With the economic development, increased urbanisation and industrial growth is clearly visible. Urbanisation rate is increasing almost one per cent annually and starting from 36 in 2000, it has risen to 47 in 2009. However, the urbanisation rate is relatively low when compared to most of the developed countries. In the USA, European countries and Japan, it is approximately 80 per cent or 90 per cent.

With economic growth, the ratio between urban and rural incomes has widened from 2.78 to 3.31 in 2008. Furthermore, the genic coefficient reflects the income inequalities. The value of genic coefficient has risen from 41per cent to 47 per cent within the last 7 years. In the aftermath of successful economic rise, new challenges are now coming from widening economic inequalities in China. This has created significant problems for the Chinese government. The discontent caused by the economic imbalances may also cause social instabilities which could further increase political difficulties. The political difficulties may in turn affect the outcome of future economic development. Therefore for China, continuing with the economic transformations is an imperative.

The questions that arise now are: how and whether the Chinese economic and social issues complement each other and would they proceed steadily; how long would the high economic growth persist and how stable and perceptible it would be to the people? Essentially , it is not a problem of economic growth. The problem lies in equitable distribution of the GDP progressively. For a more equal economic distribution of the GDP across the country, the Chinese government will have to establish mechanisms for 'distributional equalities'. The mechanism to improve distributional inequalities may involve market revamp and review of laid down policies. Here, actually the transformation would need to be an ongoing process.

First of all, the market driven mechanism is essentially reflected in flexible and better pricing.With accumulation of capital, productivity of labour will also grow with time. That must get reflected in the rise of wages also. As long as the wages keep getting adjusted, to reflect the higher productivity of labour; that essentially will result in reduction of income inequalities in the country. It is occurring already. In the last two years, Labour Contract Law has been imposed. Starting from June this year, the wages in coastal cities have also risen. This would help in reduction of income inequalities.

Furthermore, rise in wages especially in the coastal cities, will cause the industries to move frequently Some of the industries have already started moving towards the west or to less developed areas. In this case, because most of the industries are labour intensive, taking advantage of low wages in less developed areas, would be more profitable. The rise in wages in the coastal areas will make the more labour intensive industries to move to the rural areas leaving behind capital intensive industries in the coastal cities.

Firstly, this would enhance specialisation in the Chinese economy and would also help in the development of rural areas. On the other hand, as far as the policy leg is concerned, the 12th Five Year Plan, talks of improving 'equality' in the country as 'the top priority'. One of the major processes in this would be urbanisation. Presently, there is a requirement of imposing some policy changes to remove distortions created during the past 'central planning era'.

In the past, the land was not owned by the private sectorEssentially, it was owned collectively. Therefore, land could not be transacted freely. In China, most of the people in rural areas cannot benefit from land transactions. Furthermore, the Huko System has created differences between the rural and urban populations. Essentially the rural population cannot move to a city freely or they cannot benefit as much as their urban relatives. Therefore, right now, China needs to peg certain actions to remove the distortions created by the past policies. Some actions have already been put in place in a few cities to test their efficacy.

The first one is 'land reforms'. Land reforms are essential to re-establish the land market. Thereafter, land can be transacted freely. The second one is to make reforms in the Huko system. Reforms in the Huko system would increase the people's mobility between rural and urban areas, together with regional development policies that would increase urbanisation in the country

There are some distortions in the financial sector also. Most of the banks in the country are large nationalised banks. Most of them finance the needs of big enterprises and national businesses onlyTherefore, that creates financial difficulties for poor people in the rural areas and also for small enterprises in the rural areas. The big banks simply inhibit the economic development of the rural areas. Therefore, it would be crucial to develop more local and small banks to make the financial markets more accessible to the rural population and small/medium businesses; especially in the rural areas. These two steps would be really helpful for the development of the rural areas and reduction of urban and rural inequalities.

Overall, notwithstanding whether it is a market driven or a policy led mechanism, essentially, it will reduce the income gap between urban and rural areas. It will increase urbanisation and growth of the middle class in the country. By ensuring better economic balance, China can become socially more stable and that would be the key to their economic growth in the future. Economic balances in the country would create social stability and that will also reinforce political stability. Political stability would help in reaching social stability and that would result in further economic prosperity Therefore, to achieve long term stability and prospective economic growth, top priority for the Chinese government should be to maintain a stable and peaceful environment instead of going in for military expansionism and other hegemonistic activities.

Development of the Chinese economy would also benefit the world. The economic benefits from a stable Chinese market would be shared globally. Firstly, from the rise in wages, exports will become more expensive; and with improving productivity the Renminbi will also appreciate. Since China has the largest population in the world, development of the Chinese economy will create larger demand for imports from all over the worldAll of this could help in reducing global fiscal imbalances with China. The growth and maturity of the Chinese economy will mutually benefit the whole world. It would reduce global imbalances because China possesses the largest market in the world. China, therefore, will be a crucial key to the economic growth of the global economy.

Imposition of drastic actions, like putting restrictions on China' exports would not be good for the development of the Chinese economyIt will also not be good for the growth of the global economy . Progressive growth of the Chinese economy would create a more peaceful and stable environment around the country and also all over the world. Rest of the world could also share the benefits of the Chinese economic growth and political stability

In conclusion, I would simply add that globalisation is an unavoidable trend in the world today . All the countries are closely interrelated. In a globalised world, as we can see from the global financial crisis, all the benefits, setbacks and shocks can be shared globally . Therefore, we should seek mutual benefit for all. These days, peace certainly is the key to everlasting economic development and should be desired by all people across the world.

Session 2: Third Paper

Mr Prem Shankar Jha

We have just heard two very interesting points of view. The morning session was devoted almost entirely in trying to understand, what China wants to do or is likely to do on the global stage. Mr Mohan Guruswamy has discussed the forecasts of 'China's Future Economic Growth' and Dr Yu Ning Hwang showed us other side of the picture. However, these forecasts depend upon continued stability in China, which requires a number of reforms; Dr Hwang has spelt them out very clearly. The question is whether these are possible and in what timeframe? In a sense, that is going to be the key question. What I am going to try and do is to bring together China's politics and economics to project what we should be watching out for. To do that, I will go back to the original title of the seminar; 'China's Quest for Global Dominance: Reality or a Myth?'

At the starting point, we have had two things that cannot be doubted. First one is China's economic power. It is a growing economic power and we have seen the projections already. The second is the tendency towards 'growing arrogance' and an arrogant use of power . Until this tendency became very apparent, the general impression was that China is basically a status quo power and it is seeking its position in the world order , without wishing to actually change the world order. Now, people are actively asking: is China trying to change the world order to suit its national interests? Both these questions are wrong ones to ask because they are based upon a questionable premise that the Chinese State has sufficient control over what happens within it and around it, for it to be able to translate its intentions into actions. If we were to judge China solely by its intentions I have no doubt whatsoever that China would be in fact a 'status quo' power that has a very strong interest in world peace. The reason is quite simple and we need to understand this in a historical context.

China has the largest reserves of free liquid capital in the world and it is growing at the largest pace than anywhere else — almost everyone else is running in deficit. If you go back to the study of capitalism, you will find that the political power of capitalism depends upon the State's access to and control over liquid capital. In this respect China is phenomenally beyond anybody else. China's potential for using that capital, whether in a soft way to extend its influence and expand its hegemony or as hard power militarily is greater than anything that the world has really seen so far.

China has a very strong reason for using only soft power; because it owes its growth to globalisation and not to the development of capitalism internally. Two-thirds, almost about 60 per cent, of China's foreign exchange reserves are earned from what they call 'trade in processed goods' i.e. last stage manufacture and assembly of products originating in the rest of East Asia. If you look at China's countrywise trade figures, you will find that it has a vast trade deficit with East Asia as a whole; and a correspondingly large trade surplus with the USA and Europe. China being a mid-station, in a huge river of global trade; much like the gigantic thermo-haline current in the Atlantic Ocean, which has been flowing now for the past 60 years. Earlier, it used to be directed from Japan and the East Asian countries to the US and Europe and now it comes through China. China has been incorporated into that. It is earning middleman's profits. This is not a new development. If you go back to the 13[h], 14th and 15th centuries, the entire rise in power of Venice was based upon its middleman status between the orient, whose riches had been discovered by the crusaders, and the European markets, which were hungry for all these goods. Venice became so rich through in 1420 that the budget of the city of Venice exceeded the budget of the entire Kingdom of France. China is in a very similar position today . However, precisely because of this reality, it has a bigger stake in the continuation of this great trade flow uninterrupted than any other country has had in history Therefore, if you were to judge China by intentions alone, it would be a profoundly peaceable country.

If that is so, why is China behaving in this very strange way? Let me go through my list of the way China is now dealing with the rest of the world. There have been 'seven examples' in the last nine months of China taking drastic unilateral action; and saying, we do not really care about what the other countries, negotiation partners or the treaty partners have to say.

The first was this categorical 'refusal', during the last minute talks between Obama and the G4 basic countries at Copenhagen, to accept international monitoring verification of its own independently set carbon emission reduction targets. This is something all the other countries had agreed to. China said 'No' and, therefore, the wording in the Agreement, had to be changed at the last minute to become sufficiently vague for China to be able to sign on.

The second was the manner in which it 'disrupted' the US-South Korean naval exercises in the Yellow Sea, originally scheduled for the end of June. If you recollect, without any ado, China announced live ammunition firing naval exercises to take place in the mouth to the Yellow Sea, precisely at the time when these exercises were supposed to start.

The third was this 'casual announcement' that it was going to supply Pakistan with two more plutonium based and virtually unsafeguarded nuclear reactors in the face of the Nuclear Suppliers Group which had refused to endorse this.

The fourth was its 'threat to stop contracted exports of rare earths to Japan; that is very recent you know about that.

The fifth was 'dispatching of Chinese soldiers into Pakistan administered Kashmir', ostensibly to help in flood relief; not only without recognising that it is a disputed area, but also without the courtesy of at least informing India.

The sixth is the fact that they have on their own started 'building five dams' on the Brahmaputra river, with a capacity of 40000 MW. We do not know of their plans of diverting some of the river streams northwards.

The last of course, is the 'enormous reaction in China', orchestrated against the Dalai Lama as a Tibetan before the Beijing Olympics and against the award of the Nobel Prize to Zhu Sha Bo.

All of these have a certain 'in-your-face' character. The question is, where is it coming from and why? It is coming from a particular form of the 'economic power' converging into 'political power', which comes at the end of every cycle of capitalisms expansion, when there has been a struggle for hegemonic status between the declining hegemon and the rising hegemon. At present, it reflects in the decline of the US and Western hegemony, and 'China stepping in, to fill that gap'. The Chinese arrogance is something that actually reflects their hyper-nationalism; which is a source of danger, but the danger arises on two counts. One is that the decline/collapse of Western hegemony is faster than it may have been because they gave up the doctrines of 'peace through deterrence' in favour of 'peace through pre-emptive military action'. Pre-emptive military action has caught them in a succession of wars without end and this has bled them dry. The USA has spent $ 3 trillion dollars, since the Iraq war began, on a succession of pre-emptive military actions. There is no end in sight because it could now be Iran, it could be North Korea, Israel and Gaza and this thing is going on. With the rise of China, an adjustment of power balances and hegemonic spheres was inevitable; but if one side collapses and the other side expands faster than anticipated, then there is a vacuum that needs to be filled; and it is that expansion which is a source of danger.

The second and more important source of danger is what   Yu-Ning referred to, as the political consequences of the rapid economic growth in China. The political consequences have been internally destabilising. China can still trigger conflict; even war, because wars are seldom a product of rational calculation. The vast majority of wars started through miscalculation, especially due to miscalculation of an adversary's response. In spite of its extraordinary stake in global peace, Chinas recent behaviour suggests that it is in some danger of making precisely this miscalculation.

Is this because of an urge to redress the wrongs of the past or is it being driven by internal developments that its leaders are unable to control? My considered view is that it is the latterChina is making its bid for hegemony in a particularly aggressive manner because the Chinese Communist Party is facing a crisis of legitimacy at home, and it is stoking hyper-nationalism of its newly empowered middle classes to consolidate its hold. In short, it is being threatened with losing its 'Mandate of Heaven'. Therefore, rather than going in for democratic reforms that everyone assumes will automatically happen, what it has chosen is to go for hyper-nationalism.

Regrettably this is making China more unstable and, therefore, more of a danger to regional and world peace. The internal crisis of the Communist Party is reflected in more than 100000 incidents of mass protests that are now taking place in China every year . These protests reflect a growing willingness amongst the people to confront their rulers.

Mass protests in China occur when something that is a part of the Confucian state, the right to legitimate resistance, is ignored by the rulers. That is what has been happening in China during the last 20 years. It is a very serious thing and a challenge for the State. These protests reflect a growing willingness in the people to confront their rulers in the Confusion system, a generalised increase in discontent is taken as a warning signal for the Emperor i.e. the rulers to reflect on wrong things they are doing and mend their ways. The sharp rise in protests, from mere 8700 protests in 1993 is the surest indicator that the rulers, in this case the Communist Party of China, are in imminent danger of losing their 'Mandate of Heaven'.

This warning was given in completely unambiguous terms by Yu Jan Rong, the Director of Social Issues Research at the Chinese Academy of Social Sciences. There has been a lot of writing on this. I will, however cite only one of his warnings because of the importance of what he said. He gave a public lecture in Beijing on December 26 th. last year. It was a long lecture. In the last part he warns, "deepening social fractures were caused by the Communist Party's obsession with preserving its monopoly on power through State violence and ideology rather than justice." Although Yu Jan Rong was a key member of the Chinese Academy of Social Sciences, when he spoke to an audience in Beijing; to the best of my knowledge, he has neither been removed nor has he been sent into exile.

Growing social tensions in China have been commented upon extensively, however, what is not understood is that these are a product of the very same causes that underlie its dazzling growth; and this is what we need to understand. Even today bulk of the actual investments in China are made by enterprises that are not owned by the Central State; but by one or the other 70000 to 80000 central and local governments owned State agencies. These are run by the cadres of the Communist Party   . These cadres are salaried employees who bear none of the risks of making wrong investment decisions and for whom the supply of capital is virtually free of cost. What is more, all of them can to varying degrees command the largely State owned banking system to provide them with the loans that they need for their pet projects. This has led to huge surge in investment because when things are good, everybody invests, you had that happening in 1984 to 1988, you had it even more dramatically from 1991 to 1996 and then you had it again from 2002 to the beginning of 2007.

Each time at the end of such sur ges, there is a huge excess capacity . Thereafter, there is a sudden decline and people stop investing. If you look at the input data (not at the GDP output data which are regularly fudged particularly in recession periods), there are very sharp declines in the use of inputs, including energy. This has happened three times; it is all there to be seen in the data. The problem is at the local government levels, township and village administrations, counties etc. The 7.87 million State and locally owned enterprises that were set up by 1996, tended to go 'belly up'. In fact, during the recession between 1991 and 1997, about 2 to 3 million did go belly up. The pressure of all this comes upon the rural areas and upon the people in the rural areas. This is one of the main reasons for a 'very large and rising income differential' in the country— particularly between the town and rural areas.

The social discontent arises out of this. What Yu Jan Rong's lecture actually shows is that, in the last two years, it has spread to organised labour in the industrial units also. This is important because Andrew Walder had written a very perceptive piece questioning, 'What makes China Stable?' He said, "The social discontent is confined to socially marginalised groups." He wrote this in 2006. This year, he modified the lecture to say, "But, if it moves into the core areas and if there is an external shock, which makes the people feel it as a national humiliation; that could make the people to suddenly stop believing in the Chinese regime." This could make the Chinese regime to fall. This is the precise danger thatYu Jan Rong is pointing to and saying that the solution lies in democratisation only

What are the implications of these issues? What are the possible causes that could trigger conflict in China, which is now relying upon hyper-nationalism for maintaining its internal political stability and giving legitimacy to the Communist Party? What would make it go into an external conflict? First is, anything that disturbs its position in the great river of trade. For example, one thing which would not be acceptable beyond a point is, 'heavy pressure, backed by threats of sanctions, to revalue the   Yuan.' I do not favour this. China should in fact gradually allow the Yuan to go up. But, the basis of this revaluation proposal is Ricardo' s international trade theory . The truth is that Ricardo's international trade theory is no longer operative in its original form where manufacturing has crossed boundaries and capital movement is entirely free. Both these factors were not there in the original theory or in any of the modifications that have taken place over the last 150 years. Therefore, we should be careful about this.

The second equally dangerous thing would be that if China does not do this or things get worse the trade imbalance would worsen, people would start imposing taxes under some pretext. In the USA, non-tariff barriers and a carbon tax is being talked about already. These are major threats.

A third area for China, which affects us, is their inability to assimilate Tibet and Xinxiang. The Chinese do not have in the Confucian system any concept of federalism or making accommodation with the minorities. The only way they deal with minorities is by signifying and bringing them into the value and cultural system of the Han people. They have failed to do this with Tibet. If they continue to fail, they will always point their fingers towards India because of the asylum given to the Tibetan people and the Dalai Lama in India.

Session 2: Discussion (Part II)

Issue Raised (By the Chairman)

My own observation is that China is not a monolith and the Chinese Communist Party also is not a monolith entityYou can see the diference in the pronouncements ofWen Jiabao (when he talks about political transition being a must), and the PLA, which is talking a dif ferent tone altogether. There are clear divides within the Chinese people whereas we keep assuming that China echoes one voice, everything is sorted out and they have got clarity in whatever they want to do. I do not agree with that. There is still a clear possibility that there will be a more liberal part of the Chinese Communist Party and the establishment. Maybe it would be led by the Shanghai people who are far more pragmatic, business minded and not in the business of throwing their weight around like the Beijing and the northerners are. The Shanghai people might just still win because, there is a great realisation in China that their cart is inextricably linked to the global horse; and if they do fall foul of the global order, then they will not achieve what they want to achieve. In the background of such distinct difference in perceptions amongst three segments, the Chinese establishment is gaining an upper hand.

Response

First, you can get a little bit of empirical evidence from the Internet. The evidence on this is absolutely overwhelming. All our sinologists have it. They are in touch with others and there is also enormous amount of secondary writing based upon the original stuff. I will give you some very specific examples of this. In 2008, when the Dalai Lama had convened the 49 [th] Anniversary Commemoration Ceremony of his fleeing to India, there was trouble in Lhasa (in the monasteries) and it had spread to Guangzhu. Greater Tibet is 25 per cent of the land area of China, therefore, when anything spreads out of theTibet Autonomous Region (TAR) into the adjoining areas; it becomes a very serious threat to the Chinese. At that point in time, there was a sudden and total outburst of Chinese reaction on the Internet. The word used about India was that it is 'an evil' country. One of the other things that was said was, "India needs to be taught a lesson."

Next thing was in Xinxiang, last year. At that time, a Chinese lady in Urumchi had lamented to a BBC correspondent, "We converted this place into a paradise and look, how ungrateful they are, why are they trying to destroy it? 'Ungrateful' was the word on all the websites when they referred to Tibetans; and 'evil' was the word used about India. Lastly , there are several other actions, which reflect that these are not the actions of a country that is willing to keep in mind other peoples' sensitivities and that it intends to maintain peace with others. These are the actions of people who want to show to their own people that they have the power to intimidate others and get away with it. That is hyper-nationalism.

Five years ago, a 42-year old lady had written a little book about Confucius. She was a school teacher and was using it to teach. It was suddenly picked up by the Chinese Government and she became a National icon. This book was printed 'in the millions' and sent out, because it emphasised one part of Confucian doctrine to the people which was 'the absolute duty, to obey'; and ignored the second part of Han Confucianism called "Imperial Confucianism" which comes from Mentius which says, "It is the duty of the Emperor to be virtuous and, when he faces generalised discontent, to first reflect on where he may have gone wrong." This idea was embedded in the most serious crisis that the Chinese faced during Tiananmen Square protests of 1989 referred to, as the 'Tiananmen Square Massacre' by some westerns and as 'June Fourth Incident' by the Chinese.

Chairman's Remarks

Does anyone want to add anything more to that or a different view regarding China's hyper-nationalism? Is it the dominant tendency in China today or is there a trend of any other possibility in the future?

Response

Essentially, the military actions of China are an indication of defending themselves, instead of attacking others. This is one of the reasons why

Chinese military acts in that way. I would like to mention two possibilities pertaining to political instability in the country or in the region. If the country is essentially 'socially unstable' domestically, it could lead to political difficulties. There is also a possibility of partisan politics resulting in arousal of the Chinese National vision.Another thing I would like to point out is that actions of the Chinese Government and the Military are essentially dependent upon different voices domestically. As long as there are causes for social instability in the country, there would be a possibility of some kind of conflict or political tensions. Essentially China is acting to 'defend itself instead of playing an active role to take offensive action outside the Country.

Issue Raised

There are two different views on China's economic development versus social inequality. The first one is that, since economic development continues to raise people's quality of life in China, it gives legitimacy to the Communist Party rule. However, according to Samuel Huntington, in most of the developing countries, if their GDP level reaches around $5000 per capita there is likelihood of the social instability rising even further.In the face of these two conflicting views, what are the future prospects of the Chinese economic development and the rise in social inequalities in the country?

Response

On the question of economic development versus social stability, I would agree with the first view. Right now in China, most of the people are in the 'labour phase' and there are still inequalities and differences between the rich, wealthy and the poor But, as long as they continue to give a better life to the poor, they would have stability.Therefore, future economic growth in China will make the society more stable in that Country

Issues Raised

One of the Panelists had talked about land reforms in the rural areas of China. Is that true or is it still incomplete? In this context what is the present status of the regularisation of Huko in urban situations?

Responses

(a) Land reforms are not happening all over the country as yet. Presently, land reforms are essentially taking place in some parts like Chengdu and in rural areas. Land reforms are coming in, to enable the market mechanism to work in the land transations. Firstly , there is need to assign land to the people in rural areas. Thereafter, either the Government can purchase the land from them or they can sell the land through market transactions. The people and investors, who are interested in developing this region, can do so simply by going to the market to buy land tickets; and then to propose a (development) plan for starting development in the region. This is how at present land market is being established in Chengdu region. In the long run, maybe the land market mechanism would be established all over the country However, it is not likely to happen in the near future.

(b) As far the Huko system is concerned, right now it is essentially between two parts i.e. the rural and urban areas. The people in these two areas are completely separated. They cannot shift or change their Huko very freely. Therefore, if your Huko is in rural area, and you also find a job in the urban city—you cannot change your Huko. This means that you cannot benefit from the social welfare programmes that the urban residents are entitled to. This stipulation would cause difficulties for some people who work in the cities, and move back to the rural areas to take care of their lands and agricultural production. It is an obstacle for people's mobility between the rural and urban areas.The Huko system, therefore, needs some reforms. This problem in the social welfare programme has already been recognised and the Huko system is being reformed gradually

Issue Raised

What is your view or estimate of the PRC's economic development in the short term i.e. the next five years?

Response

In the short term, the Chinese economic development will continue with its current projected growth rates. I am also confident that in the next five years, same pace of economic development would be maintained as it has happened in the last ten years.

Issues Raised

In early part of the 21 st Century, Hu Jintao had announced W estern Area Development Programme. However, in 2008, there were riots in Lhasa; and in 2009, there were disturbances in Xinxiang. Is there any co-relation between the 'development programme' that was launched in early part of this century and the 'social instability' being witnessed in the last couple of years?

Response

On the question of reliance of the regime upon growth for stability: whether this would be successful, and to what extent it is viable? The first is that, reliance on growth for stability policy is a post-Tananmen Square protests (1989) happening. It was actually based on a paper that Jiang Zemin wrote in 1990; it was called a kind of neo-liberalism in China. He said, "Combine nationalism with rapid growth in order to marginalise the people who are being hurt by economic liberalisation". This was the understanding arrived at post-Tiananmen threshold, where the losers of the mid-1980s had come out on the streets (including students, workers and a lot of the cadres themselves) because they were on fixed salaries and inflation was destroying their incomes in front of their eyes. This policy was not challenged within the Communist Party till about 2000.

In 2000, the Central Committee received a detailed report prepared by the Central Party School over the previous four years. It was a survey of 'Cadre versus People' relations. Most of it was just never released. Three years later, after Hu Jintao and Wen Jiabao had been anointed, one thing was released to the public. They had found that all the Party cadres looked upwards for orders and had lost complete touch with the masses. This is what really scared them and that is where the origins of Hu Jintao's 'social harmony' programme lay. In 2005, when the rise in protests had gone up to 87,000 from 8700 in 1993, Hu Jintao used the data of Survey done in 2000 to begin his 'social harmony' policy. This clearly shows, there is already a great understanding in the China Central Committee (CCP) that 'growth by itself does not provide political stability'.

The Blue Book of Chinese Academy of Social Sciences also pointed out that, on an average the number of people per demonstration in 2005 was 10 times the number in 1993. This means that there was a 60 fold increase and that was just the beginning. Nowadays, the scale of discontent is much larger. This obviously reflects that the Chinese have not been able to find the right answers to the problems agitating the minds of the people.

Basically, there is only one answer; which in fact is, 'decentralisation of power, away from the Communist Party'. This aspect has been brought out clearly by MacGregor in his book 'The Party'.

Issue Raised

My question is related to the Chinese hyper-nationalism and greater assertiveness in various fields being witnessed by the world. This may result in China getting a misperception of its capabilitywhich could in future trigger a situation which may go out of control. Is this perception being allowed to be generated deliberately or is it happening on its own?

Response

I agree with you completely. In China, destabilisation could come from a feeling of 'national humiliation'; because, the Chinese have increasingly begun to rely upon 'nationalism' to hold the Party together and to assert its legitimacy.

Issue Raised

Is there a land market system operating in China?

Response

In spite of the fact that between 50 to 70 per cent of the residential and office space (that has been built in China in the last 10 years), is still 'lying vacant', this continues to be the most 'bounding sectorof investment today. It is bounding despite every effort possible by the Central Government and major banks to slow it down. Surprisingly , all the constructed space gets sold, although it may remain vacant for a long time. The reason is that 'money in the bank is getting very low or actually (in real terms) negative returns.' Since the middle class in China is getting very rich, buying an apartment is one sure way of getting a permanent title to use a bit of land or apartment. The way Chinese are wondering and worrying about, how to keep their savings intact is entirely different from us. That is why the Chinese real estate sector continues to maintain its 10-15 years old 'bubble'.

Session 2: Chairman's Concluding Remarks

Dr Rajiv Kumar

Let me just end the session by a couple of insights. One is that in China today 'net exports demand' contributes 10 per cent of the GDP; whereas, it is negative one per cent in the case of India. Their domestic consumption is 35 per cent. Their savings rate is above 50 per cent. That sort of a model does look increasingly vulnerable in a global economy which is trying to find a new balance and norm. There are clear signs that in the coming decade the global economy would not be growing at the same rate as it has done in the past because there are problems in Japan, in the USA and in Europe. How successful China would be in raising its share of domestic consumption and lowering its dependence on the external market is a key issue. Here we need to take note of the perceptive remarks often made that 'so far it was not China which exported to the USA, it was the USA which imported from China', through companies like   Wal-Mart, Nike and so on. Is there a likelihood of them being replaced by Chinese companies and being successful? That would be difficult. It is also difficult to believe that this switch from external demand to internal demand would be made easily because creating internal demand also requires negotiating your way through the whole bureaucracy which is quite large in the Chinese situation. The aspect that needs consideration is that continuing with the rate of growth of 10 per cent in the next five years or so could be difficult; with the people in business wanting correction in the global imbalances.

The second remark is about the inequalities that have come up in China. Perhaps the Chinese Communist Party would be successful in developing the central and western provinces because there is a huge focus on shifting infrastructure development westwards. They are giving massive incentives to their firms to make investments in the central and western provinces. It is a fact that the 20 million or 22 million people who went out of jobs with the recession were sooner or later absorbed within the system, without there being a great disruption. That part of the Chinese actions breeds confidence. The uncertainty lies in, whether the Chinese would be able to switch from external to internal demand, as rapidly as they would wish to do.

At the end of the day, what we need to take from whatever has been said, comes from a Chinese proverb; " *We all expect to live in ver y interesting times*". In the coming days, we will all be watching how China grows in the future.

As for India, of course, the next 20 years are critical.We need to have internal stability and a benign external environment because we need to achieve 10 per cent rate of growth as we go forward. Our key priority today is our economic growth. I just hope that we would not find anything happening on our northern borders or from our western neighbour to disturb our external environment, because we need peace and stability for our growth. We have to actually exercise all our ingenuity and intelligence to make sure that we maintain a balanced relationship with China which would give us a window of opportunity for growth in the next 20 years.

With that ladies and gentlemen, allow me to close this session and thank the panelists on your behalf also.

Third Session

Development of China's Military Capability (Part 1)

Opening Remarks	Lt Gen PK Singh, PVSM,AVSM, (Retd), Director, USI
Chairman's Introductory Remarks	Lt Gen Vinay Shankar, PVSM, AVSM, VSM(Retd)
First Paper	Vice Adm H Kaneda (Retd), Okazaki Institute, Japan
Second Paper	Brig Gurmeet Kanwal (Retd), Director, CLAWS, New Delhi
Third Paper	Vice Adm AKSingh, PVSM, AVSM, NM(Retd)
Fourth Paper	Dr Ming-Hua Tang, Taipei
Chairman's Concluding Remarks	Lt Gen Vinay Shankar, PVSM, AVSM, VSM(Retd)

Session 3: Opening Remarks

Lieutenant General PK Singh, PVSM,AVSM (Retd)

Yesterday, in Session-1 we discussed 'China's Grand Strategy' and in Session-2 we looked at 'China's Economic Future'. Today the thread between the 'strategy' and the 'economy' would be inter-linked and that would be connected with developments in the military field. Since issues related to China's military modernisation are of great interest to the USI members and our Services fraternity we decided to cover this in two sessions.

The first session is being chaired by Lieutenant GeneralVinay Shankar. He is not only a distinguished member of USI, he is also a Member elect of our Council. Earlier, he was the Director General ofWeapons and Equipment of the IndianArmy and the Director General ofArtillery. After his retirement he has been a prolific writer on matters of security. More importantly, he has been advising the private sector about getting into the defence field. What is not known to many of us here today is that he also participated in the 1962 operations and that is a separate storyHe participated in the 1965 and 1971 wars also. It is my privilege to introduce him to you all.

The panelists in this Session areVice Admiral Kaneda from the Okazaki Institute, Japan; Brigadier Gurmeet Kanwal, Director of CLA WS, Delhi. We also haveVice AdmiralAK Singh, the former FOC-in-C of theAndaman and Nicobar Command. He also commanded the Eastern Naval Command, the Indian nuclear submarine and was the Director General of the Coastguard. The last speaker is Dr Ming Hua Tang from Taipei. I would now request General Vinay Shankar to commence the proceedings.

Session 3: Chairman's Introductory Remarks

Lieutenant General Vinay Shankar, PVSM, AVSM, VSM (Retd)

Yesterday morning, China' s 'Grand S trategy' was discussed and it was indeed very insightful and absorbing. Today, as the Director said we are taking the thread forward. Looking at the PLA would be a long session. It is relevant and pertinent that this subject be discussed exhaustively because over the years a mystique and myth have tended to surround the PLA and we need to demystify that somewhat. W e need to understand the PLA much better, particularly in the Indian context. For us in India, the PLA is a very important subject. We have a 4057 km long border with China, most of it is disputed. Lot of the areas are claimed by the Chinese, which led to a war with them. I was there during that war; and in the deliberations that took place yesterday, there was a talk of bringing the spirit of China into this auditorium. I will try to bring the spirit and ghost of the PLA into this auditorium because I was involved in direct combat with them for a short period, around this time 38 years ago - from November 14 -18, 1962. Even today in some areas, we are in eyeball to eyeball contact with the Chinese and the PLA. In many areas patrols are meeting each other very frequently and on quite a few occasions the meetings are not so friendly. We have territorial issues about, what we believe is our territory and these manifest in many irritants that we are exposed to from time to time. Therefore, to us and to quite a few in the audience: Japan, Taiwan, South Korea, Vietnam, PLA would be a matter of serious concern.

I will briefly go back to PLA 's Nanchang Uprising of 1927, that is when the Red Army was born. During the 1934-35 Long March of the Communist Party of China, it was bloodied and it went through all kinds of experiences which are a legend to date in the PLA. During those days, of course, it was the Red Army. In 1949, when the PRC came into being, the Red Army became the PLA, the National   Army. Groomed entirely on guerrilla warfare tactics and a peoples war approach to warfare, it performed creditably in the Korean War from 1950-53. Its achievements there were pretty impressive. Subsequently in 1958-59 it was ruthless and efficient in suppressing the Tibetan rebellion and then occupying Tibet. Thereafter, in 1962, India suffered a humiliating defeat. Clearly, the PLA's performance right upto 1962 is something noteworthy Post-1962 the PLA got intimately and seriously involved in the Cultural Revolution and Nation building within China.

The first negative exposure of the PLA was in 1979, when they moved into Vietnam. From that experience, they learnt many lessons. Then they embarked on improving and modernising the PLA which till then had been a predominantly infantry oriented organisation. It is from 1979 onwards that they started modernising, building up their industrial base and looking at warfare more holistically.

Truly we have got to look at the PLA since then. What are the recent issues that have attracted attention where the PLA   is concerned? T ake 1996, when they did the famous war-game and lobbed missile across the Taiwan Straits. Subsequently in 2001-2002, they did not hesitate to bring down an American plane which had violated its air space. Since then onwards; we are witnessing, what is happening today or has happened over the last six months, seven months to a yearIf you look at all this, obviously there are many issues pertinent to the PLA that need to be flagged. Yesterday's discussions arrived at some kind of a consensus that the 'Role of the PLA' is diminishing in influencing Chinas national policy and strategy and national objectives. I do not know whether the panel here, now and subsequently, will agree to that position. It is a debatable issue.

Next, I will flag off a few issues which we need to delve in and discuss as we go along. First is this business of 'tantalising catch phrases' that we have been alluding to for many years - 'people'   s war under modern conditions', 'limited war under hi-tech conditions', 'informationalisation' and whatever other phrases. Whenever we heard those expressions, at least when I was in service, the Chinese grew a few inches taller because we were very impressed by these catch phrases. But, there is a serious case to analyse them as to, how these translate into specific military actions? What do they mean? When we delve into them, then maybe we will come to conclusions whether they are abstractions or are they just phrases to a 'theory kind of a formulation', i.e. something they use as a benchmark? What are they? One lesson that is very clear is that the Chinese do look at war as a 'whole nation approach'. The term 'People's war' it says, 'is people's war under modern conditions'; and if you read Mao Tsetung and his various quotations that are attributed to him, this message comes loud and clear throughout his statements. In a 'people's war', people are the most important ingredient. 'People' in their term is the whole nation. So, how does the whole nation get integrated into what the PLA wants to achieve, is a big question.

The second point I want to flag is this business of, 'China becoming a Global Military Superpower.' Now let me compare China with the USA. The USA today has a defence budget of US $700 billion. China's budget today is US $100 billion; the ratio is 7:1. Chinese budget has been growing at the rate of 10 per cent annually over the last 22-23 years and let me extrapolate that it is going to continue to grow at that rate. By 2025, it will go up to approximately US $350 billion. That ratio is, again, and even if the USA does not increase its budget, still a ratio of 2:1. The USA is looking at a force level total of approximately 1.5 million as against 2.2 million of the Chinese. Apart from that is the issue of 'technology'. The Chinese are severely constrained from this 'businesses' of 'access to technology'. Therefore, even if they have the money even if they want to pump in more money, where do they get the 'technology' from? Earlier, the Israelis were close to China and were giving technology till the Falcon deal was called off, and technology inflows were prohibited. Same is the case with the European Union, the European nations and of course the USA. So, presently their access to technologies is from, maybe Turkey, Pakistan, or somewhere else clandestinely. The Russians have also withdrawn technology from 2000 onwards. Therefore, if you do not have access to technology, even if you have the money, you have a long journey to cover if you want to move forward. That is the next challenge.

Therefrom, arises the question of China's superpower status, in terms of its economy and military power. Economically, China will perhaps, if it keeps moving as we are projecting, surpass the   American economy by 2030. But, what matters is, what happens militarily? The next question is about Superpowers. The Soviet Union and the USA were militarily equal but economically the Soviet economy was a 'third world' economy; yet for 50 years the Soviet Union, together with the United States, was a Superpower. Now, when we have a changing dynamic, where economically China will become comparable to the USA, but whether militarily also, is questionable. Therefore, how do we define comprehensive national power and how do we deduce whether China is a Superpower? Unless, of course, we deduce that 'credible nuclear deterrence' largely neutralises conventional military superiority. So, that is the next big question.

Third issue is the point that came out yesterday. The Chinese and the PLA 'appearing to be 10 ft tall'. My take is, they are definitely not. But, it is when we address those catch phrases and we analyse them deeply   , then we will be able to draw a better deduction of, what exactly the PLA is all about?

Lastly, from my point of view 'China's Rise' is inevitable; however, there is a big question mark whether it would be peaceful or otherwise. More so, because the Chinese have till date never baulked and never hesitated to use military power. Therefore, if this kind of brinkmanship is natural to them; when would the things run out of their control, that also is difficult to predict. Having made these introductory remarks, now I will request Vice Admiral Kaneda to kindly take the floor

Session 3: First Paper

Balance Of Power in the Western Pacific

Vice Admiral Hideaki Kaneda (Retd)

China announced a national defence budget for FY 2010 of approximately 519 billion Yuan, about 9.8 to 10 per cent up from the previous year Thus, China's official defence budget recorded a growth of over 10 per cent for 22 consecutive years in terms of the initial defence budget. This pace of increase in official defence expenditures means that the defence budget doubled every five years, and that the official national defence budget of China has nominally increased eighteen fold over the last 20 years.

China has been giving top priority to handling of the T aiwan issue, more specifically to improving their capability to hinder the independence of Taiwan and foreign military support for   Taiwan. Furthermore, in recent years, China has begun to work on acquiring capabilities for specific missions other than the Taiwan issue.

As regards a long term plan for China's military modernisation, China proclaims it will lay a solid foundation by 2010, basically to accomplish mechanisation, and make major progress in informationalisation by 2020; and then to almost accomplish the goal of modernisation of national defence and armed forces by the mid-21st century.

China has reduced the number of its military personnel, mainly in the army, and has been modernising equipment of its entire armed forces, especially its naval and air forces, and nuclear and missile capabilities.

As for ground forces, China is improving i t's mobility by switching from its past regional defence model to a nationwide mobile model, working to mechanise its infantry and, in addition strengthening its airborne troops and special operations forces.

The Chinese Navy has introduced modern submarines to enhance its submarine force; added surface combatant ships with improved air defence and anti-ship missile capabilities, and increased and improved its landing ships and supply ships. Through those improvements, it is believed that, China is trying to build-up their maritime capabilities to operate in distant areas far away from China's shores. Moreover, several high-ranking military officials have expressed positive views on acquisition of aircraft carrier battle groups.

The Chinese Air Force and Navy have approximately 1,950 combat aircraft in total. The number of 4^h generation fighters is rising steadily such as domestically produced (J-10), under license-produced (Su-27) fighters, and imported (Su30) fighters equipped with improved anti-surface and anti-ship capability. In addition, China is making continuous efforts to improve its in-flight refuelling capabilities, early warning and control systems. Moreover, China intends to import a number of large cargo aircraft from Russia. It has also begun to enhance electronic warfare and intelligence gathering capabilities.

China has continued independent efforts to develop nuclear capabilities and ballistic missile forces, seemingly with a view to ensuring deterrence, supplementing its conventional forces and maintaining its voice in the international community. China has already acquired a large number of nuclear weapons and ballistic missiles, and is working to increase performance by extending ranges, improving precision, introducing Multiple Independently Targetable Reentry Vehicle (MIRV) and other new means such as ASBM (Anti-Ship Ballistic Missile), while updating liquid type propellant to solid type propellant to improve survivability and readiness.

China continues to put forth eforts for Space development. As it appears in China's Space development, military and non-military sectors are related. There is a possibility that China utilises Space for military purposes; such as information gathering, communications and navigation; and offensive weapons, such as ASAT. China is reported to be having strong interest in Cyber Warfare and they are believed to have oganised huge Cyber Warfare-specialised units.

As stated before, although China has begun to work on acquiring capabilities for missions other than theTaiwan issue. China is undoubtedly giving top priority to handling of theTaiwan issue. Chinese core strategy for achieving that purpose is called as "Anti-Access/Area Denial (A2/AD) Strategy."

The overall military balance between China and Taiwan is clearly shifting in favour of China. In view of the fact that China is enhancing its missile, naval and air forces specifically the Taiwanese military needs to modernise its equipment. The US government decided to sell P AC-3, AH-4D attack helicopters in 2008, and PAC-3, UH-60 helicopters and Osprey-class mine sweepers in 2010, but Taiwan still wishes to buy submarines and F-16C/D from the USA.

Session 3 : Second Paper

China's Military Modernisation and Emerging Doctrine

Brigadier Gurmeet Kanwal (Retd)

Information warfare and electronic warfare are of key importance, while fighting on the ground can only exploit the victory. Hence, China is more convinced (than ever) that as far as the PLA is concerned, a military revolution with information warfare as the core has reached the stage where efforts must be made to catch up and overtake rivals.

**General Liu Huaqing,
Vice Chairman, Central Military Commission [1]**

Introduction

India's unresolved territorial and boundary dispute with China and an un-demarcated Line of Actual Control (LAC) on the Indo-Tibetan border do not augur well for long-term peace and stability between these two Asian giants. Territorial and boundary disputes that are carried over from history and left unresolved carry within them the seeds of future conflict. The next major incident on the LAC could possibly lead to a localised border conflict, as either Indian patience with Chinese intransigence wears thin or the Chinese could view Indian attempts to build infrastructure and develop the border areas as adoption of an aggressive forward posture. Hence, in the foreseeable future, a limited border war between the two Asian giants, though improbable, cannot be entirely ruled out. China's continuing opposition to India's nuclear weapons programme; its nuclear and missile collusion and intimate defence cooperation with Pakistan; its support to the military regime in Myanmar; its covert assistance to the LTTE (Liberation Tigers of Tamil Eelam) in Sri

Lanka and increasing activities in the Bay of Bengal; its attempts to isolate India in the ASEAN Regional Forum (ARF); and, its relentless efforts to increase its influence in Nepal, Bhutan and Bangladesh; are all pointers to a carefully orchestrated plan aimed at the strategic encirclement of India.

PLA's Modernisation Thrusts

The People's Liberation Army (PLA) is rapidly modernising itself and is known to be preparing to fight a 'limited border war under hi-tech conditions'. China is engaged in developing a "revolutionised, modernised and regularised people's army with Chinese characteristics (it is) endeavouring to transform its armed forces from a numerically superior to a qualitatively superior type and from a manpower-intensive to a technology-intensive type, as well as to train high-quality personnel and improve the modernisation of weaponry in order to comprehensively enhance the armed forces combat effectiveness."[2]

The Gulf War of 1991 had brought about a rude awakening as China realised that there was a wide gap between its technological capabilities and those of the West. In August 1991, President Jiang Zemin said, "The Gulf War let us further realise the importance of technology in a modern war. Although we believe that the decisive factor in winning a war is human power not firepower, advanced weaponry is very important and we cannot neglect (the impact of) science and technology (in a modern war). Despite the rhetoric about 'human power', the Chinese military planners were forced to accept that the PLA was still in the so-called 'people's war' groove and that it would be quickly out-gunned, out-manoeuvred and hopelessly upstaged electronically if it were to face a modern army or , air force and navy, for that matter. Since then, the Chinese defence budget has witnessed a double-digit rate of growth.

Land forces are receiving the least priority in the PLA modernisation plans. The Chinese are engaged in developing rapid deployment capability with strategic airlift for the PLA. One rapid reaction division is being given to each Military Region. The PLA is improving its air defence capabilities, EW systems, mobility for its field formations and logistics support to them.

Heavy investments are being made in introducing better C4I2SR systems at the tactical, operational and strategic levels. Para-military forces have been downsized consistently over the last two decades. The PLA is steadily improving the logistics infrastructure inTibet. With the inauguration of the Gormo-Lhasa railway line, it can now pre-position large war-fighting stocks in Tibet over a single season to obviate its difficulties in building-up for and then sustaining a ground conflict. The road infrastructure in Tibet is also being improved and new airfields are rapidly being built. With regard to China, India faces what Professor Raju GC Thomas calls a "capabilities-intentions" dilemma.[4] China is rapidly creating enhanced capabilities for trans-border offensive operations. While the intentions appear to be benign at present, these can change virtually overnight, as has often happened in history.

Military Doctrine: Active Defence and Local Wars under Conditions of Informationisation

Since China's ignominious incursion intoVietnam in 1979, PLAdoctrine has evolved from Mao's "people's war" to "people' s war under modern conditions" through a "limited/local war" phase to the current doctrine introduced in 1993. The new doctrine is more assertive than the previous one and is not bound by any restrictions to confine and limit future conflict to within China's national boundaries. Underpinning the new professionalism of the PLA is the basic doctrine of "active defence" *(jiji fangyu)* that seeks to conduct "people's war under modern conditions" better understood as "local wars under hi-tech conditions" – *gaojishu tiaojian xia de jubu zhanzheng.*

The 'active defence' doctrine calls for integrated, deep strikes – a concentration of superior firepower that is to be utilised to destroy the opponent's retaliatory capabilities through pre-emptive strikes employing long-range artillery, short-range ballistic missiles (SRBMs) and precision guided munitions. The new doctrine and the strategy and tactics associated with it have been influenced by the lessons of Gulf War I in 1991 and the Iraq War of 2003, both of which have been extensively studied by Chinese scholars. The doctrine requires the creation of a capability to project force across China's borders through rapid deployment, conventional SRBMs and cruise missiles, information warfare, electronic warfare, precision-guided munitions, night fighting capabilities and other advanced military technologies. Beijing has defined the following five likely limited war scenarios: Military conflict with neighbouring countries in a limited region; military conflict on territorial waters; undeclared air attack by enemy countries; territorial defence in a limited military operation; and, punitive offensive with a minor incursion into a neighbouring country.

The PLA expects to fight the next war under conditions of what it calls "informationisation" or "informationalisation"[5] In the White Paper on National Defence issued in 2004, informationisation was explained only in general terms, but bears repeating: "T o adapt itself to the changes both in the international strategic situation and the national security environment and rise to the challenges presented by the RMA worldwide, China adheres to the military strategy of active defense and works to speed up the RMA with Chinese characteristics:[6]

(a) To take the road of composite and leapfrog development.

(b) To build a strong military by means of science and technology

(c) To deepen the reform of the armed forces.

(d) To step up preparations for military struggle.

PLA analysts have called the ongoing RMA an "informationised military revolution"[7]. It emerges that informationisation "clearly relates to the PLAs ability to adopt information technologies to command, intelligence, training and weapon systems. This would include broad investment in new automatic command systems linked by fibre-optic Internet, satellite and new high-frequency digital radio systems... The PLA can also contest the information battle space with its new space-based, airborne, naval and ground-based surveillance and intelligence gathering systems and its new anti-satellite, anti-radar, electronic warfare and information warfare systems...there is increasing 'information content' for new PLA weapons as it moves to link new space, airborne and ELINT sensors to missile, air, naval and ground-based 'shooters' to enable all its services to better use new precision-strike weapons."[8] According to the 2004 White Paper, "In its modernisation drive, the PLA takes informationalisation as its orientation and strategic focus." The PLA has adopted what it calls a "double historical mission" and a "leapfrog development strategy" – accelerating military informationisation while still undergoing mechanisation.[9]

Cyber-Warfare Challenge

Developing Cyber Warfare capabilities is seen as presenting a level playing field in an otherwise David versus Goliath scenario as Chinese hardware is no match for the weapons technology fielded today by the USA and its allies. Recent cyber -attacks directed against T aiwan and the USA is indicative of the efforts to develop new techniques, viruses and logic bombs. Information warfare will be crucial in the opening phases of a war aimed at the re-unification of Taiwan or a border conflict with India as it will be important to knock out the adversary' s communications infrastructure by cyber as well as physical means. A private army of young civilian hackers on whom the state can bank during crises is being developed for this purpose besides the employment of regular PLA personnel.[10]

Conclusion

Compared with China's historically reactive stance of luring the enemy in deep and destroying him through strategic defence, the present doctrine is essentially pro-active and seeks to take the battle into enemy territory . It also strives to achieve surprise in a pro-active manner that is demonstrated by new 'quick-strike' tactics. The aim is to catch the enemy unprepared in order to inflict substantial damage on strategic targets and disrupt logistics to gain psychological ascendancy . While the land frontier is expected to continue to generate some local tensions, the Central Military Commission (CMC) has identified space and the oceans as the new areas where future conflict might take place.

China is modernising rapidly and steadily enhancing its military capabilities. The military gap between China and India is growing as India' military modernisation is constrained by its low defence expenditure, which is now less than 2.0 per cent of the GDP . The Chinese are continuing to drag their feet over resolving the territorial and boundary dispute with India. Hence, China poses a long-term strategic challenge to India as a competing regional power inAsia, but will remain a military threat till the territorial and boundary dispute is resolved. India needs to take this reality into account and distinguish between what China professes, i.e. peaceful co-existence, and what it actually does. I n the near future, a situation of tenuous peace and tranquility is likely to continue to prevail along India'Himalayan frontier. It will be punctuated increasingly by patrol face-offs, Chinese incursions and intrusions across the LAC and new claims on Indian territory   , as it happened in the Finger area of the Sikkim plateau in May-June 2008.

Endnotes

1 General Liu Huaqing, Vice chairman of the Central Military Commission, in Edward Timperlake and William C. Triplett III, *Red Dragon Rising: Communist China's Military Threat to America* (Washington, D.C.: Regnery Publishing, Inc., 1999), p. 121.

2 White Paper on *China's National Defence in 2000*, www.china.org, October 2000. Issued by the State Council, Beijing.

3 Pr esident Jiang Z emin in Andr ew Lai, "Pr eparation f or High-Tech Regional Wars: Beijing's Strategic Shift in Military Policy and its Impact on the Modernisation of China' s Arms", *Institute for National Str ategic Studies – Strategic Forum*, Washington D.C.

4 Enunciated by Pro f. Raju G. C. Thomas during a lectur e on "I ndian Security Policy after Nuclearisation" at the United Service Institute, New Delhi, on November 5, 1998.

5 Western governments and analysts are using both the terms "informationisation" and "inf ormationalisation" inter-changeably. It has not been possible to get an exact equivalent to the corresponding Chinese phrase from an authoritative source. From the point of view of language aesthetics and phonetics, the term informationisation is preferred here. It is also to be noted that the Chinese themselves now increasingly prefer the term informationisation in their writings.

6 *China's National Defence in 2004,* White Paper on national defence published by the Government of the People's Republic of China.

7 Zhou Fangyin, "The Impact of Information Revolution upon Military Affairs and Security", *Contemporary International Relations,* 7 (2001), p . 28.

8 "China' s M ilitary P ower: An Assessment f rom Open S ources", Testimony of Richard D. Fisher, Jr., International Assessment and Str ategy Centr e, before the Armed Services Commit tee of the US House of Representatives, July 27 , 2005; www.strategycenter.net.

9 Ka Po Ng, *Interpreting China's Military Power: Doctrine Makes Readiness"* (Abingdon, Oxon: Frank Cass, 2005), p. 109.

10 Mac William Bishop, China's Cyberwarriors, *Foreign Policy, September/October 2006,* http://www.foreignpolicy.com/story/cms.php?story_id=3553

Session 3 : Third Paper

Vice Admiral ArunKumar Singh, PVSM, AVSM, NM (Retd)

China's Four Modernisations

After Chairman Mao passed away in 1976, Deng Xiaoping embarked on the following four modernisations inthe undermentioned order of priority:-

(a) Agriculture.

(b) Industry.

(c) Science and Technology.

(d) Defence.

Though defence was initially , the lowest priority , the Chinese were pragmatic enough to take advantage of the 1991 collapse of the USSR, to hire about 5000 scientists and specialists in various fields ranging from space, missiles, aviation, ship and submarine building, nuclear propulsion, tanks, artillery etc. The Russian government took action to get these specialists back by 2000, by which time China, despite sanctions on armaments from the USA and the EU, managed to get significant indigenisation done, though hi-tech weaponry still eludes them.

China's economic growth is based on exports of various types and imports of large quantities of oil and gas. Hence, rapid growth of Chinese sea power was inevitable. In addition to its claims ofTaiwan, and territorial disputes in the South and East China seas, China had to use innovative measures to overcome its 'single coast' location, and the 'Malacca dilemma'.

China's Eleven Challenges

China faces the following eleven challenges, which require it to dedicate considerable funds, manpower, and focus: -

(a) Insurgencies in Xinjiang and Tibet provinces.

(b) Labour unrest (e.g. Sichuan province in 2010).

(c) China concentrates a lot of its military capability on its territorial claims on Taiwan, the South China Sea and the East China Sea.

(d) In addition it earmarks forces for its boundary dispute with India, and also for securing its SLOCs e.g. sustained three ship anti-piracy patrols in the Gulf of Aden since January 2009.

(e) Uneven economic development.

(f) 150 million floating population.

(g) Environmental pollution.

(h) Growing energy demands.

(j) Natural disasters.

(k) Allaying fear of neighbours.

(l) Managing risk in large scale financial investments abroad. e.g. loss of about 480 billion US dollars in US treasury bonds.

(m) Water shortage and potential water wars with neighbours e.g. Vietnam, Cambodia and India.

Chinese Sea Power Linkage to Economic Rise

China's economic rise is dependent on exports and imports of large amount of raw materials (steel) and energy (oil and gas). All this requires China to invest heavily in becoming a two oceans (Pacific and Indian oceans) sea power. The following are noteworthy aspects of China's focus on the sea:-

(a) China is the world's largest fishing nation.

(b) It is the second largest oil importer (mostly by sea).

(c) It has a very large merchant fleet, both International and Coastal.

(d) Over 52 major seaports and 16 major inland river ports connected to the sea.

(e) China has 492 shipyards with 288,000 workers.

(f) Chinese yards contribute 84 per cent to domestic shipping (Indian yards 2 per cent).

(g) China has a Navy of about 930 ships and submarines. By 2020, will exploit space for sea power linkage.

Comprehensive National Power and Global Power

In 2007-08, China's Academy of Social Sciences (CASS), promulgated a list of 10 countries in order of their Comprehensive National Power (CNP) where the USA is at No 1, China at No 6 and India at No 10. The basic inputs for CNP are a combination of a nation's hard and soft power, along with its scientific and industrial base, and other factors like the genius of its people, geostrategic location, the political will and strategic vision of its leadership, and demonstrated capability along with military potential. The CNP list is as follows –

(a)	The USA	-	First
(b)	The UK	-	Second
(c)	Russia	-	Third
(d)	France	-	Fourth
(e)	Germany	-	Fifth
(f)	China	-	Sixth
(g)	Japan	-	Seventh
(h)	Canada	-	Eighth
(j)	South Korea	-	Ninth
(k)	India	-	Tenth

In September 2010, a new list of 'Global Power   ' nations was promulgated by a joint report of United States National Intelligence Council (USNIC) and European Union Institute for Security Studies (EUISS). This joint report made the following list of 'Most Powerful Nations/Blocks" wrt 'Global Power' for 2010 and 2025:—

(a) 2010 (Most powerful nations)

    (i) USA   -   22% global power (GP)

    (ii) China   -   12% GP

    (iii) India   -   8% GP

(b) 2010 (Most powerful blocks)

    (i) USA   -   22% GP

    (ii) European Union -   16% GP

    (iii) China   -   12% GP

    (iv) India   -   8% GP

    (v) Russia, Japan and Brazil - Less than 5% GP.

(c) 2025 (Most powerful nations)

    (i) USA   -   18% GP

    (ii) China   -   16% GP

    (iii) India   -   10% GP.

(d) 2025 (Most powerful blocks)

    (i) USA   -   18% GP

    (ii) China   -   16% GP

    (iii) European Union -   14 % GP

    (iv) India   -   10% GP

(v)   Brazil (rising) and Russia, Japan (both declining) - 5% GP

New Military Doctrine of 1990s

In China the Central Military Commission (CMC) issues guidelines to the military. The Chinese gradually evolved and promulgated the concept of 'Active Defence' in 1956, 1964, 1971, 1980 and 1993. Over the years, the concept of Active Defence has retained the two undermentioned principles:–

(a) It must be 'Active Defence' and not 'Passive Defence'.

(b) Seize initiative early in the conflict.

Active Defence has evolved as follows:-

(a) In 1956, the then Chinese Defence Minister Peng Dehuai, suggested the concept of 'Active Defence' to the CMC.

(b) In 1964, the CMC adopted Active Defence, as a concept of "luring the enemy deep, fighting people's war, fighting annihilation warfare, and fighting movement warfare". This was done to face three threats viz from the East (USA), from the North (USSR) and from the South (India).

(c) In 1971, to focus only on the threat from the USSR, the CMC, changed to only "Active Defence and luring the enemy deep".

(d) In 1980, with growing confidence on its ability to "fight the enemy at the border", the CMC, deleted "luring the enemy deep" from Active Defence.

(e) In 1993, the CMC promulgated a "Hi-tech warfare   doctrine of two modernisations" known as the "Military Strategic Guidelines for the New Period". This new guideline implies the creation of a capability to project force beyond China's borders through rapid deployment, conventional SRBMs and Cruise Missiles, IW, EW and PGMs.

(f) In 1993, the Chinese promulgated "two modernisations" as follows:–

(i) To convert the Armed Forces to fight local wars under modern conditions.

(ii) To change the Armed Forces from being based on quantity to quality.

(iii) Subsequently, IW, networking, jointness, ideal man-machine interface were also added.

(g) In 2010, a new concept of "Non-Contact W arfare" (NCW) was being discussed. NCW envisages, demoralising and "teaching the enemy a lesson" or defeating the enemy "without fighting directly", by using a combination of cyber and electronic warfare, economic warfare, precision strikes by ballistic and cruise missiles on targets with low probability of collateral damage and surgical strikes by air power-cum special forces. NCW is also known as a doctrine of "shifting from a war of annihilation to a war of paralysis".

In addition, the Chinese have focused on jointness, "informationisation" (a combination of RMA and network centricity), hi-tech force multipliers, Cyber Warfare and Information Warfare.

Chinese Navy Modernisation

The Chinese Navy (PLAN) has about 930 ships and submarines (about 100 of them are blue water capable), 800 aircraft, 58000 marines and manpower of over 257,000. China hopes to cross the undermentioned milestones by the times indicated below:-

(a) By 2010, to be capable of handling situations in Taiwan and China sea, i.e. "first island chain",

(b) By 2020 to be capable of power projection beyond 1000 nautical miles, i.e. "second island chain".

(c) By 2050 to be capable of power projection in the Pacific Ocean upto "third island chain" and also the Indian Ocean.

PLAAF, RRF, IW & EW, and Space

The CMC directive is for the Chinese Air Force (PLAAF) to have quick reaction integrated combat capabilities. The PLAAF with over 393,000 men has 3400 fighters (mostly 3rd generation). It has the following capabilities:-

(a) Provide Maritime support upto the 2nd Island chain, with air refuellers and anti-ship cruise missiles.

(b) With ALCM strike targets in South Korea and beyond Tokyo.

(c) Airlift one Division (15000 men) in one go.

(d) Carry one Para Regiment (3000 men) for para drop in one go.

(e) Carry two battalions (1600 men) by helicopters in one go.

(f) During Exercise "Stride - 2009" moved 50,000 men, rapidly, 1200 to 1600 kms, by a combination of airlift and high speed rail from major regional commands (stationed in the cities of Shenyang, Lanzhou, Jinan and Guangzhou).

The Rapid Reaction Force (RRF), also known as REMCF (Resolving Emergency Mobile Combat Forces), can deploy three divisions (43rd, 44rth & 45th Paras) within 36 to 48 hours to counter any threat to Chinese national interests. This RRF is expected to expand, and is likely to be the spearhead of any Chinese offensive action against Taiwan, Vietnam, South Korea or India. The RRF is under the direct control of the CMC.

China has a very capable Information Warfare (IW) and Economic Warfare (EW) organisation in place and the impact of its cyber warfare are felt worldwide.

In Space, China presently has 40 satellites for various civilian and military tasks. It expects to become a global Aero Space Power by 2020.

Chinese Ballastic Missiles

The Second Artillery is responsible for holding and exploiting all China's land based Ballistic Missiles (with conventional and nuclear warheads). Of the 1900 ballistic missiles of all types (SRBM,MRBM, IRBM and ICBM) only about 200 are IRBMs and 100 are ICBMs. The number of newer DF-31 ICBMs and JL-2 SLBMs is not yet known, as these missiles and the Jin class SSBN is not yet fully operational.

Chinese Cruise Missiles, ASAT, BMDS and SAMs

China has over 1000 cruise missiles of various types, including   ALCM, ground launched, ship and submarine launched. These are capable of anti-ship and land attack functions.

On 11 Jan 2007, China successfully tested an interceptor missile (possibly a modified DF-21D) against a low earth orbit satellite.

On Jan 2010, a modified DF-31D missile successfully intercepted an incoming ICBM in the 2nd (mid-course) phase outside the earth's'atmosphere. Earlier only the USA had demonstrated this capability.

The S-300 SAM system of Russian origin has a range of over 150 kms, and covers the entireTaiwan straits. China is also building a indigenous version.

Chinese Land Forces

Chinese PLA (Army) has strength of 1.6 million, with modern tanks, artillery air defence and rockets.About 400,000 troops are earmarked oppositeTaiwan for amphibious operations in support of the Marines.

In addition to the 40 infantry divisions, China has 60 divisions of the 'Peoples Armed Police', who are basically disbanded PLA units.

In Tibet, the Chinese have enough infrastructures (including airfields, railways and roads) to induct, support and maintain about 20 divisions. Logistics dumps have been created in advance, along with good roads, upto the 4000 km long border with India.

Chinese Soft Military Power

The Chinese have a concept of demoralising the enemy to "win without fighting" or "win small battles to gain big victories". The three facets of Chinese "Soft Military Power" are as follows:-

(a) Public Opinion Warfare. Incite ethnic nationalism, lower the possibilities of international intervention and intimidate the enemy

(b) Psychological Warfare. Destroy enemy morale.

(c) Legal Warfare. Justify and legitimise its provocations for war.

Two Nuclear Armed Proxies of China

As is well known, China has the following two nuclear armed proxies:-

(a) East Asia. North Korea to keep South Korea and Japan "pre-occupied".

(b) South Asia. Pakistan to keep India in South Asia.

In addition, given its energy requirements, China may try to improve relations further (to get a strong foothold in the oil richMiddle-East), with Iran and Saudi Arabia by supply of missiles and even nuclear weapons.

Chinese Defence Budget

China's defence budget is opaque and is   about 2 to 3 times the budget actually promulgated in March every year In 2000 the promulgated budget was US$14.6 billion or 121 billionYuan. In 2004, it was US$ 25 billion. In 2008, (US $ 57.22 billion), in 2009 (US$ 70.27billion) and in March 2010 (US $ 78 billion). Analysis indicates a 1 1-12 per cent growth (inflation adjusted) against a national GDP growth of 9 -10 per cent (inflation adjusted).

Chinese Defence Budget-Allocation Estimates

The Navy gets the pride of place with an estimated 35 per cent allocation of the Defence budget. The Army and Air Force get 29 per cent each, while the 2nd Artillery (Strategic Forces) get an estimated 7 per cent.

Chinese Navy Force levels

Since Commander Sandeep Dewan of USI is presenting a detailed paper on the Chinese Navy in Session 4 today, I will cover this aspect briefly. As Eastern Fleet Commander , I visited Shanghai in September 2000, and conducted basic exercise with the Chinese Navy . I also visited an export version of a Frigate, which had very modest technology.

The Chinese Navy, like the Indian Navy is still in a period of transition to genuine blue water capability and may achieve this by 2025 -2030. More disturbingly since 2005, China has built long range HF radars (Ground wave with a range of 200 kms against ships and aircraft, while the Sky wave type gives ranges of 4000 to 6000 kms and covers the large parts of the eastern Pacific and the Bay of Bengal along with south-south western parts of the Arabian Sea, and parts of the Indian Ocean, south of Indonesia.   As mentioned earlier, the Chinese Navy has only about 130 blue water capable ships and submarines. Its first aircraft carrier the 65,000 ton Shi Lang (ex-Varyag) is expected to sail by 2015 and it will take 10 to 15 years for China to master the art of carrier aviation.   Two more 50,000 ton carriers are expected to be inducted by 2020. China is today producing eight different types of destroyers/frigates, theYuan class conventional submarine, the yet to be proven Shen class SSN and the yet to be provenJin class SSBN (with the JL-2 SLBM having a range of 7200 kms). LSD has been built and was deployed for three months in the Gulf ofAden anti-piracy patrols.

PLA Navy Fleet Commands

(a) The PLA Navy North Sea Fleet HQ is based in Qingdao, and also has a part of the nuclear submarine force.

(b) The PLA Navy East Sea Fleet HQ is based in Ningbo.

(c) The PLA Navy South Sea Fleet HQ is based at Zhanjiang. It has nuclear submarines and the new Sanya Naval base (on Hainan Island) in its jurisdiction.

Chinese Navy - Trends in Overseas deployments

In the decade 1980-1990 China sent two   Task Groups (TGs)   to four countries. During 1990-2000 it was 10TGs to 30 ports in 20 countries. And from 2000 to Oct 2010, it's 15 TGs to 30 countries.

Chinese Aero Space Power

China has about 40 satellites for various civilian and military tasks. By 2011 it will have a regional GPS, and by 2015, a global GPS. It expects to be true Aero Space power by 2020.

China's Over the Horizon Targeting

As mentioned earlier, China in an attempt to overcome its geographical limitations of sea power has made innovative attempts to detect ship targets at long ranges (and possibly target them with long range ballistic and cruise missiles), by the introduction of Over The Horizon Targeting (OTHT), High Frequency (HF) Radars. It has a OTHT (HF- Ground Wave) radar chain to cover the Taiwan and Taiwan straits with a range of about 200 kms. For the Asia Pacific, Indian Ocean (south of Indonesia), Bay of Bengal, and south west Arabian sea, China has built three to four OTHT (HF- Sky Wave) radars, with a range of 4000 to 6000 km. Australia and Russia also have similar HF-Sky Wave radars, while the UK has one HF-Ground Wave Radar.

String of Pearls

To reduce the risk to its SLOCs in the Indian Ocean Region (IOR) China has embarked on the 'String of Pearls' concept of creating   port facilities from which it could pipe oil and gas, and also move goods by road and rail to and from China. The list includes the undermentioned:–

(a) Pakistan. Gwadar port on Pakistan's Baluchistan coast, was built by China, and is located just 360 miles from the Straits of Hormuz. In 2005, Pakistan signed a 40 year contract with PSA (Port of Singapore Authority) to enable PSA to operate the port. Now in 2010, Pakistan has initiated steps to cancel this agreement and hand over the port to

China. Gwadar port is being linked by road, rail and oil pipeline to Xinjiang province in China, through the Karakorum pass.

(b) Bangladesh. China is building two deep sea container terminals at Chittagong port, and wants to connect Chittagong by a motorway and 111 km railway to Yunan province via Myanmar. In addition, it's building the brand new Sonadia port at Cox's Bazaar.

(c) Myanmar. China is building Sittwe port and also has an 'Electronic Listening Post' in Cocos island.

(d) Sri Lanka. China is building Hambantotha port (3 times larger than Colombo), and the nearby Mattala International Cargo Airport. In September 2010, China has also won a contract to build a new container terminal at Colombo port.

PLA Multi-National Exercises

China has been carrying out military exercises with Russia, Pakistan and the SCO. It has been carrying out very basic exercises with the Indian Navy and Army, and may exercise with the Indian Air Force in future.

Future Developments

By 2018, China may begin induction of a fifth generation fighter, advanced tanks, artillery SAM systems etc. By 2020, it may induct a large 20,000 ton, indigenous SSBN type submarine capable of launching 20 to 24 SLBMs, and also induct two indigenous, 50,000 ton aircraft carriers.

Implications

The implications of China's economic and military rise are self-evident, even though their maybe an element of bluff with regard to the actual capabilities or operational induction of   some systems. As recent events indicate, China will create tensions to advance its interests and territorial claims in the South and East China seas, and also against India. Its GDP (expected to cross 20 trillion US dollars) may overtake USA by 2035, and it should become a true super power   with a two oceans Navy by 2050, if there is no political turmoil.

China is also aware that at 9 per cent GDP growth, India may overtake China's GDP by about 2045, and India too could become a superpower with a two oceans Navy by 2050. Hence China will continue to aid Pakistan, and find new allies in the IOR to keep India 'within South Asia, and in a state of low equilibrium.'

After 2030, India could expect an increased   presence of Chinese warships and intelligence trawlers in the IOR, with the attendant risk of minor incidents escalating into conflict.   The options available to India include : amending its 'no first use' nuclear policy, increasing its sea power and spending more on national security.

Session 3: Fourth Paper

Dr Ming-Hua Tang, Taipei

Today, I would like to introduce the security environment, military strategy and defence transformation inTaiwan, in five parts. In the first part, I would like to introduce the 'international strategic environment'. After the Cold War, many scholars agree with the global situation as follows:-

(a) Global strategy to oppose the USA the only superpower , is the multi-power including the EU, China, Russia and India.

(b) The larger scale or full scale war is not likely to happen globally. But, war in some flash points is still possible to break out.

(c) Each country has to deal with arms proliferation, sovereignty disputes, famine panic, climate change, energy security and economic development through cooperation by the international and regional organizations.

(d) With the China rising in economic and military power the surrounding countries feel the pressure and the threat, especially in Japan, Korea, India and even Taiwan.

In the second part, I will introduce the 'trends' that China pursues. What does China feel about its security environment and sovereignty dispute? With reference to the US policy of 'regional containment', if you look at the North EastAsia region, they have a US-Japan mutual cooperation and security treaty. They have military cooperation through joint military manoeuvres and get togethers. In South East Asia region, the US has strengthened cooperation with Asia, e.g. in this year the Secretary of the US S tate Department Hillary Clinton said "South Sea China is the core interest". That is a hint we need to take a look at. In the SouthAsian region, the USA wants to strengthen its cooperation with India and Pakistan; e.g. the US will sell arms to India worth more than US$1000 billion in the next six years. They also have better economic and trade relations with the USA. In Middle Asia also they have set up several operations e.g. they have established military bases in Uzbekistan and Afghanistan to have better relations and cooperation between the regional countries. So, we can conclude that what US has done is not just aimed against China; but, the strategic deployment is meant to somehow to contain China.

Now I will take a look at countries that might have a conflict with China:-

(a) Japan. They have the East China Sea problem and Senkaku Island.

(b) India. The Indians have a border dispute with China. The India specialists will know all this and about the PLA military expansion in the Indian Ocean.

(c) China's claim on the South China Sea. The island sovereignty is a very important issue and as mentioned by the US Secretary of State, 'South China Sea is the core interest for the USA '. That is a flash point. We know that Taiwan, Mainland China, Vietnam, Philippines and Malaysia are the countries that have a claim on 'all' or 'part' of sovereignty in the South China Sea. In the last few decades they had 12 military conflicts with each other Taiwan seeks unification, but do the Beijing authorities want to do this? But for Taiwan, I want to say that, in this situation do not be in a hurry for unification with mainland China.

(d) USA. The US military power is involved in the dispute in Korea, Japan, Taiwan and South China Sea issue. So, that is the reason mainland China will create the so called uncertainty and deny that.

(e) Korean Peninsula . Many military conflicts have happened on the Korean Peninsula. They also have the North Korea issue.

China's National Interests. We can see the Chinese economic interests. It wants to enhance its Comprehensive National Power (CNP) to ensure the safety of their global economic strategic interests and guaranteed access to energy and strategic resources. On the issue of security interests, China seeks peaceful and stable environment and enhanced comprehensive national security. Most importantly, China wants to ensure the integrity of its national territory. The third issue is its political interests. China wants to keep the domestic politics stable and enhance its economic prosperity in the national interest. That would enhance the Chinese influence in the international field to keep its position as a leading power.

The Chinese Defence Policy and Militar y Strategy. The Chinese Defence Policy has ensured peaceful and guaranteed national development peacefully. For Mainland China, it is very important that they have a peaceful environment to make the military modernisation possible. That would make the defence and military force build-up to conform to the national interest. Third is: 'Strengthening and Force Building in the Information W arfare', both for protecting itself and contesting others. The military strategy towards 'active defence' issue.

Insisting on the Self Defence Nuclear Strategy. The policy is to use it for self-defence - they don't want to use it for 'first strike'. The next issue is to create a security environment that is beneficial for national development peacefully. The military strategy of 'active defence', strategically insists on defence and self-protection and to gain advantage by retaliatory strikes only after the enemy has struck.The second is 'limited war' under conditions of 'information invasion'. Third is to deal with the various security threats and to achieve the capability of implementing various military missions. Next point is: 'Strategy of the Military Modernisation.' Originally Deng Xiaoping proposed this idea/philosophy. Right now, it is economic policy and until Hu Jintao they combined together the economic and defence modernisation together. So, we know the three stages of military modernization. He hoped to set up a firm military foundation by 2010 and then by 2020, to carry out best possible modernization and to make great progress in informationalisation capabilities. Third part is to achieve the goal of military modernisation by the middle of 21 st century. He also hoped that in the third part i.e. until middle of the 21 st Century, they also want to catch up with the middle countries like France, the UK; and to have the GDP rise may be US$ 30,000.

China's Defence Transformation and Force Build-up. First, we take a look at the Army. For Mainland area defence, China wants to enhance its mobilisation capabilities to transfer forces rapidly across different military regions. On the other hand, talking of their ability to carry out multiple functions smoothly, it wants to develop 'joint air-land'operations; and also 'first strike' and 'special operations' capabilities.

Second part is the Navy . China wants the 'of f shore' defence to transfer to the 'far sea' defence and also spruce up its two oceans strategy. The Navy wants to enhance its defence potential by improving:-

(a) Blockade Capability.

(b) Anti SLOC's Measures.

(c) Maritime Land Attack Capability.

(d) Anti-ship Capabilities.

(e) Marine Transfers Protection.

The third part is theAir Force. The strategy for homeland defence has two functions defence and attack.The Air Force wants to enhance following capabilities:

(a) Reconnaissance and early warning.

(b) Air strikes.

(c) Air defence or missile defence.

(d) Promote its 'strike projection'capability.

The Second Artillery now wants to have the capability of, 'Limited Nuclear Deterrence Capability'. It wants to use its conventional nuclear weapons firstly as a 'deterrent'; and secondly it follows the strategy of 'no first use of nuclear weapon' as policy.

The last part is to look at the Chinese 'defence transformation and force build- up'. The current developments indicate it wants to strengthen it's 'anti-access' and 'area denial' capabilities. That is very important for them. Last month, we had a conference in the   Taiwan where we talked about A2 and AD capability. Some American think tanks have created the term 'counter anti-ASATs concept. That is very important from the US side, to counter anti-ASATs. The second one is strengthening of 'long range and air-sea power' and 'precision strike' capability. My American friends worry much about the Dong Feng 21D, which is an anti-ship ballistic missile. The third one is 'setting up a satellite system' and 'anti-satellite weapons' (ASAT). That is how China wants to strengthen its military operations other than war. The military operations other than war include anti-terrorism, anti-piracy, anti-aviation, security, protection, disaster relief, and Space cyber warfare for safety and security. Finally, I will say that China's PLA wants to transform its defence forces from 'quantity' to 'quality' performance and from 'labour' to 'technology' intensive.

To conclude, the PLAmilitary strategy point is very simple. It wants to enhance its nuclear deterrent capability by enhancing its surveillance system and Aero-space capability. It wants to get some long range precision strike weapon and develop the 4th generation fighter and the future generation air operations support aircraft. Also expand the range of air defence missile and air to air battle missiles, aircraft carrier and deploy the new surface underwater combat ship and strengthening their warfare capability and send special operations and reconnaissance force. Last thing they want to develop is information operations capability and cyber warfare capability

Session 3

Chairman's Concluding Remarks

Lieutenant General Vinay Shankar, PVSM, AVSM, VSM (Retd)

Ladies and gentlemen, instead of opening the house for questions and answers right now, the Director has suggested that we do all the questions and answers after the second stage of the presentations. It will be prudent to address all the issues together after we have heard the next panel of speakers.

I will not try and summarise what the Panelists have said because most of what has been said does not need to be summarised. But, I will flag just three issues. One is a question I have for Admiral AK Singh and another to Dr Tang. They both said that China is looking at 'assimilating Taiwan' and that it is their first immediate strategic objective, the question I would like to ask is: What is the timeframe? Do they have a timeframe in mind? That is very relevant. The second is: All panelists have talked about the enormous arsenal of missiles that the Chinese have developed. Whereas the range is in large numbers, the point to be taken note of is that till now only conventional warheads are being used, if you do a cost benefit analysis of the destruction at the target end the lethality of the warhead, its accuracy the sum that will emerge is something that we need to look at very carefully Therefore, are we drawing the right conclusions on this extensive massive use of missiles only with conventional warheads and their impact at the other end? The third issue is what Brigadier Gurmeet mentioned about the 'precision guided systems' and that the Chinese arsenal is limited in this context, and while they are trying to build-up on it, where will they get the technology from? Because, in some types of missiles the technologies are complex. I will leave it at that.

Fourth Session

Development of China's Military Capability (Part II)

Session 4 : Opening Remarks

Lieutenant General PK Singh PVSM,AVSM (Retd)

In this Session we continue with Part II of our discussion on, 'Development of China's Military Capability'. The Panelists from different countries will present their views about China's enhanced military capability and also the response of their own countries to it.We will also hear the Indian viewpoint through Indian scholars and others' responses to them. This Session will be chaired by Air Commodore Jasjit Singh.

The panel consists of Professor Ma Cheng Kun from National Defence University (NDU) Taiwan, Commander Sandeep Dewan, a serving Indian naval officer who is a scholar at the USI, Professor Changhee Park from Research Institute on National SecurityAffairs (RINSA), South Korea and Professor Srikanth Kondapalli from Jawaharlal Nehru University (JNU). I will now requestAir Commodore Jasjit Singh to take over the proceedings.

Session 4 : Chairman's Introductory Remarks

Air Commodore Jasjit SinghAVSM, VrC, VM, (Retd)

Ladies and gentlemen, General Sinha, former Army Chiefs, distinguished people on the Panel, looking at the time factorI am not going to say anything right now. If there is anything that I have to contribute I will try and say something at the end. Therefore, may I first request Professor Ma Cheng Kun to initiate the discussion.

Session 4 : First Paper

China's Anti-Ship Ballistic Missiles

Professor Ma Cheng Kun

Ladies and gentlemen, it is my pleasure to attend the USI's conference and give my presentation to all of you today . The subject of my presentation- 'China's Anti-Ship Ballistic Missiles' (ASBM) is attracting much attention these days. This is a very hot topic. Recently, two countries have begun to pay full attention to the development of China's ASBM capabilities. One of them is the USA and the other is India, because both of them have aircraft carriers. Secondly, probably in the future, India and the US Naval power will face challenge from China in the Western Pacific Ocean and the Indian Ocean. Therefore, it is necessary to study the development of China's ASBM capabilities today. Basically my presentation will be based on the Chinese perspectives, which would be quite diferent from the Western perspective.

First of all, I want to talk about the 'most important considerations' for China to develop ASBM. Maybe, the Western observers think that China wants to develop ASBM capabilities in order 'to deter the American naval force from entering the Taiwan Strait area' during a conflict in the future. In addition to this, China still has another three considerations to develop ASBMs. First, ASBM is a cheaper and faster way than building aircraft carrier as a strategic weapon to deter the US Navy from approaching China's maritime periphery. So far, China has tried to develop two weapon systems, in their strategy to counter the US Navy The first one is an aircraft carrier However, to build an aircraft carrier is a very expensive project and would take a long time. As we know, China purchased the Russian made aircraft carrier Varyag, in 1999. Although 11 years have already elapsed, still the first indigenously built aircraft carrier is not available to the PLA Navy. The Chinese understand very well that to build an aircraft carrier is a very complex project. Therefore, by deciding to develop Second Artillery Force they have chosen a cheaper and faster weapon system than the aircraft carrier. That means they have converted their original DF21 MRBM into ASBM to speed up the development of their anti-ship capabilities.

The second consideration is that, ASBM is a more practical and asymmetrical weapon system to counter the US Navy in the Western Pacific Ocean. The Western observers would have to worry more when the PLA Navy would have aircraft carriers, because they will use them to counter the US aircraft carriers in Western Pacific Ocean. The Chinese understand that even when they can build their own aircraft carriers they would basically be incapable of conquering the US aircraft carriers because the US aircraft carrier technology is far more advanced and has operational experience for more than half a century. Therefore, China is convinced that it is neither possible for them to surpass the US aircraft technology nor to match their operational warfare capabilities. Consequently, to develop and use ASBM instead of aircraft carrier through asymmetric operations is a more practical way to counter the US Navy. They have realized that this is the best way to deter the US aircraft carriers from approaching the Taiwan Straits.

Last consideration is the 'internal competition' between the Services in the PLA, especially between the Navy and the Second Artillery Force. The bureaucratic competition among the different Services in the PLA is quite intense. Different Services try to increase their political influence, among the military in order, to get more budget allocation and to increase their say on political decisions of the CCP leadership. Therefore both, the Second Artillery and PLA Navy, use the development of a 'strategic' weapon as a pretext to get more budgetary allocations and to increase their own political influence among the PLA. That is why, over 10 years ago, the PLA Navy claimed that they want to build an aircraft carrier. Soon, thereafter, the Second Artillery Force also claimed that they want to develop ASBM. It is very interesting that both, weapon systems have similar purpose of 'deterring the US aircraft carrier force'. Surprisingly, although they have the same strategic purpose, China has separated the resources and budget into two dimensions to develop two different strategic weapon systems.

The only answer for this dichotomy is the bureaucratic competition between different Services among the PLA. So, that is the Chinese perspective.

The Western observers' interpretations of the Chinese 'main considerations' for developing ASBM are different. To begin with, we should take note of the technology issue. Even though China has decided to develop this kind of strategic weapon system, they still need to overcome (especially) some technological difficulties. The first difficulty they need to overcome is the technology of 'terminal guidance'. The DF 21 basically is a 'ground to ground' ballistic missile. Its flight (in attack) is dependent on the initial transitional trajectory. But, to strike a moving tar get on the surface, you need to change the flight of the warhead in the terminal stage. For the terminal stage, basically the altitudes are less than 40 metres; because the speed of the warhead flight is very fast (it will roughly reach Mach 7 or Mach 8) it would have less than 20 seconds during the terminal stage. Therefore, changing the trajectory of the warhead during the terminal stage is very difficult. Therefore, some additional device on the warhead is needed to achieve this. The first technical difficulty is of web transparent material for the guidance communication and 'data linkage' between the headquarters and the warhead in the terminal stage. The first requirement is to develop the web transparent material on the warhead. Second requirement is to put on the warhead the 'active target seeker' and the third is to put a guidance synchronization device on the warhead. There is also a need to have an expiry date on the warhead. What is the possibility of China overcoming these difficulties? The answer is positive. Dong Feng 15P can strike with terminal guidance. If we look at the parade held last year in China, they demonstrated the Dong Feng 15P in it. This type of missile is equipped with GPS system and circular laser These kinds of devices can get digital pictures from GPS to match the target and that can modify the direction during the attack stage. The warhead is basically equipped with an auxiliary tail, which helps in the function of changing the trajectory of the warhead. In the future, China's ballistic missile strike accuracy is likely to be reduced to less than 15 metres.

In addition to this, in short range and medium range (SRBM and MRBM) missiles also they have developed this kind of technology successfully. The DF 21C, displayed in last year's parade, has a long range of 1700 km and is also equipped with 'millimeter wave terminal guidance system' for high altitude middle course flight. They are also equipped with the GPS system and circular laser and auxiliary tail in order to change the terminal flight trajectory of the warhead. This was the first technical difficulty China needed to overcome to develop a successful   ASBM. So far, they have already displayed two types of missiles with terminal guidance system. In conclusion we can say that basically they have now overcome this technological difficulty.

Now we come to another technological difficulty they need to overcome: How can they extend the range of the ASBM in order to hit a moving target on surface with precision? DF 21 is a medium range missile. After the launch, it takes 20 minutes to reach a moving target. During these 20 minutes, a US aircraft carrier navigating at the speed of 30 knots, would move away upto a distance of 20 kms from its original position. The purpose of this missile is to deter and paralyse the aircraft carrier instead of destroying it. Therefore, they would not load it with a nuclear warhead. When they load it with a conventional warhead, they need to strike the target precisely otherwise it would lose its purpose. The problem lies in getting the missiles in flight to strike a target which moves away from its original position upto 20 kms in 20 seconds. The only way to extend the warhead's attack range is to try to extend the middle course flight above the atmosphere i.e. roughly 200 km altitude. China has tried to overcome this problem by using a way we call 'post glide skip wave' twice or thrice in order to extend the flight of the warhead in the orbit and in the middle course.

Therefore, to develop this kind of technology successfully they need to develop three things successfully: First, a manoeuvrable re-entry vehicle; second, the thrust action booster; and third, vector thrust. Whether they overcome these problems or not, can be found from Senso 5 Manned Space Flight-operated in 2003. Basically it shows that China has already succeeded in controlling the orbit changing technology and China has also developed orbit switching technology. China has claimed publicly that they have already successfully developed this kind of orbit switching technology. They view this as a breakthrough in their Space technology development. Therefore, it is clear that China has already overcome the two technological difficulties it faced for the ASBM development.

The third technological issue is C5SR.To operateASBM for attacking the surface moving targets is not an easy operation. Basically, it is a very complex operation and which needs linkages between different command and control unit or systems. All these units are spread across the Space, in the orbit, to the satellite receiving station, UnmannedAerial Vehicle (UAV) and the ground based radars, e.g. the 'over the horizon' (OTH). Basically the operations are organised by several units, just like a network. It is not an easy thing to do, especially with the present Chinese organisation due to existing rivalry and bureaucratic competition. China has used at least one OTH radar in South Eastern coast province. This radar is monitoring distances over 3000 km. Since OTH radar has already surfaced on duty, it shows that they are gradually overcoming these difficulties. In Space, China's Space based Reconnaissance System has launched eight satellites into orbit this year; which includes two reconnaissance satellites, three positioning and navigation satellites, and two other communication satellites. China has launched 10 remote controlled Reconnaissance Satellites in the last five years - half of them equipped with Sympathetic Aperture Radar (SAR). China's Satellite system can overlap the area between Ground Receiving Station and the Space, which means that, if China wants to use ASBM to strike a moving target in the area overlaid by the Ground Receiving Station, they can conduct these kinds of operations. Of course, this would also include North India.

In conclusion we can say that, if China wants to develop the DF 21D they do have a theoretical model to do so. The launch range will be under 1700 km because Dong Feng's long range is 1700 km. But since you need to put a lot of complex devices on the missile, the weight of the missile will increase which would reduce the range.

Two last questions: First the Bomb DispenserWarhead; because of so many complex devices on the warhead, the warhead needs to be small. How to make this possible is the first requirement. Second, whether the 'vector thrust' would be effective, is doubtful. Finally, in conclusion I would say that China's ASBM development still faces three limitations: First is bureaucratic contradiction, especially between the General Staff Development and the General Staff Armament, because the General Staff Development is in char ge of 'W arfare operations' but the General S taff Armament is in charge of 'Space activity'. Whether these two departments would be able to coordinate, is doubtful. The second weakness in their satellite system is that, China's satellites have 'very low revisit rate'which raises doubts whether they can operate ASBMs successfully. Third is the 'integration of horizontal and vertical ascent' with different ascents to establish the data linkage. It is not clear in what timeframe these limitations would be overcome.

Session 4: Second Paper

China's Quest for Seas Beyond It's Shores

Commander Sandeep Dewan

Humanity's interest and attention are increasingly turning towards the seas for a variety of reasons. Whilst the gradual resolution of conflicts on land, depletion of land resources and growing energy needs are contributory factors, it is the imperatives of globalisation and the extremely 'connected' world that are literally taking the world 'out to sea'.

With maritime issues receiving greater attention in recent years, in stark contrast to clear land-oriented pre-occupations of the past, the varied dimensions of maritime security have indeed come into the limelight and assumed greater significance. This has also influenced naval force development plans.

Unlike concepts of land power or air power which are generally defined only in military terms, sea power can never be quite separated from its geo-economic purposes. Navies may be the palpable armed element of sea power, however, maritime shipping, seaport operations, shipbuilding industry undersea resources, other forms of commerce and communications through fluid mediums are equally important and can all be seen as integral to a nation's sea power.

For those who question rising naval expenditures on national economies, the enduring relevance of Sir Walter Raleigh's dictum continues to hold good, "Whosoever commands the sea commands trade; whoever commands the trade of the world commands the riches of the world, and consequently the world itself." Today, the world is increasingly being integrated through hyper-globalisation and the maritime dimension is gaining quantum importance because of the '70-80-90 concept', which is:-

(a) 70 per cent of the world's surface is covered by the oceans.

(b) 80 per cent of the worlds population is moving closer to the ocean littoral, and the majority of the worlds major cities, industries and urban populations lie within 200 kms of the coast.

(c) 90 per cent of international trade, by weight and volume, including most of the strategic cargo is carried over the oceans.

(d) Also, international law provides for freedom of the seas in which any nation can use the open ocean for purposes of trade or defence without infringement on another's sovereignty, subject, of course, to certain international agreements.

Sea Power is best leveraged by those who have the resources and will to use them effectively. While international law may provide for equal access to trade and resources, the means to defend such access against interdiction call for effective maritime forces. This has been the primary driving force behind the quest of nations for naval power.

The importance of a navy rests on twin pillars: its ability to influence events on land and its ability to control use of the sea.   Technology has enhanced the reach and lethality of naval weapon systems which can now strike deep into enemy territories.   The world's growing dependence on international trade and ocean resources has driven nations to build capability to 'control' ocean areas of interest. With this dependency in a globalised economic system, naval power assumes greater importance.

In the words of President Theodore Roosevelt in a 1902 address to Congress - "A good Navy is not a provocation to war It is the surest guaranty of peace". Paradoxically, however, the number of ocean going navies has shrunk over the last decade. This process commenced with the disintegration of the Soviet Union. The United States continues to maintain a superpower-sized navy and some nations are quite satisfied with the evolution of this international system and see little political reason to maintain an ocean going navy. For others, the economic cost of raising and maintaining a navy is simply unaffordable.

Traditionally, the roles of the navy have been classified as - military, constabulary and diplomatic. In recent times, the benign role of the navy has assumed not only greater importance but also international acceptance, as it addresses humanitarian aspects.With changes in the political and geo-strategic environment, a particular role assumes pre-eminence.

The maritime history of China dates back to thousands of years, with archives existing since 7th century BC about the ancient Navy of China and the various ship types used in warChina became a leading maritime power around the 10th century AD, but the Chinese fleet shrank tremendously after its military, tributary and exploratory functions in the early 15th century were deemed too expensive.

The modern day PLA Navy or PLAN was founded onApril 23, 1949. From 1949 to 1955 it set up the surface ship force, coastal defence force, aviation, submarine force and Marine Corps, and established the objective of building a light maritime combat force. From 1955 to 1960 it established the three Fleets successively. From the 1950s to the end of the 1970s the main task of the Navy was to conduct inshore defensive operations. Since the1980s, the Navy has embarked on a strategic transformation to offshore defensive operations.

This paper shall examine 'China's Quest for Seas beyond It's Shores' through the PLAN's aspirations and modernisation under the following:-

(a) China's naval modernisation strategy in the backdrop of its stated policies and guidelines.

(b)PLAN's missions and deployment patterns and the likely trends.

(c)Implications of PLAN modernisation and deployment for the region.

China's Naval Modernisation Strategy

In accordance with China' s strategy for the PLAN' s modernisation, the PLAN in the past couple of decades operated in accordance with the offshore active defence strategy. This was to achieve an end state to win local wars under high tech conditions. This led PLAN to develop offensive capabilities to conduct limited sea control operations to enforce sovereignty and territorial claims in the East and South China Seas. This requirement has changed slightly over the intervening years, to fighting and winning a "local war under informationised conditions".

As per China's 2008 White Paper on national defence, China pursues a national defence policy which is purely defensive in nature. China places the protection of national sovereignty , security, territorial integrity , safeguarding of interests of national development and the interests of the Chinese people above all else. It goes on to add that the PLAN is a strategic service of the PLA and the main force for maritime operations. It is responsible for such tasks as safeguarding China' s maritime security and maintaining the sovereignty of its territorial waters along with its maritime rights and interests.

Much has been written and spoken about the Chinese defence budget, its opaqueness and the sizeable allocation to the PLAN. China' s, like any other nation's, growing global economic reach and its consequent increase in military power are inextricably linked. National development is tied to global factors and expanding interests that demand increased defence capabilities.

The two contradictions that can be seen here are the stated Chinese peaceful rise and the quantum of force and weapon acquisitions; and secondly, the gap between Chinas stated aspirations and its present capability verses its force levels in the near future. While some of us would like to or are coerced to believe that China aspires to oust the US naval presence in her maritime vicinity or in areas that concern or comprise her core interests, my personnel opinion is otherwise. China is asserting herself like never before, but her current or envisaged near future maritime capabilities do not afford her the ability to operate credible maritime forces to power project in distant waters.

PLAN's Missions and Deployment Patterns and LikelyTrends

China has decided to build and deploy apparently Asia's most diverse and capable naval force. PLAN commanders seek to realise the capabilities inherent in the party strategic guidelines over the next decade by:-

(a) Becoming a viable strategic arm.

(b) Developing maritime strike packages to conduct and sustain "blue water" offensive naval combat operations out to the "first island chain".

(c) Providing combatants and support assets capable of limited force projection operations in distant seas beyond peripheral waters.

(d) Providing leadership, doctrine, tactics, and training for integration into joint and multinational operations.

China, as part of fulfilling its aspirations of becoming a world power has embarked on the path of augmenting its 'Comprehensive National Power' (CNP) through political, economic, military , technological and diplomatic means.As a means to the end, it is increasingly focussing on the waters that not only adjoin but also go way beyond her shores. This is in consonance with her quest for becoming a regional, political, economic and military power with global aspirations and an important player of the global strategic environment. China is conscious, more than ever before, that maritime trade, its security and naval supremacy will play a key role in its eminence as a global power.

Towards achieving this ambition, the PLAN aims at a gradual extension of its strategic depth for offshore defensive operations and enhancing its capabilities in integrated maritime operations. This shift in its strategy has been necessitated primarily due to its trade and energy security concerns. Ensuring that its Sea Lines of Communication (SLOCs) remain open, safe and secure at all times has become an even more important Chinese maritime interest. These SLOCs stretch almost 9,600 kilometres from the Persian Gulf to the East Coast of China and currently transport 80 per cent of China's energy imports. This, thus, becomes the basis of China extending its maritime defensive perimeter and consequently improving its ability to influence and protect initially regional and subsequently global SLOCs.

The latest deployment patterns of and the routes taken by the Chinese Flotilla seem to be in consonance with a three stage strategy in the PLANs' modernisation plans as indicated in the White Paper on China's National Defence. The Navy has been developing capabilities of conducting cooperation in distant waters and countering non-traditional security threats in order to progress the overall transformation of the service in consonance with its new strategy of far sea defence with long range capabilities.

Through its three staged strategic transformation, the PLAN aims to further develop into a technologically modernised and networked naval force capable of operating within the 'first islands chain' comprising islands that stretch from Japan in the North toTaiwan and the Philippines in the South. The second stage aims to transform the PLAN into a regional naval force that can operate beyond the first islands chain to reach the 'second islands chain' that includes Guam, Indonesia and Australia. Finally, in the third-stage, the PLAN seeks to transform itself into a global force capable of true blue water operations by the middle of the 21st century.

Admiral Mike Mullen, Chairman of the Joint Chiefs of Staff, said he was worried by China's "heavy investments" in sea and air capabilities. He added "A gap as wide as what seems to be forming between Chinas stated intent and its military programs leaves me more than curious about the end result. Indeed, I have moved from being curious to being genuinely concerned." This probably is a sentiment that a lot of nations echo but may not say so in so many words.

With a presently limited capability in shore based maritime air and naval aviation capability, China has to necessarily rely on its missile armed submarines and shore/ship basedASMs for control of waters in and around its shores. This affords it the capability of pursuing a strategy of limited sea denial rather than outright sea control. Even with its naval force build-up plans, it lacks the numbers to effectively deny over extended periods of time areas like the South and East China Seas or theYellow Sea. However, with its potentA2/AD strategy and its growing numbers of short and medium range ballistic and cruise missiles deployed on coastal and maritime units,

China has slowly begun to flex its muscles not only in waters adjacent to her coast, but in those well beyond it as well.

China's gradual aggressive posture has been made possible due to its bolstered capabilities in ASBMs, ASAT, reliable indigenous satellite navigation, high quality satellite imagery and C4ISR. Some of these capabilities are still unproven and untested fully, but their mere possession and in an advanced stage of development have given China the much desired deterrent capability

Chinese capabilities to conduct sea control operations further from its shores will become a reality if Anti-Ship Ballistic Missiles (ASBM) deploy and prove as effective and potent as many analysts fear, and PLAN submarines become increasingly capable of long, extended deployments. PLAN's nuclear attack and ballistic missile submarines are deploying to new basing facilities in Hainan Island. In addition to the aircraft carrier induction programme, the PLAN is in the process of inducting new classes of indigenous destroyers and frigates. These destroyers are designed to ameliorate the PLAN's most glaring maritime force projection shortfall namely the shipborne area air defence and the capability to conduct long-range anti-surface warfare missions with supersonic ASCMs. The PLAN's new frigates also incorporate much-improved fleet air defence systems and stealth design technology.

The PLAN is also in the process of inducting a large number of fast-attack missile platforms with a stealthy, catamaran hull design. These will further bolster a range of missions in littoral warfare. Deployment of these vessels in swarm tactics as done by the Sri Lankan Navy in the Elam war could successfully support combat operations in a Taiwan theatre or a South China Sea conflict, as well as anti-access or area denial operations against US or allied forces.

The PLAN anti-piracy missions in the Gulf of Aden further demonstrates the seriousness with which Beijing views the security of its SLOCs. The Chinese task force has been operating far from home and that too for extended periods of time, putting its crew and ships under a lot of strain. Such considerations off late have led to calls for the establishment of overseas bases in East Africa, the Middle East and or South Asia.

An important debate among security strategists concerns the protection of the Chinese trade and energy resources that flow through the Straits of Malacca and the South China Sea. While current and pending capabilities may allow China to negotiate from a position of strength regarding territorial and resources claims in the South China Sea, China has very limited ability to respond to large-scale threats to Chinese shipping in the Straits of Malacca and distant reaches of the South China Sea, leave alone the Gulf.

China's thinking of 'slowly opening up its forward deploymentin order to showcase its naval presence in the Pacific and Indian Oceans, from the hitherto South and East China Seas, is a natural consequence of the Country' desire to be a global maritime power. Modernisation apart, it has come to realise that naval power is more benign than land power . Navies by themselves cannot occupy or fortify areas at sea and thus, must do far more than just fight. They need to protect not only trade and energy supplies, but also secure the routes and vessels that transit the same.

The past incidents of harassment of the US Navy surveillance ships by Chinese fishing vessels in the South China Sea and Yellow Sea and the recent incident with the Japanese Coast Guard illustrate what one high-level US official describes as "strategic mistrust" based on inadequate military-to-military relations between China and the US and its other Asia and Asia Pacific maritime neighbours.

Despite all indicators on China's maritime build-up and modernisation, China has a long way to go in becoming a real maritime power. Maritime nations recognise that ships and submarines alone do not make them a maritime power. I carry this agument in accordance with whatAlfred Thayer Mahan defined as the essentials which determine the potential of a nation to become a maritime power . The first essential was the requirement of a good number of ports and easy and unhindered access to the sea. In addition, a two-coasts configuration provided inherent advantages. Most importantly in order to be a truly credible maritime power, a country has to be able to dominate important SLOCs.

While China comes good on two other of Mahan's stated criteria i.e. geography and population size, it comes a cropper as far as seafaring character of its people and its access to open seas is concerned. China's access to 'open seas' can be constrained in the North by Japan, in the centre by Taiwan and in the South by Philippines.The East and South China Sea SLOCs carry a considerable amount of global trade, especially energy China does not dominate these SLOCs like India geographically does in the IOR as also the energy lifelines from the Gulf.

Implications of PLAN Modernisation

China's stated or otherwise naval build-up and modernisation and its articulation of the South China Sea as a 'core national interest' increases the complexity of the issue. These could have a direct bearing not only on regional and global trade, but on its security as well. The Chinese envisaged A2/AD capability could have far reaching security implications not only for the region but on the global front also.

Given China's unique interpretation of sovereignty in its maritime zones combined with a willingness to use force to support this stand is a destabilising factor for the security in theAsian region. China is also displaying growing assertiveness in the pursuit of its stated 'core national interests'.The sustained emphasis on the modernisation of the PLA Navy without any accompanying transparency in its strategic goals also causes concern. Though there has been some expectation that with China's growing power will come, willingness for playing a greater role in global security and international order, but this is yet to be demonstrated. On the other hand, China's growing economic and military power appears to be making it more assertive as has been indicated by its apparent desire to divide the Pacific Ocean with the US.

This aspect was echoed by many Chinese scholars and PLA officers during the Xiangshan Forum in Beijing a fortnight back. General (Air Force) Ma Xiaotian while delivering the opening address at the forum stressed on China's peaceful rise and its commitment to peaceful development. He stressed on the fact that China's rejuvenation was in consonance with the 'tide of the times'. He added that China's military build-up was to aid regional stability and world peace. He also brought out that China was the only big country in the world that was not fully unified. He stood by the Chinese belief that it was the country' s policy rather than military strength that displayed its defensive nature. He, during his 40 minutes speech, repeated at least five times that China was not hegemonic in its policy as believed by many nations around the world. He substantiated this by saying that China was the only country amongst the five permanent members of the UN that neither had any overseas military bases nor stationed any troops abroad.

Many Chinese PLA participants were of the firm view that China was neither a super power nor aspired to be one. They bluntly put it that China was not ready to shoulder international responsibility that accompanied super power status and added that as per their belief the word super power had a very negative connotation. Well so much for the Chinese denial.

Other states in the region are also looking towards greater military self-sufficiency. An arms race has begun, thanks to Beijing, and it has been intensified by the qualitative leaps that modern technology has permitted. This reverberation of China's economic rise and enhanced military capability is quite visible across Asia and as far as mainland USA Asian countries are responding to China's military might by building suficient deterrence against possible escalation of disputes. Although several Southeast Asian militaries have security dialogues, military-technical cooperation and bilateral security arrangements with China, but they are concerned about the growing Chinese assertiveness particularly in South China Sea. The South East Asian naval and air forces are miniscule both in terms of quality and quantity when compared with China's maritime forces and are uging the US to get engaged in regional security affairs much to the consternation of China. They also seek cooperative agendas with India and Japan, the other major   Asian powers, to contain China.

As far as India is concerned, China does not appear to take India as a serious rival and underplays its standing by looking down upon its economic problems and inability to take on reforms in all fields. The Chinese are critical of India's democratic process which has led to a very poor pace of change but agree on the fact that perhaps this provides India a degree of stability which may see it through in an economic crisis whereas China may not be able to do so in a similar case. China is keeping a close eye on India' growing political and economic sway especially in the   Asian region. It considers strong India a challenge to its natural strategic space which it is endeavouring to carve out for itself not only in the entireAsian region, but beyond that as well. At present, outwardly, China reflects more concern about Japan, the USA and Taiwan and asserts that it wants to have peaceful and stable relations with its neighbours.

Conclusion

To conclude, I would say that reading too much into PLAN modernisation is going to serve no purpose. Countries, which have the wherewithal and ability will continue to progress and modernise, both economically as well as militarily Aren't we doing this as well? So, why are we losing sleep over China 'and more so PLAN's modernisation. The question we need to address is: whether over a long period will all these increasing numbers, (without much proven or visible capabilities, combat experience and well-orchestrated war plans) be sufficient or sustainable? China, while presently on a song, will soon have its own internal contradictions which will eventually get her to rethink on this feverish building-up of capacity

In the long run, whether this resolve would also translate into using the maritime power to enhance Chinese national interests is something that remains to be seen. A mere building-up of platform numbers without demonstrated or tested fighting capability; or a three ship extended period deployment or a ten ship foray within the first islands chain; or beyond without the ability to effectively control air space in the immediate vicinity; does not translate into maritime power Therefore, while Chinese presence in seas beyond its shores is possible, it will not be credible. Indeed, without any substantial maritime partnerships and involvement in any future security architecture in the region, it would be counterproductive.

Almost a century ago, Sir Julian Corbett warned, "To aim at a standard of naval strength or a strategic distribution which would make our trade absolutely invulnerable is to march to economic ruin." He could not have said it better.

Session 4 : Third Paper

China's Military Strategy and Capabilities

Professor Changhee Park

I am happy to be in incredible India, to present my views on China military affairs. My topic is 'China's Military Strategy and Capabilities'. I will focus more on its implications and prospects because we have already heard much about China's basic military strategies and capabilities. My arguments can be summarised into four points. The first point is that China's strategy and capability is quite offensive oriented rather than defensive. According to offence/defence theory, if the offensive part is more dominant and adventurous, the possibility of war will increase. The second point is PLA military modernisation is now going beyond, what they need to protect their national interests. It can cause a security dilemma and an arms race that could make the regional military balance 'unstable'. The third point is Beijing's current assertiveness is based on military confidence, which can be seen in several cases. In July, China's Foreign Minister, Yang Jie Chi mentioned at a meeting of ASEAN leaders in Hanoi that South China Sea is a core interest of China; and also later in August they clearly opposed the ROK-US joint military drill on West Sea (Chinese call it Yellow Sea) which was scheduled to respond to North Korea' s torpedo attack on South Korea' s ship. We also saw that in last September they showed very harsh response to Senkaku island incident. So, this kind of behaviour can be a threat to neighbouring States. The fourth point is that PLA 's 'anti-access' strategy can weaken the security commitment of the USA to its allies. Therefore, why don't we start multilateral talks to solve security dilemma and to discuss arms control immediately?

Now, let us take the overall relationship between the strategic environment and doctrine of the PLA. Currently , China's strategic environment consists of three factors. Maybe, there could be other factors also; but these three influence the doctrine of the PLA. China is now a rising power and is expanding commitments to regional players to secure its national interests. In the interim the local war doctrine of the PLA is still valid and effective. The face of future wars has transformed from mechanization to 'informationised warfare'. PLA cannot sit idle and that is the reason why, '2004 to 2008 Defence White Paper of China' mentioned that PLA should have the capability to win the local war under informationised conditions. But there is a clear problem for PLA to catch up with the Western style armies. It could take much more time. That is the reason, why the PLA has pursued symmetric strategy until they get full capability for informationised warfare. These characteristics of the doctrine actually stipulate the current military strategy of active defence.

What is PLA's military doctrine? PLA's current doctrine consists of both local war under 'high tech' conditions and local war under 'informationised' conditions, doctrined together The High Technology War Doctrine, introduced in 1993, actually postulates mechanised warfare and its main target is Taiwan and its neighbours. But the Informationised Warfare Doctrine, introduced in 2004 Defence White Paper, of course, reflected serious ongoing debates among party leaders, including Jiang Zemin and Hu Jintao. The new doctrine actually targets the threat of the US military and its allies. However, these two doctrines cannot be separated because they go side by side. So, today , maybe the High Technology War Doctrine is more dominant than Informationised War Doctrine; but, as time goes by the Informationised Wafare Doctrine will be more dominant, and in 2015, maybe it will totally substitute the previous war doctrine.

Now, I will talk about the 'military strategy guidelines'. Throughout history, there have been several changes in PLA 's strategic guidelines. Currently the military strategy guidelines conform to 'active defence' which were introduced in 1993. Earlier the requirements were met through High Technology War Doctrine. The question that arises now is: What would be the new guidelines for the 21st century i.e. after the current guidelines for informationised war conditions? Unfortunately, I don't know the answer.

According to 2008 Defence White Paper, the 1993 Strategic Guidelines are still effective. But in PLA, there is a serious ongoing debate about: What would be the future of the 'Informationised Warfare'? We can infer, maybe, new guidelines would be coming out soon. The new guidelines would stress the importance of 'pre-emption' and focus more on swift and decisive warfare, asymmetric strategy, power projection and long range strike capability; all of which means that PLAs military strategy is becoming more and more offensive rather than defensive.

In this context, let us consider China's naval strategy and capability. The PLA's strategic concept is 'offshore active defence' and the operational boundary is expanding from 'coastal area to offshore area'. What is offshore area? Actually the definition of offshore differs between scholars. I had a chance to meet two PLA generals last year in a public place, so I asked them to clarify this question. They answered that it cannot be defined in terms of distance. Actually, it is very flexible and can vary according to the situation and mission capabilities. My conclusion is that current thinking in the PLA about the meaning of the offshore boundary is changing from 'first islands' to 'second islands' chain. The boundaries of the operational area of PLA Navy, for the past few years, have been extending beyond the 'first islands' chain and are now getting closer to the 'second islands' chain.

Now we will discuss the PLA Air Force (PLAAF) strategy and capability. The strategic concept of PLAAF is to have modernisedAir Force with offensive and defensive capabilities. In the past, only the PLA Navy stayed up to cover their territorial area in the air. They actually did not go beyond their boundary. They just remained defensive in the air because of their doctrine of Peoples War. But, after the Gulf War, especially, they realised that they should employ theirAir Force more offensively. So, they are now stressing on pre-emptive and surgical strike to secure control and dominance over Taiwan. The operational area of Sukhoi LM 27 and 30 can reach beyond the 'first islands' chain, and some bombers including Hun-6 can reach to the 'second islands' chain.

What are the SecondArtillery's strategic concerns? They are changing from 'hiding' to a 'fighting' force. Until 1980s, they just focussed on survivability because they did not have any ICBMs and their ballistic missiles number was very limited. But since 1990s they actually began to put more emphasis on war fighting aspects which meant they would retaliate more actively after the first strike from the enemy . Their strategies are contemplating tactical nuclear battles, emphasising on sea based launching platforms and also conventional missile warfare.

Many panelists have already spoken about China's Asymmetric Warfare Strategies, so I would not cover that aspect now . I will, however, discuss the implications of PLA's military strategy, which is more ofensive oriented rather than defensive. Throughout history, every time a new power rose, there was a war. Except 1890s when the USA rose to power, (at that time there was no war); but otherwise there was always war . Presently, when China is rising: What would be the situation in the future, maybe in 2050? Actually, to 'maintain internal stability' and 'to deter attacks from outside' China needs to protect its Sea Lines of Communication (SLOCs). However PLA's military capability is much beyond their minimum requirement for China's defence. Then the question arises: What would PLA do with this surplus military power? That would make for a very unstable situation, because, as the Chinese power grows the rulers would tend to get more confident militarily; which would mean, they could come to depend more on their military prowess rather than diplomatic tools.Also, the Chinese people can ask PLA then, as to why did you build-up the military forces so-much? Then, maybe, the PLA and the CCP leaders could rationalize the build-up by 'making a conflict' or 'exaggerating threats' from outside sort of things. So, we should be very careful about these developments in China.

To conclude, my assessment is that at present the PLA does not have enough capability, nor would it have it in the near future, to dominate the world unhindered. The point to take note is that there is not much change in China's grand strategy at this point of time. Their 'tar get year' to do so would be around 2050, and this would provide sufficient opportunity to engage and to talk with China. However, if we do not address our concerns about growing military capability of China responsibly that could cause security dilemma amongst the 'regional states'. So, why don't we take new measures

of arms control like Washington Conference, in Asia also? Actually
Washington Conference was concluded in 1922 between Great Britain and
the USA, Japan and Italy; but, it failed because of breach of faith amongst
the countries after the   Agreement. But nowadays we have better inter-
communication system, better surveillance capabilities, and better global
network for cooperation amongst countries. So, why don't we get together
and discuss about these matters frankly to safeguard the interests of regional
states in the vicinity of China?

Session 4 : Fourth Paper

From Hiding to Showcasing: Enhancing China's Military Capabilities

Professor Srikanth Kondapalli

A number of developments in the recent period indicated that the Chinese military capabilities have been enhanced substantially as compared to the previous period when the People's Liberation Army (PLA)'s forces were looked down upon for their poor capabilities and miserable performance in the last war it waged – the Sino-V ietnam War of 1979. These new developments include across the spectrum improvements in the PLA 's capabilities.[1] In October 2006, a Chinese conventional submarine trailed USS Kitty Hawk near Okinawa, while a decade ago the same US vessel was trailing a Chinese Han-class submarine in mid 1990s near Qingdao.[2] This naval engagement with the more advanced forces reflected to the new-found confidence in the PLA's naval forces. Next year on January 11, 2007, China conducted an anti-satellite test with a ground-based missile destroying one of its retired Fengyun satellite located at about 860 km in orbit.[3] Later, on the same day in 2010, China successfully conducted an interceptor missile test for beefing up its ballistic missile defence network. The Chinese Air Force had unveiled newer versions of multirole aircraft (J-10), while acquiring others from Russia (Su-27 and Su-30) and a stealth bomber J-20 in January 2011 at Chengdu[4], even as its commander-in-chief Xu Qilian proposed plans for furthering the offensive capabilities of not only the Air Force but also in the Space arena.

Further, the Chinese Navy sent ships for Somalia counter -piracy operations in the Indian Ocean from December 2008 and its naval officers argued for "permanent supply bases" abroad, including in Oman, Yemen and Pakistan – a measure indicating the ability to sustain forces abroad far away from the home ports[6] China inApril 2009 also organised an international fleet review – underlining the global tasks of its naval forces. At Qingdao naval parade, to mark the 60th anniversary of the PLA Navy on April 23, 2009, China displayed new vessels including the latest "Lanzhou" missile destroyer, warship 115, warship 527, warship 528, hospital ship 886 and some submarines.[7] In the same year, the US Admiral Keating was told by the visiting Chinese admiral on dividing the Pacific Ocean – with east of the Pacific remaining in the US hands, while the Chinese intending to hold sway over the west Pacific Ocean and the Indian Ocean.

In July 2010, the maritime engineering capabilities of China were reflected when it developed Jiaolong submersible which planted the Chinese flag in South China Sea at a depth of 3,759 meters. In December 2006, the PLA has also indicated in its 'white paper on national defence' that China would increasingly deter regional conflicts from breaking out and would manage conflicts in the short to medium term.   According to a Japanese Kyodo news feature in January 2011, China is also revaluating and lowering its no-first nuclear use pledge during "critical" situations[8].

Further instructions for Revolution in Military   Affairs' (RMA) applications were issued through the 2008 white paper on national defence. In the Beijing parade on October 1, 2009, China unveiled 52 new weapon systems, consisting of 8 DF-31ICBMs (as against 3 in 1999 parade), Dong Hai 10 (DH-10) long-range land-attack cruise missile (LACM), new PLA Marine Corps blue camouflage Infantry Fighting Vehicles, DF-11 and DF-15 missiles, sea-skimming YJ-83 anti-ship missiles, J-10, J-11 multi-role aircrafts, UAVs, Satcoms and AEWC platforms. In January 2011, during the visit of the US Defence Secretary Gates to China, it was revealed that the Chinese anti-ship ballistic missile DF-21D capabilities have reached initial operational capability.[9]

The above developments in the PLA are a reflection of the level of China's military capabilities in the last decade, and indicate to decades of preparations by the country in this regard.[10] The above developments also show that across the board, the PLA   forces, viz., ground, air , naval and strategic forces are undergoing major modernisation trends with new found confidence in matching advanced forces. [11] This paper traces these developments in some detail and argues that China had reached a level that indicates it could pose challenges to the established and advanced militaries in the not too distant future; and as China is rising in economic and technological prowess, these developments reflect structural and long-term changes in the world today.

Bean Count of the Capabilities

According to a Chinese military yearbook's assessment in 2005, the comprehensive combat capabilities of the Chinese Armed Forces rank third in the world after the USA and Russia, while its integrated military capabilities rank fourth after the USA, Russia and France. Likewise, in the nuclear field China's capabilities rank fifth in the world after the USA, Russia, France and the UK, and seventh in the overall conventional military capabilities; while its ground forces rank second after Russia; naval capabilities are sixth after the USA, Russia, the UK, Japan and France; and the air force capabilities also rank sixth in the world, but in the order of the USA, Russia, France, Germany and the UK. [12]

Ground Forces

The London-based International Institute of Strategic Studies (IISS) in its Military Balance had outlined the "bean count" of the PLA forces. Based on these estimates, China has nearly 1.9 million armed force personnel divided among the ground, air, navy and strategic forces. [13] In the ground forces are about 18 Group Armies directing manoeuvre forces of about 44 infantry divisions (including five mechanised infantry divisions with two amphibious assault units and 24 motorised infantry divisions), three rapid response units at national and nine RRF units at regional levels. The 15th Airborne Army (with plans to raise another the 16th Airborne Army) provides for limited airborne missions. Two amphibious assault units and the strengthened Marine Corps provide for the amphibious operations of the PLA forces.

After Russia, clearly China is the second largest in the world today in terms of ground forces. China's ground forces command about 7, 580 main battle tanks and 1,000 light tanks in addition to 4,500 armoured personnel carriers, 14,000 towed artillery 1,200 self-propelled guns, 2,400 MRLs and 381 helicopters although most of these are obsolete.To enhance the ground force capabilities, China had undertaken several measures, including improving the battlefield survivability of the armour, enhancing firepower, targeting systems, crosswind sensors, third-generation night sights, computerised fire control systems, mobility of the vehicles, provision of the Global Positioning Systems, and others. [14] The latest models of MBT s (from Type 85II) are made of welded steel instead of the previous versions of cast steel turrets. In addition, the Type 90 II indicates explosive reactive armour. Secondly, the power-to-weight ratio has been enhanced over a period of time from 14.44 hp/t in the Type 59 to 25 in Type 90II. The speed has been increased from 40-50 kmph powered by a 520 hp engine of the Type 59 MBT to about 62.3 kmph of the 1,200 hp engine of the   Type 90II with enhanced fuel capacity for longer duration operations. Among the Armoured Personnel Carriers the Type 90 and WZ 551 are improved versions compared to the previous versions of Types 77, 85, 63 and WZ 523 in terms of steel armour 320-360hp diesel engines that provide higher power-to-weight ratio. Rapid response nature of future war meant importance shown to the wheeled types of APCs rather than that of the tracked ones.The latest versions also exhibit enhanced mobility at 95 kmph driven by turbo-charged engine of 320 hp and with an enhanced combat range of about 800 km.

China's artillery forces rank only next to Russia and North Korean forces in the world today and have witnessed an upgradation in the capabilities.[15] Relatively, the mechanisation levels of the Beijing, Shenyang and Jinan Military Regions (MRs) are higher as compared to the other MRs. Shenyang MR, with an estimated 250,000 troops, has four Group Army's, one mechanised brigade, two armoured, four motorised, besides others. Beijing MR, composed of 300,000 troops, has five Group Army's with two armoured, one mechanised, and five motorised divisions, besides others. Jinan MR has 190,000 troops with three Group Army's, two armoured, one mechanised infantry and others. Nanjing MR, with focus on T aiwan operations has two armoured brigades. Other MRs has either one or no armoured units and are relatively less mechanised.

Naval Forces

China's naval capabilities are being enhanced and a number of countries are concerned about this development.[16] With oceans becoming an important arena for economic and military expansion in the recent period, China has been paying considerable attention in this field – even terming the naval, in addition to the air and strategic forces as "strategic" in the white paper on national defence in 2008 (but released in January 2009).[17] Specifically, power projection force such as the Navy was emphasised by China. [18] Towards executing anti-access and anti-denial operations, the Chinese Navy had made certain preparations and could be employed first in the Taiwan Straits, towards Japan and South China Sea, the Pacific and the Indian Ocean. Recent estimates by the IISS indicate that China is building more naval vessels than many of the advanced forces, including the US.[19] Today, China's naval forces consist of about 255,000 personnel, with two strategic (1 Xia SSBN and 1 Jin SSBN), six SSNs (2 Shang and 4 Han-class) and 54 tactical submarines, 29 destroyers, 45 frigates, 331 patrol and coastal combatants, 52 amphibious vessels, and about 700 naval aviation aircraft. New warships are under construction including Yuan class submarines, new nuclear attack SSNs and strategic nuclear submarines (SSBNs), with the latter poised to enter Yulin base in southern Hainan province[20]. New combatant programmes include Luyang-II (052C with HHQ-9 long range SAMs), Luzhou-class (051C with Russian SAMs) destroyers and Jiangkai-II (054A) frigates, Jiangwei III frigate (export version F-16U), refitting of aircraft carrier Varyag, etc.[21] China had been emphasising on the following naval capabilities: enhanced firepower, endurance capabilities and reach of the naval vessels and weapon systems and training programme of the naval troops have been made. The mobility of the ships has also increased noticeably thanks to the gradual transition into gas turbines and nuclear propulsion. The endurance capability of the submarines was also enhanced. Acquisition of a large number of Kilo-class submarines could definitely alter naval capabilities of China in the future. The firepower of the destroyers, frigates and submarines (54 Moskits, Gadfly's, HQ & YJ-series SAMs & SSMs, etc) show substantial improvement. Automation of SAM launchers is another significant advance.

Air Forces

The PLA Air Force (PLAAF) has one of the most active programmes in Asia and the world.[22] China's Air Force has about 400,000 personnel, with six bomber regiments, 39 fighter regiments and 24 regiments for ground attack missions, 290 planes for reconnaissance or ELINT roles, one A-50 I AEW, 513 transports and about 100 helicopters.[23] Major modernisation efforts have commenced in this force as well.   [24] China had emphasised on the following capabilities in the recent period: multi-functional air superiority with advanced fire control systems, electronics, stealth, beyond-visual range air-to-air missile systems, and air-to-ground assault systems. Other areas in which China has shown keen interest are AWACS, in-flight refuelling, anti-missile defences, ECMs, automatic command and control facilities. While the Su-27 aircraft rolled out of the licence-manufacturing aircraft factory at Shenyang and re-christened as J-1 1, the agreement with Russia saw new additions of Su-30 MKK ground-attack versions of aircraft, transports and helicopters. Plans were also made to acquire   A-50 I Mainstay AWACS, Zhemchoug radar systems, R-73 and R-27R AAMs, AL-31F engines, SA-20 SAMs, etc.

The quantitative and qualitative improvements made in the PLAAF are the most noticeable in this regard. These are expected to change the regional strategic situation and air environment in East Asia and Southeast and South Asia in the next two decades. Quantitatively the PLAAF intends to enrich its battle order by modern aircraft. Given the preparations in this regard, this claim can hardly be doubted. With about 300 Su-27s, 100-150 Su-30 MKs, 150-200 J-10s and 100 FC-1s for the Naval Aviation, upgradation of large number of J-8IIs, transports, S-300 PMU SAMs, acquisition of 3 to 4 AWACS and air refuelling capabilities, the PLAAF is clearly destined to surpass the air power strengths in the region. With over 6.5 metric tonne carrying capacity, aircraft like the J-10 is a suitable answer to replace the functions of additional bombers in the PLAAF inventory

In qualitative terms also the PLAAF has been making a significant dent in the region. Licensed manufacture of the advanced AA-12 (R-77) active radar guided BVR missiles for Su-27s/Su-30s, and possibly for other aircraft underdevelopment, (which has a clear edge over the Mirage 2000-5s MICA air-to-air missiles) is bound to enhance PLAAF's offensive capabilities.[25] Similarly other air-to-air missiles from Russia, likeAA-11 (R-73), AA-10 (R-27R) are also expected to boost beyond the vision combat capabilities of the PLAAF. Enhancing its transport fleet of IL-76 and 78 could go a long way in bridging PLAAF's airborne capabilities. Soon after the Sino-Russian August 2005 exercise, PLAAF reportedly has shown interest in placing an order for nearly 30 Il-76 transports from Russia, in addition to some Il-78s and backfire bombers.

Strategic Forces

In addition, the strategic weapons capabilities of China (including nuclear and ballistic missiles) have shown improvements in quantitative and qualitative terms. With an estimate 48 ICBMs and 1700 IRBMs, China is emerging as a major force in international strategic relations. Its January 1, 2007 test of an anti-satellite weapon, by knocking off one of its own Fengyun satellites through a ground based missile, indicated its capabilities in this crucial field. The Second Artillery, the custodian of the strategic weapons of China, has focussed its efforts in the recent period on enhancing its missile capabilities in the following fields: emphasising on building new and veritable range ballistic and conventional missiles, solid-propellants, multiple independently launched re-entry vehicles and land mobile forces. Besides strategic missiles, China is also involved in development of several versions of cruise missiles. It has produced for the domestic and external market several such missiles including SY-1, HY- series, FL-series, YJ-series and C-701 and C-801. Chinese strategic weapons capabilities surpass that of India's programmes. While China has deployed a wide variety of missiles, India is yet to deploy enhanced IRBMs, and its short-range missiles are hardly able to deter China. On the other hand, China's DF-3/DF-3A and DF-21 deployments in Qinghai and Yunnan regions pose security concerns for India. Some suggest that about 50-60 Indian cities, strategic hubs or transportation links are being targeted by China. Given the debates and changes in the nuclear doctrine of China, as outlined above, security concerns in India are logical According to Vijai K Nair, citing US Air Force National Intelligence Centre's declassified documents and Russian reports, China has been upgrading its nuclear and ballistic missiles to target India. Not only are the numbers of CSS-2 missiles at the 53rd Army at Jianshui, with a range of 3,100 km, not changed, but the training programme of the crew at Kunming training area is being enhanced, in addition to the probable replacement of CSS-2 by CSS-5 Mod1. Large-scale training activities were reported from Datong field garrison, Haiyan training facility in the 56^h Army (with missile bases at Da Qaidam, Delingha and Xiao Qaidam). The interconnecting communications between the missile bases from Jianshui-Kunming-Yunan-Chengdu-Lhasa-Haiyan-Datong are being upgraded for faster mobility.[26]

Software Capabilities

Acquiring military equipment is one significant aspect of the military capabilities of a country but not the only one. Training and exercises also constitute a major portion in these capabilities. The PLA leadership offers a variety of training programmes to conventional and strategic forces in their effort to enhance combat capabilities. These are undergoing major transformations in content and method in the light of new challenges and revolution in military affairs (RMA). Taking a cue from the recent wars waged by the USA and others in Iraq, Afghanistan and Kosovo, the PLA has been attempting to change the training manuals inherited from the Soviet days. The PLA is currently training its troops in offensive operations to pose challenges to the neighbourhood Although the geographical orientation of these training programmes still emphasise Taiwan, South China Sea and Senkaku Islands, there has been a gradual increase in the training orientation towards India as well. In terms of subjects, RMA aspects like electronic, information and Space-based warfare methods are being imparted to the PLA forces. These training programmes are aimed to prepare troops at "winning" rather than simply "waging" future local wars under informationised conditions.

China has introduced the concept of combined arms exercises

[*duobingzhong lianhe yanxi*] to suit the need of high-tech wars.   A few important aspects of combined operations include improving the integrity of command organisation, means of command and introduction of guidance legislation. In the process, the PLA leadership stressed centralisation of the command of all participating forces, compatibility , comprehensiveness, timeliness, and adaptability of the means of command. In the joint operational training, officers of various armed services were urged to "widen" their field of vision about other services and develop joint formation, joint tactics and joint training. In 1959 PLA leadership began codifying the combat regulations under the leadership of   Ye Jianying. Subsequently , several modifications were made including the latest Jiang Zemin' s issuing of "Essentials of Combined Operations of the first generation".   Chinese combined-arms exercises are intended to enhance the role of "combat operation, joint operation" [*hetong zuozhan, lianhe zuozhan*] of the troops. Simulation methods and training are also being utilised extensively in the PLA to enhance its capabilities.

In the recent period, the PLA conducted several military exercises to test its capabilities. On an average about 200 such activities are noticed per annum in the recent years. Major military exercises include, "Swirl Wind 082" of Shenyang Military region in 2008, "Lianhe 2008" drill byWeifang Military Training Coordination Zone in Jinan, "Libing-2008" [Sharpening the Troops] Exercise open to foreign military attachés, "Beijian 2008" [Northern Sword 2008] of Beijing, "Qianfeng-2008" (Vanguard 2008) by Jinan, Stride (*Kauayue*) 2009, Airborne Movement (*Kingjiang Jidong*) 2009 and Vanguard (*Qianfeng*) 2009, besides Peace Mission exercises with Shanghai Cooperation Organisation member states.Also, in early 2009, the Guangzhou Military Region reportedly drew up a tactical plan to seize the disputed South China Sea Islands. It included use of bombers for flattening adversary's defences and amphibious operations through the deployment of 18,000 tonne Kunlunshan vessels.[27]

Conclusion

Military capabilities are a sum total of all the military assets that a country can muster, including its hardware (troops, military equipment, resources, manufacturing and S&T prowess, etc) and software skills (training, morale, previous combat experience and the ability and will to exercise force, leadership qualities, etc.) in an organised application and in pursuit of perceived and stated goals of the State's interests. Several of these capabilities have been outlined in the above analysis. However, measuring accurately with any precision such combat capabilities of any armed force of a country is a difficult task. In the case of China such problems are still more visible because the Armed Forces have hardly taken part in any major war after the 1979 war with Vietnam; while earlier it had waged four wars against the US/UN forces in Korea (1951-53), India (1962) and the USSR (1969).   The Air Forces had participated in all these wars except the Korean War, in which they operated under the Soviet guidance. In the naval skirmishes with the Taiwanese in the 1950s and with the South Vietnamese in 1974, however, the naval forces did take part in operations. Howeverlarge-scale use of air, naval and strategic forces in actual combat operations have been largely absent, with the exception of peace-time military training and exercises in different parts of the Country in addition to simulated scenarios. Nevertheless, attempts were made in assessing the combat capabilities by analysing the force structures, 'bean count' of the equipment and weapon systems, deployments, efficient integration of weapon systems, and so on.

As mentioned above, China's military capabilities in terms of global ranking had been generally upgraded by different W   estern, Indian and Chinese estimates. Individually and cumulatively such capabilities have been enhanced with concerted attention from the leadership, modernisation efforts, upgradation and innovations as well as higher defence budgetary allocations. Significantly, the responses worldwide about these Chinese military capabilities are also increasing in terms of the alarmist predictions and their probable impact on regional and global security[28] All the above conclusions indicate that instead of "hiding capabilities and biding for time"[taoguang yanghui], as Deng Xiaoping cautioned the leadership in the 1980s, during the reigns of both Jiang Zemin (1989-2002) and Hu Jintao (2004-2012), the PLA has been displaying its capabilities and raising concerns among the neighbourhood and beyond.

Endnotes

1 Part of the analysis below is based on revisions and updating of Srikanth Kondapalli, "Chinese Military Capabilities in 2000-2010" in K. Santhanam and Srikanth Kondapalli (eds) Asian Security and China 2000-2010 (New Delhi: Shipra Publications, 2003) pp. 182-201. See also Larry M. Wortzel, China's Military Potential (Strategic Studies Institute, U.S. Army War College, Carlisle, 1998) and Roy Kamphausen and Andrew Scobell ed. Right Sizing The People's Liberation Army: Exploring The Contours Of China's Military (Strategic Studies Institute, U.S. Army War College, Carlisle, 2007)

2 See for the 1990s Srikanth Kondapalli, China's Naval Power (New Delhi: Knowledge World, 2001)

3 On the subject, see Srikanth Kondapalli, "China's Space Program: Problems and Prospects" in Subrata Ghoshroy and Gotz Neuneck Eds. South Asia at a Crossroads: Conflict or Cooperation in the Age of Nuclear Weapons, Missile Defense, and Space Rivalries (Berlin: Nomos Publications, 2010) pp. 171-83 and Srikanth Kondapalli, "China's Space Programme and Asia" in Kai-Uwe Schrogl et.al eds. Y earbook on Space P olicy 2008/2009: S etting New T rends (New York: SpringerWien, 2010) pp . 286-299

4 Ac cording to Y ang Minqing, f ull oper ationalisation of the J-20 wi ll r equire nearly 10-15 years. See " J-20 fengbo- Meiguo Riben sanbu zhongguo junshi weixie lun" [The J-20 Storm- United States and Japan spread China military threat theory] Sina.com January 24, 2011 accessed at <http:// news.sina.com.cn/c/sd/2011-01-24/171221867190.shtml>. Rodger Baker suggests that China needs more time to integrate and deploy effectively such stealth capabil ities. See R odger B aker, "China's Mil itary Comes Into Its Own" Str atfor.com January 18, 2011. Others suggested such a test is sure to change the balance of power in the region. See Dan Oaks, "Chinese fighter 'has changed power balance'" The Australian January 15, 2011

5 Jonathan Holslag, "Embracing Chinese Global Ambitions" The Washington Quarterly Vol. 32. No. 3 (July 2009) pp. 105-18

6 For instance, according to Admiral Yin Zhuo, a senior researcher at the Chinese navy's Equipment Research Centre, permanent base in the region would help supply Chinese ships. Yin said: "We are saying to fulfil our international commitments, we need to strengthen our [nav al] supply capacit y." Yin cited by Malcolm Moore, "China ma y build Middle East nav al base" The T elegraph December 30, 2009 at <http://www.telegraph.co.uk/news/worldnews/asia/ china/6911198/China-may-build-Middle-East-naval-base.html> . According to Shen Dingli, a noted nuclear physicist and academic at Fudan University, China should protect its international assets and for this "we need to set up our own blue-water navy and to rely on the overseas military bases to cut the supply costs." See Shen Dingli, "Don't shun the idea of setting up ov erseas military bases" January 28, 2010 at <http://www.china.org.cn/opinion/2010-

01/28/content_19324522.htm> See also the opinions of several Chinese, including fr om the na vy, Yu Dong, "Where Will the Chinese Navy B uild it s Overseas Supply Points?" *Guoji Xianqu Daobao* April 14, 2010 NewsEdge Document Number: 201004141477 .1_1bd10359d1406ce4 World News Connection File Number 985 Accession Number 297401581; Saibal Dasgupta, "China mulls setting up military base in Pakistan" The Times of India, January 28, 2010 and Richard Weitz, "Global Insights: China T ests Waters on First Overseas Naval Base" World Politics Review January 5, 2010

7 Liu Gang, "Introduction of Ship Formation Equipment Displayed in Maritime Parade" Liberation Army Daily April 25, 2009 NewsEdge Document Number: 200904251477.1_ 92a800a5f5e93bf1

8 Jason Miks, "China Rethinks Nuclear P osture?" The Diplomat January 7, 2011. See also, M. Taylor Fravel and Evan S. Medeiros, "China's Search for Assured Retaliation: The Evolution of Chinese Nuclear Strategy and Force Structure" International Security Vol. 35, No. 2 (F all 2010), pp. 48–87 and Junichi Abe, "China Will Not Join Global Nuclear Disarmament" AJISS-Commentary No. 75 at <ht tp://www.jiia.or.jp/en_commentary/200909/25-1.html >

9 See Dean Cheng, "Chinese Military Modernization: The Future Is Arriving Much Sooner Than Expected" The Heritage Foundation December 30, 2010 WebMemo #3090. Howev er, ac cording to Liang Guangl ie, China's def ence minister receiving Gates on January 10, 2011 at Beijing said "The efforts that we place on the research and development of weapons systems are by no means targeted at any third country or any other countries in the world, and it will by no means threaten any other country in the world.... We cannot call ourselves an advanced mil itary country...The gap between us and adv anced countries is at least two to three decades" . See "Chinese mil itary "decades" behind US" The Global Post January 10, 2011

10 Zhang Huaibi (ed), *Junren Shouce* [Soldier's Handbook] (Beijing: National Defense Universit y, 2005) part one

11 Today, with the technological progress, China is able to build several advanced weapons and systems and seems to have turned the tables on Russia and Israel- China's traditional suppliers of military equipment. See for this assessment based on the exhibition of defence electronic components and other products at Beijing, Rafael Smith, "Report from the 2010 Chinese Defense Electronics Exhibition (CIDEX): Growing Industry – Adv ancing Technology" October 3, 2010 ac cessed at <ht tp://www.strategycenter.net/research/pubID.230/ pub_detail.asp>. On the waning Russian interest to participate in the other main exhibition at Zhuhai in November 2010, see Richard Weitz, "How China's Jets Threaten Russia" The Diplomat December 13, 2010

12 See for the various assessments and Chinese debates on China's standing in the world in military capabilities, Academy of Military Affairs*Shijie Junshi Nianqin* [World Military Yearbook] 2005 (B eijing: PLA Publications, 2005) pp.124-32; "*Shishi qiushi*" [Seeking truth from facts] at <http://junshi.xilu.com/2010/ 0220/news_334_66686.html > ; "*Zhongguo junshi nengli lishi xing zhuanxing*

jiang tisheng guojia zhanlue nengli? " [Can historical transformation of China's military capability increase its national strategic capability?] April 29, 2009 at <http://zhidao.baidu.com/question/95438314.html >; " *Zhongguo junshi shili shijie paiming*?" [Global Ranking of the Chinese military capabilities] January 14, 2010 at <http://wenwen.soso.com/z/q174453306.htm > ; " *Zhongguo xianzai de junshi shili*" [China's current military capabilities] January 26, 2005 at <http://zhishi.baidu.com/> and Anthony H. Cordesman and Martin Kleiber, The Asian Conventional Military Balance in 2006: Overview of major Asian Powers (Washington, DC: Center for Strategic and International Studies, 2006)

13 The Academy of Military Science *Shijie Junshi Nianqin* 2005 does not provide for the bean count – details of the inventory of the PLA. (see p.128)

14 See Terry J Gander and I an V Hogg Eds. Jane' s Infantry Weapons (Surrey: Jane's Information Group, various years).

15 For a recent assessment, see Richar d Fisher, Jr., "PLA Makes Big Investments In Artillery" Aviation Week October 6, 2010 accessed at <http://www.strategycenter.net/research/pubID.233/pub_detail.asp >

16 See Richard Fisher, Jr., "The Implications of China's Naval Modernization for the United States: T estimony bef ore the U .S. –China Economic and S ecurity Review Commission" July 11, 2009 accessed at <http://www.strategycenter.net/research/pubID.199/pub_detail.asp>

17 "China's Future Route to Maritime Dominance" The Independent (Moscow) January 1, 2004 as excerpted at People's Daily and reprinted at <http://www.uscc.gov/researchpapers/2004/southchinaseamilitary.php >

18 See the three series on the Chinese naval power projection plans and capabilities at Stratfor.com. March-April 2009 at <www .stratfor.com >

19 "China now has more warships than America" The Economist August 30, 2010 at <http://www.economist.com/blogs/newsbook/2010/08/daily_chart>

20 Reports indicated to the shifting of T ype 094 Jin-class SSBN (with 8,000 km range Jl-2 SLBM) and construction of several berths to accommodate warships and tunnels that could lodge nearly 20 submarines at this base. See US Department of Def ense, Annual R eport To Congr ess: Mi litary and S ecurity Developments Involving the People's Republic of China 2010 accessed at <http://www.defenselink.org> p.2

21 US Department of Defense, Annual R eport To Congress: Mi litary Power Of The People's Republic Of China 2009 p. 49 accessed at <http://www.defenselink.org> and The Military Balance 2008 (London: Routledge, 2009) p.384

22 Curie Maharani and Koh Swee Lean Collin, *Bracing For Impact: Fifth-Generation Jet Fighter Programmes in Asia"* May 4, 2010 RSIS Commentaries No. 45 (2010) at <http://ntu.edu.sg > and Phillip C. Saunders and Eric R. Quam,

"China's Air Force Modernization" Joint Forces Quarterly Issue 47, (4th quarter 2007) pp. 28-33

23 See Jane's All The World's Aircraft (Surrey: Jane's Information Group various years)

24 Xin Ming (chief ed.) *Zhongguo renmin jiefangjun junguan shouce: Hangkong fence* [Chinese People's Liberation Army Officers Manual: Air Force Part] (Qingdao: Qingdao Publications, 1991); John Wilson Lewis and Xue Litai, "China's Search for a Modern Air Force" International Security vol. 24 no. 1 Summer 1999 pp. 64-94

25 For a comparison between the relative performances of such missiles, see *Bingqi Zhishi* Issue 114 April 1997 p.31

26 Vijai K Nair, "The Chinese Threat: An Indian perspective" China Brief V olume 1, Issue 9 November 8, 2001 at <http://china.jamestown.org.html >

27 In May 2009 and July and November 2010 accordingly the PLA naval forces conducted large exercises in the area as a follow up to the plan. See for the report, Kenji Minemura, "China's scenario to seize isles in South China Sea" Asahi Shimbun December 31, 2010 at <http://www.asahi.com/english/ TKY201012300112.html>

28   For a sober assessment see Drew Thompson, "Think Again: China's Military" Foreign Policy February 22, 2010 accessed at <http://www.foreignpolicy.com/ articles/2010/02/22/think_again_chinas_military> See also Austin Bay, "China's Navy Gets Bigger — But Why?" Real Clear Politics December 29, 2010 and for the impact of the PLA capabilities on India see Srikanth Kondapalli, "Chinese Military Eyes Southern Asia" in Andrew Scobell and Larry Wortzel eds. The PLA Shapes the Future Security Environment (Carlisle Barracks, PA: US Army War College & The Heritage Foundation, October 2006) pp.197-282 at <http:/ /www.strategicstudiesinstitute.army.mil/pdffiles/PUB709.pdf>

Chairman's Remarks

Thank you very much Professor Srikant Kondapalli for an extensive, exhaustive and very complete presentation. I wish we had more time for this session.

Ladies and gentlemen, we had four outstanding presentations. I am opening the house to comments, questions and discussions. I am told there was not enough time for questions and answers in the last Session. So, these things can also be referred to in the present Session, although, we have only fifteen minutes to do it.

Sessions 3 and 4: Combined Discussion

Issue Raised

The Chinese claim to having put conventional warheads on to their ICBMs, or even theAnti-Ship Ballistic Missile (ASBM) programme appears to be a counter-productive move, as having a conventional warhead on a ballistic missile would invite nuclear response even before the missile hits the target because a ballistic missile would be tracked from the moment it takes off. What are the panelists views on this issue?

Responses

(a) In 1988, the Blue Ribbon Commission, ordered by the President of the USA and led byAlstator (with leading experts) came to a conclusion that the future lies in having ICBM with conventional warheads as their accuracy had increased so much. The USA has not yet shown any signs of implementing their own conclusions arrived at that time; but the Chinese have done that. That poses many problems, particularly to a country that has a 'no first-use' nuclear strategy because every missile that takes off, you would not know whether it is armed with a nuclear or a conventional warhead. This is what India also ought to be doing, as we have 'countries' across our borders who have chosen the 'first use' nuclear policy. But our leaders tend to see it in financial terms and say that it will cost too much money etc. However, we do need to calculate the cost of, not doing it that way.

(b) There is a way to distinguish whether a ballistic missile is armed with a nuclear or a conventional warhead. Currently, the Long Range Ballistic Missiles (LRBMs) and ICBMs are basically 'nuclear powered', therefore, they carry nuclear warheads. There are no questions about that. However, the Short Range Ballistic Missiles (SRBMs) basically would always have a conventional warhead. Therefore, we need to focus only on the 'Middle Range Missiles (MRBMs) and Cruise missiles. Presently, the PLA Second Artillery Force have their 'reserve nuclear missiles' positioned all together in one base. So, if a picture is taken from an early warning system or a satellite, to take notice of any unusual activity at the nuclear warheads serving base, launch unit or position; and if there are also reports of some combat activity, then it can be anticipated that the missiles would be loaded with a nuclear warhead. Otherwise, if the missile is launched without any linkages with this Second Artillery reserve base, then basically it would be carrying a conventional warhead.

Issue Raised

Every speaker today has spoken about the 'regional build-up of the Chinese' around the South China Sea, the Indian Ocean and certain other areas in the region. The South Korean speaker also alluded to the   Washington Conference. Is this not the right time for this region to evolve some form of 'regional security architecture'? The closest we have got to it is known as the ASEAN Defence Minister's Meeting at Hanoi in July, 2010.

Response

One of the speakers has actually proposed arms control measures and that is what you are proposing.

Issue Raised

Most of the speakers have laid a lot of emphasis on the Naval build-up of China. However, one area which has not been really addressed is the issue of 'Strategic Nuclear Assets of China'. Professor Kondapalli talked about it, very briefly. What is the reason for that?

Response

In terms of conventional and nuclear payoffs, the situation is confusing because there is really no answer to this. Except that we need to look into our own 'Early Warning Devices' to determine the efficacy and adequacy of nuclear or conventional payoffs. Presently, Early Warning Systems are the only single best defensive measure. Secondly, in terms of the Ballistic Missile Defence (BMD) preparations all countries, including Japan and India, are developing these systems.

There are four estimates related to the Chinese nuclear arsenals in terms of stockpiles increase.Albright's suggestion (Rand Corporation) and the Arms Control Disarmament Agency (ACDA) estimate that (based on the quantum of enriched plutonium and enriched uranium that they can produce) the Chinese will be able to make something like 2000 bombs by 2015. Five major estimates have been made from the stockpile that they have and from the amount they would be able to produce in the future. While China still suggests that this is their 'minimum nuclear deterrent' position; yet, these stockpiles indicate that they are actually moving towards a 'limited nuclear deterrent'. Secondly, Chinese never committed anything at the Strategic Arms Reduction Treaty (START1) and START 2 dialogue process. President Obama did make a mention of this.

Issue Raised

Most of the speakers have alluded to the threat that China is posing to our region, but I would like to seek views about the threat South Korea perceives from China.

Response

The military build-up in China can be a threat to Korean security as well as other neighbouring countries. It can be described in two terms. First is about the Chinese intention. South Korea tries to maintain peace and stability on the Korean Peninsula. But in March last year , North Korea torpedoed a South Korean warship. At that time, China just maintained a neutral stand because they did not want to disturb the Six-Party talks that were going on then. They clearly mentioned that they neither favoured the North Korean side nor the South Korean side. Later, South Korean measures to respond to North Korean military provocation were twofold: First one was, to bring this matter to the UN Security Council to facilitate denouncement of this sort of thing. But, at that time China opposed to insert the 'clause' that North Korea was the attacker. So, that was really disappointing. They also opposed the US military exercises in West Pacific Ocean. What was their intention in doing so?Actually they wanted to be on the side of North Korea. That clearly indicates the relative importance of China in maintaining peace and security on the Korean Peninsula in the future.

My second point is about the Chinese capabilityWe will get into a pact for operational control with the USA on the Korean Peninsula. Maybe, the US forces could get strategic flexibility by moving the US forces from Korea to another place in East   Asia to address all the dimensions of PLA 's asymmetric strategy etc. The US base in Korea can be a target for China's Dong Feng ballistic missiles. These are examples that clearly show that we should remain prepared for threats from China in the future.

Also, if there is a contingency in North Korea; maybe, if the Kim Jong-il regime collapses, China could intervene. Their increased military power would actually have some role in the future, in order to lead the way in the Korean Peninsula reunification process and stabilising North Korea.

Session 4: Chairman's Concluding Remarks

Air Commodore Jasjit Singh, AVSM, VrC, VM (Retd)

We have gone past the time within which we were supposed to finish and therefore practically I am not going to say anything. But, let me just mention one thing about the Chinese military capabilities and the way it is being built-up. What stands out as most important are essentially two issues: One is that the Chinese military, especially the Chinese Air force and the Chinese Navy, has gone on to conduct, for the first time in the PRCs history (doctrine strategy, equipment) exercises which aimed at 'offensive action' i.e. a long range strategic strike. That is a fundamental change that has taken place.

The Chinese Navy is going to be in the Indian Ocean; whatever you want to call them, they come for a friendly visit and they go back with something else. China doesn't have to actually start fighting the Indian Navy in the Indian Ocean. They themselves have their vulnerabilities, and we need to look at them. Why are we looking at their strengths? The second point is a much larger project: What China is doing, as part of 'China's grand strategy' is to keep the USA as their benchmark. Therefore, it is increasing its military capabilities technologically and otherwise to be able to one day catch up with the USA. This is what the erstwhile Soviet Union used to be doing. In some cases the Soviet Union over shot their position and in some cases it remained far behind. But all of these things; for example just take the central issue of using the ballistic missiles with conventional warheads. The US has a choice, at any time to use any of the ballistic missiles with conventional warhead. There is no need for them to come forth with an enunciation that they would deploy a thousand of them.

The Cruise Missiles are now coming up with a new technology from the twenty years old Tomahawk, and they are already on it. India also has supersonic Mach 3 missile, three times the speed of sound. Very soon there will be hyper-supersonic cruise missiles. We are seeing anti-ballistic missile defences growing all over the world.

There is a counter anti-ballistic missile now on the list. We used to hear and talk about it ten years ago, but basically it is a manoeuvring re-entry vehicle. A manoeuvring re-entry vehicle technology is just not available to other countries; it is just being mastered by the USA and Russia. China is claiming to do that or is certainly working towards that; which actually implies that three powers in the world will have military capability that others will not have. That has political, economic and strategic implications that we can see right across the board in this field. This question, whether the 'informationalisation warfare' is linked back to the offence-defence equation of the 'asymmetric warfare'; would take you will get into 'cyber warfare' automatically. Each area in itself is an area of both vulnerability and certain amount of strength.

To conclude, I can say that China is a rising power , not only just in name, but also in terms of its apparent capabilities. But, what it is doing today is a clear sign that in very selective key areas it is going to match the USA. It is possible for them to do so because what you need, to take one example, is 're-entry manoeuvrable vehicle'. To have that, what you need is the 'scram-jet' technology. If you work very hard on a single technology which can give you that benefit, you are not getting a 'silver bullet' as such. But that is a capability with which you can always, as Putin said in 2004, "We have now a deployable, operational, manoeuvrable re-entry vehicle which will defeat any ballistic missile defence on earth". The USA had got that technology ages ago and has been improving it all long.

So, you are already seeing a fundamental change in, how the USA in the 21st century, is going to use its military power . When new difficulties develop and the growing gap between these 'three big powers' and the rest of the world gets closer- it could be on the other side of China or this side of China, or east side of China. When would the Chinese use their capabilities in an aggressive, offensive form is very difficult to predict. On the other hand, if you do not have capabilities then your intentions are only on paper

When you have the capabilities, then you can translate your intention into capabilities and action.

Therefore, at least as military men we should look far more at the capabilities - with a cautionary word. Let us not get into 'worst case scenario' but look into these issues very carefully Here the numbers are not going to matter. For example, in the case of nuclear weapons, the numbers are not going to be the most critical factor - here technology is going to be the most critical factor. How many re-entry vehicles do you have? Does China need to deploy a thousand missiles? Yes, if the opposition has a fairly confident ballistic missile defences deployed around or in Taiwan. But the threat is very clear, for the challenge is also very clear and the response is also very clear. How the geopolitics of it will work out that is where we hope our ambassadors will find a solution for us and work out the future course of action, because in military terms we are looking at three countries – the USA, China and Russia. In economic terms, by and large you will be soon looking at three countries again; but the equation would be different - India, China and the USA.

With that let me on behalf of the participants thank the paper presenters. In my opinion although the time duration was very short, they have done an outstanding job in compressing it all into 18-20 minutes. I am grateful to you all for that, and on behalf of the panelists may I thank the audience and above all the USI.

Fifth Session

China's Strategic Posture: An Assessment

Introductory Remarks	Lt Gen PK Singh, PVSM,AVSM (Retd), Director USI
Chairman's Opening Remarks	Shri Shyam Saran, IFS (Retd) Former Foreign Secretary, India
First Paper	Dr Ashley Tellis, USA
Chairman's Remarks	(After First Paper)
Second Paper	Prof Klaus Lange, ITS, Germany
Third Paper	Shri Jaydev Ranade, IPS (Retd)
Fourth Paper	Mr Francis Yi-hua Kan, National Chengchi University, Taiwan
Fifth Paper	Prof Richard Rigby, ANU, Australia
Discussion	
Chairman's Concluding Remarks	Shri Shyam Saran, IFS (Retd) Former Foreign Secretary, India
Valedictory Address	Shri Kanwal Sibal, IFS (Retd) Former Foreign Secretary, India
Vote of Thanks	Lt Gen PK Singh, PVSM, AVSM (Retd), Director USI

Session 5 : Opening Remarks

Lieutenant General PK Singh, PVSM,AVSM (Retd)

Good Afternoon ladies and gentlemen. At the outset, I must welcome the Chief of Naval Staff for his presence here. I also take this opportunity to thank the High Commissioner ofAustralia who is also present here. Needless to say, I thank each of you for being here. The last session of our seminar will focus on 'China's Strategic Posture – An Assessment'. Let me explain the logic to you for this session and the theme. While we were discussing this seminar, we talked internally about China's strategy, its economy, military etc. We felt there was one more aspect – something which was neither published nor written about, but existed on the ground i.e. the 'posturing'. Each one of us reads that 'posturing'differently. Various incidents small or big need to be examined.At that time we felt that it would be ideal to get the views of not just the Indian experts but also of experts from other countries. That is how this panel was designed and constructed. We are extremely fortunate to have with us such an eminent panel which is chaired by none other than Ambassador Shyam Saran, India' s former Foreign Secretary and the Prime Minister 's emissary. Ambassador Shyam Saran needs no introduction so I will not spend time telling you about his achievements. I will now hand over the proceedings to Ambassador Shyam Saran.

Session 5: Chairman's Introductory Remarks

Shri Shyam Saran, IFS (Retd) FormerForeign Secretary, India

The subject is 'China's Strategic Posture –An Assessment' and the panelists will make an assessment of, what China's strategic posture would be? It is an important subject, particularly at this juncture where there are anxieties in China's own neighbourhood about, what China's recent behaviour implies. There is also a sense that perhaps we are not quite aware of China' s own thinking, and the drivers for this posture, which are emerging? This of course is of critical importance to a neghbouring country like India.

I have just come back after visiting four South EastAsian countries – Singapore, Vietnam, Laos and Thailand. I was quite intrigued to see that while there were certainly anxieties about China' s emer gence in the neighbourhood, the perceptible reaction to it was there even within these South EastAsian countries. There are differing perceptions of what China's recent behaviour implies.

So, this is an important subject. I have no doubt that the distinguished panelists will do a thorough job in making this assessment. So without further ado, may I first call on DrAshley Tellis from the USAto share his perceptions with us on the subject.

Session 5 : First Paper

Dr Ashley Tellis

Thank you once again for inviting me to this seminar I am happy to speak once again on this issue of 'China' s Strategic Posture – An Assessment'. However, I will not repeat some of the themes that I elaborated yesterday because I did speak on some of the dimensions of the posture in my first presentation. So, I will only talk about some other aspects that I didn't touch upon yesterday.

Let me start by at least reaffirming one important point that we have to keep in mind and that is – China' strategic postures are still oriented towards maximisation of power. It is this maximisation of power that is focused on attaining the range of external and internal goals. These internal goals are fundamentally directed towards sustaining economic growth in order to maintain what is laid down in the authoritarian social contract that keeps the China's Communist Party (CCP) in business. Even as the CCP is attempting to modernise itself in the face of great economic success, but also growing inequality and rising internal restiveness. So, these domestic goals cannot be overlooked as one thinks about China' s posture. I want to focus on externals this evening.

In the external area, it is very important to recognise that China' s success in maximising its National power over the last thirty years has now enabled it to move from what was its previous objective – which was protecting narrow tangibles, primarily its territorial integrity to now pursuing diffused larger national interests. What you are seeing at the moment is a classic case of a rising power – attempting to protect its prerogatives and its claims, consistent with the power that it has succeeded in accumulating and in anticipation that the existing great powers in the system might try to restrain its rise. So, there is a peculiar mix of defensiveness and offensiveness in the posture. This is reflected most clearly in the changing orientation of the Chinese military. I just want to say a few words about that.

The PLA's notion today of new historical missions encapsulates perfectly the evolving Chinese shift from the protection of tangible goals like territorial integrity to larger goals like essentially keeping strategic outcomes both within the region surrounding China and in the larger international environment. There are four broad dimensions that I would like to flag in the external realm which allow us to see the changes in Chinese posture.

The first objective is that China is focused greatly on making all the investments required to protect its interests vis-à-vis what it believes is its biggest competitor in the international system and that is the USA. These investments are taking the forms of very substantial upgrades to its strategic nuclear capabilities because nuclear deterrence is more important to China today than ever before, great investments multi-dimensionally and across the services in anti-access, anti-denial capabilities and simultaneously continuing a very vigourous engagement with the USA.

So, the first thing to bear in mind when one thinks of China posture is that the USA still remains central to its power political calculations; and much of what it is doing in the economic, strategic and military realms is focused on an effort to protect its interests vis-à-vis Washington. There is a second dimension to this posture and that is, China is preparing to deal with the powers on its periphery particularly what its beliefs are - its peer powers and that too from a position of strength. It will pose certain challenges to the interests of countries that lie on its periphery and it will no longer be content to simply manage those challenges through diplomatic means. Of course, diplomatic means are preferable at all times but should they fail, China wants to be able to put in place the capabilities it has to protect its interests vis-à-vis these peer players. A very important aspect of this is the way China treats disputes with its peers. No longer is China interested in resolving the disputes that it has with its peers. It happens to resolve disputes that it might have with its political inferiors but not with its peers, because the disputes that it has with its peers are really substantive disputes. China seems to believe that it would be able to resolve such disputes in its favour the longer it waits and as it accumulates greater powerSo, when one thinks of key disputes involving real competitors, like India and Japan, it is in China' strategic interest to delay any final resolution of these disputes because of its expectations that its own continuing growth and power will actually advantage it – when it has to deal seriously with the management of these disputes. In order to sustain this strategywhat China has embarked upon, is a very comprehensive conventional force modernisation. You see this unfolding in all dimensions of Chinese capabilities.

I am briefly going to highlight a few aspects of this modernisation. With land forces, the focus is on rationalising China' capabilities – reducing the numbers of the force but simultaneously raising its combat capability, improving its logistics and more importantly, improving its command and control mechanisms to enable the Chinese state not simply to use forces in particular military regions but actually control forces across multiple military regions.

Where Naval Forces are concerned, China is now moving towards the capacity to undertake open ocean operations of the kind that were simply impossible for China to do for most of its independent spree. Its greatest investments are actually not in its platforms, even though it is making those investments, but in a very serious effort to understand the maritime environment. The resources that China is putting to understanding the oceans, into building the capacity to fighting different realms in the oceans suggest that this is more than just a haphazard effort at building capabilities that can appear and can be identified.

As far as the Air Force is concerned, their focus is very much on rationalising the force structure, i.e. having a smaller air force but having greater combat capabilities and supplementing that with the ability to control information. Two new dimensions that China has made investments are in Space and the Cyber Space. And for those of you who follow these issues, some of the developments there are quite disturbing.

There is a third dimension of China' posture that I think is very important to keep in mind and we should not forget – i.e. the need to consolidate internal control over restive provinces. Even as China looks to manage the world outside its borders, it is constantly reminded of the fact that the task of state building inside is not complete. So, China has focused great attention and will do even more after the exit of Hu-Jin Tao to really consolidating control in the interior and in the western areas. It will do so essentially in four ways. An economic strategy that focuses very much on trying to shift resources from the coastal areas into the interior - a very concerted effort at improving living standards and finally a pervasive upgradation of internal security forces – primarily the Peoples   Armed Police and the Reserve Forces.

The fourth dimension of China' s changing posture is the ef fort now being made to transform the Chinese economy for what they believe would be increasingly a post western liberal economic order This transformation again will be very consequential. It is a transformation that is focused on changing the Chinese economy from its current presence of manufacturing for export to emphasis on innovation, looking to move the macro economics from investment to consumption, shifting from rural development increasingly to urbanisation and finally moving from social neglect to creating structures of social security.

So you see, China's postures are essentially undergoing transformation in all four dimensions. I will summarise this by saying that as a country China is moving rapidly from a position where it was shaped by the world to actually attempting to shape the world. As a military force, it is moving rapidly from simply focusing on the defence of territory to procuring and servicing much greater strategic interests over a bigger geographic space. China is not yet a global power but I see it increasingly becoming a serious multi-dimensional competitor, not only to the regional states but also to the USA.

Chairman's Remarks

Thank you very much Ashley for giving us a very broad brush view of China's strategic posture today, and as I had stated earlier, focusing on the 'drivers' behind that strategic posture. You mentioned 'space' and 'cyber space'; perhaps, one should also look at the very 'pliant way' China is moving towards asymmetrical development of its power potential, rather than simply trying to equate itself in dif ferent sectors of power. It is also trying to develop areas which in a sense, gives it the possibility of exploiting the vulnerabilities, both of the USA and other powers.

I will now give the floor to Professor Klaus Lange of Germany.

Session 5 : Second Paper

Professor Klaus Lange

Ladies and gentlemen, my task is to give an impression of the European feelings, attitude and assessment of the Chinese strategic posture. This assessment has gone through different stages. I am starting with the 1960s. I would like to mention a book *Power Formulas*' by Dillon Fox, published in 1967 which very much influenced the thinking of strategic experts in those days. In this book Fox tried to assess the power-political status of a couple of nations, among others China, by looking at certain parameters like steel production, energy production, demographic development etc.At that time Fox quite surprisingly had already come to the conclusion that 'China would be the number one power in the world by the year 2020 approximately'. This view of looking at China had a profound influence, for the next 10-15 years, on the European assessments, expectations, fears and hopes. One could summarise that China was considered to be a 'sleeping giant', that China had a good chance of becoming a leader of the third world and would even cut off the 'first world' from indispensable supply of raw materials. Lastly, it was expected that China would take over lead, sooner or later of the so called socialist kin. European feelings towards China were very much influenced by certain fears.

Later on, when it became clear that Chinese development had entered a period of economic stagnation, interest in China faded apart from some sections of the European Left who considered Maoism as an answer to the evils of capitalism. The fear of Chinese aggressive activity , at the end of 1960's and beginning of 1970's, was nurtured by two events: one very well known is the clash between China and the Soviet Union at the Ussuri River the second one is less known, and I am referring to the attempt by China to place Ballistic missiles on the territories of a European allyAlbania. It was only due to historically very remarkable early cooperation between the

Warsaw pact countries and the Western countries (NATO) that Albania, in the final analysis considered that to be a risky undertaking. This Chinese attempt was neutralised by this joint intervention.   Anyway, it left a very deep impression in the minds of European security experts.

Many things about China have been said already Presently, in Europe there are fears, that hopes of economic cooperation from China, in comparison with other countries, are smaller . I would say 90 per cent of European hopes and fears are concentrating on the 'economic' aspect of the European - Chinese relationship and may be at best only 10 per cent of possibilities are determined by 'security' considerations. The general credo in Europe is that in order to maintain internal stabilitywhich is synonymous with power, China needs high rate of economic growthAnything that could jeopardise such growth rate must be avoided in the interest of the Communist Party agenda and power position.

China is therefore considered to be a highly 'risk averse' country due to this over placed aim of high economic growth rates. If we look at the military developments and armament politics, European experts try to stress that for example, by looking at their land forces: regarding tanks and artillery of course old models have been there for quite some time – they are removed far more quickly than the new ones being put into service. Then we have this reduction of troops: there have been two figures mentioned this morning, one was 1.6 million and another was 1.2 million.As far as I could find out, European planners assessments are arriving at a figure of 1.25 million. It is clear that there is not much transparency , but Europeans do not see any dramatic development when they look at their Land Forces.

Somewhat different impression prevails in Europe, when we look at the development of the Chinese Navy . Again, I have to repeat what has been said already. About 50 per cent of Chinese ships can be considered as 'obsolete'. However, one must take into account the ship building capacities which do indeed give much food for thought. Here again, Chinese programmes are not transparent at all. There are many indications that production figures and units go up 'year by year ' in a very steep curve.

It is also interesting to look at the Chinese Naval build-up from the European point of view. It is seen that the Southern fleet is apparently the most important one. It is confirmed by the fact that this fleet is commanded, to the best of my knowledge, by a Vice Admiral, whereas the Eastern and Northern fleets have Rear Admirals in command. May be, this is a bit too far fetched but may be it is also not. Anyway, the PLA Navy in European assessment is looking in the middle and long term at the global south. When we are talking about a timeframe of 10 to 20 years, the Chinese are very much concentrating on the development of submarines. Although the European experts feel that the Chinese technology is far behind in comparable times and distance. Technologies, particularly the noise levels of even the Chinese nuclear submarines, are no match to respective W   estern counterparts.

Looking at the Air Force, again we have the phenomenon that the Chinese Air Force has embarked on a trend to a cosmopolitan set of quantity One could say that China is anticipating asymmetric warfare instead of a symmetric conflict in future, which I feel is quite interestingAlthough deficits in actual and painted capacities would lead one to the conclusion that one must not exaggerate, (in European eyes) the threat posed by the Chinese Air Force. Of course, people in India and T   aiwan and elsewhere in the region would view and comment on this in a different way but, faraway Europe feels safe.

As far as Nuclear Strategic Forces are concerned, European experts point to the thesis of the 2002 White Paper on Defence. This White Paper defines the aim of the developments in that sector. It is reporting a 'steady improvement of second strike ability'. I don't want to go on into numbers. On that I fully agree with what has been said this morning. There is no difference in assessment of technology and so on.

Let me now give you some examples of what the Europeans are really scared of. At this hour, the Chinese investments in the infrastructure of weaker European states is causing concern. I will give you a few examples. Chinese investments in tiny Moldova is already about 10 per cent of that country's GDP. The Export Import Bank of Chinas Finance Institute quotes its heavy investments in airports and industrial zones in Serbia, Croatia and Bulgaria. The Chinese Development Bank is about to invest more than one billion Euros in the Romanian agricultural mining and enegy sector. In Poland, a subsidiary of Chinese Railway has won two public contracts funding an outlet being financed by the European Development Investment Bank to the tune of approximately 500 million dollars; Chinese offer has been 30 per cent cheaper than the offers by their competitors. In Greece, the Chinese Maritime price group which fought for the contract in 2008, has already been commissioned to refurbish a major part of the container Port of Piraeus and the same is about to happen in the Port of Salonike. One could quote numerous examples of the Chinese economic advancement into Europe and the adjacent regions. In places such as Turkey for instance, China is busy investing all in all about now 28 billion Dollars in a huge Railway coaches project. This is quite surprising. There are great political concerns related to Chinese economic activities; namely in the guise of courting the economically weaker countries.

China creates an impression in those countries that their future must not necessarily be based on future European integration and that they can eventually go alone. In other words, under given conditions, China has very well the capacity to seriously question extended European integration, which is about to experience a great boost after the end of the Cold War. This in the eyes of European political decision makers – is the most urgent and immediate challenge to Europe by China. In my view, for the Europeans, this is the number one problem. The answer to this problem is still not visible and we are still struggling to find an answer to that.

Session 5 : Third Paper

Shri Jaydev Ranade, IPS (Retd)

In the past couple of years China has occupied the centre stage of political and geostrategic discourse not only because of its rise, but more because of its assertive policies and what they portend.

Since around 2008, when China opted for a more assertive style, there has been a strong suggestion of military muscle in its diplomatic efforts to further national interests. The decision to adopt an assertive stance reflects the assessment of China's leadership that its national capabilities are now poised to merge with intentions, enabling China to overtly push on issues benefiting its national self-interest.

The assertiveness now seen in China' s policies is reflective of the newfound confidence of the Chinese leadership and people. This has been generated largely by China's consistent double-digit economic growth over three decades and ensuant international adulation. The Chinese Communist Party leadership's confidence particularly, stems from its view that: (a) the Party's successful policies have raised the nation to its present level of military strength and economic prosperity; (b) that the country is much wealthier as visible in its high share of international trade, huge US$ 2.4 trillion foreign currency reserves etc and that the majority of the people are vastly better off than before as evidenced by their approximately US$ 4,000 annual per capita income; (c) that the Party has generally maintained stability and law and order in society , including to a fair extent in the restive Autonomous Regions of Xinjiang and Xizang; and (d) that the Party's position currently remains unassailable.

In contrast, Chinese analysts assessed that the US military was over-stretched consequent to being embroiled in the wars in Iraq and Afghanistan and that the world' s major economies, especially the US, had been considerably weakened because of the deleterious effects of the international economic crisis.

Chinese leaders, therefore, perceived the current time as opportune for China to make its bid for pre-eminence in the wideAsia-Pacific region. Its success in coercing European countries to resile from long-held positions on hitherto contentious issues, like Human Rights and T ibet, encouraged Beijing. China's assessment seemed to have been substantiated when Hillary Clinton, during her first visit to Beijing as the US Secretary of State, failed to raise Human Rights,Tibet and Democracy in her meetings with Chinese leaders. Obama's declining to meet the Dalai Lama during his visit to Washington was additional confirmation of apparent American weakness. In this backdrop the joint statements issued after the two summit meetings between Hu Jintao and Obama, in September and November 2009 respectively, took on greater significance for the Chinese. They assumed that the USA was now willing to let China exercise the role of regional hegemon while retaining for itself the mantle of global superpower

Meanwhile military modernisation had proceeded apace during the last three decades. The foundations were laid by Deng Xiaoping who anticipated a large role for the PLA in the coming years. For example, he commenced the process of revising the PLA's doctrine which today is one of 'Winning short-duration Local Wars under Hi-tech Informatised Conditions'. Successive Chinese leaders ensured adequate funds for military modernisation and the defence budget received double-digit hikes each year since the early 1990s (except in 1993). Conservative estimates peg China' current defence budget at around US$ 90 billionAs Chairman of the Central Military Commission Hu Jintao particularly paid attention to the PLA 's modernisation and preparedness to fulfill its tasks. Safeguarding of national sovereignty and territories is the primary task of the PLA, and this includes the 'recovery' of 'lost' or claimed territories.

The PLA Navy is another example of Deng Xiaopings prescience. As far back as 1982 he selected Liu Huaqing, the only senior PLA officer with experience of the sea and rank ofAdmiral to build and modernise the PLA Navy. Liu Huaqing laid the foundations for today' s PLA Navy and also prescribed its doctrine. He defined 'coastal waters for the Navy, with Deng Xiaoping's approval. The definition is significant and relevant. It includes 'the Yellow Sea, Eastern Sea (East China Sea), the Southern Sea (South China Sea), the Nansha Archipelago and Taiwan, the seas on this side and that side of Okinawa, as well as the Northern Region of the Pacific. Today the PLA Navy is in the vanguard not only of China's efforts to protect its sea lanes of communication, but also to enforce its maritime territorial claims in the South China Sea and with Japan.

Vivid demonstrations of the use of military muscle to reinforce diplomatic efforts involve the PLANavy. In March 2009, PLANavy vessels confronted the US survey ship 'USNS Impeccable', which was accused of intruding into China's EEZ. Another incident occurred in Subic Bay of the Philippines coast on 11 June 2009, when a Chinese submarine hit an underwater sonar array being towed by the destroyer ' USS John McCain'. Since late 2007-08 Chinese Navy vessels have also clashed with V ietnamese craft while enforcing their maritime territorial claims and stand-offs have occurred with Japanese vessels around the Senkaku, or Diaoyu, Islands. In fact, relations between Japan and China have been strained since July/August 2010 due to maritime territorial disputes.

It is during this period that China adopted an assertive posture with India too. While border negotiations and official-level contacts between India and China continued, military pressure along the 4,057 kms long undemarcated India-China border increased as did the number of intrusions. China re-opened the hitherto settled issue of Sikkim and enhanced the profile of its territorial claim on Arunachal Pradesh and, more recently, raised the ante in Kashmir.

A relatively new element has been recently added to Chinese diplomatic posturing contributing to this perception of assertiveness. This is the increasing incidence of comments by former, or serving, military officials which, at times, appear to deviate from stated policy . A number of such officers are employed in military-affiliated think-tanks and hold posts equated with military ranks. Had they not been given licence to speak they would undoubtedly have been punished. This particularly when the Party and the

Party General Secretary, Hu Jintao, retain such a tight grip on the PLA. No reports have, however, been noticed to suggest that any punishments have been meted out. On the other hand some of them are known to have received promotions!

There are other instances where China has assertively pushed its self-interest disregarding the articulated valid concerns of other nations. One example is that of rare earth exports to Japan. A more serious issue that impacts on the livelihoods of millions of people relates to the construction of dams on the upper Mekong River thereby reducing water flows downstream. Another serious issue having a similar impact is the proposed diversion of the Brahmaputra river waters to China's arid, but populated, north.

In conclusion, China's assertiveness is proving to be counterproductive and recently received a setback. The USA-ROK military exercises in the middle of this year were correctly interpreted in Beijing as indicative of US intention to ener getically re-enter the Asia-Pacific and maintain its dominance. Beijing has taken note of the apprehension regarding future Chinese policies in capitals in the region.The US President Obama's speech recently in the Indian Parliament would have amply reinforced this assessment. The public offer of support by US Secretary of State Hillary Clinton to Japan in the current dispute with China over the Senkaku, or Diaoyu islands together with the US overtures to Vietnam, Indonesia and South Korea have not gone unnoticed. Commentaries in the official Chinese media have described these as attempts at 'containment' of China and specifically warned India, Japan,Vietnam and Indonesia against falling into the US trap.

There is debate underway in China, though, as to whether the discarding of Deng Xiaoping's policy of *taoguang yanghui* , or 'lie low , bide your time', was premature. Articles discussing this occasionally appear in the official media like the Peoples' Daily and Guangming Daily and these are also exploring the possibility of Beijing reverting to its earlier policyA few Chinese commentators have candidly acknowledged that China's policy of 'peaceful rise', modified to 'peaceful development', had apparently not found many takers. They suggest that Beijing revert to its earlier policy and bide its time.

Whether and how China's leadership will try to retrieve its position and refurbish the image it had sought to assiduously cultivate earlier is unclear but it will not be easy. There are no indications yet to suggest a reversal in policy in which Hu Jintao's probable successor, Xi Jinping, would also have been involved.

Session 5 : Fourth Paper

Mr Francis Yi-hua Kan

Introduction

The whole world is now witnessing a rapidly emerging power gradually capable of competing with the existing sole great power for regional or even global supremacy, an extraordinary case that could only possibly happen once in a few centuries. While China's ascendancy has become a hotly debated topic concerning its benign or malign sides of its rise, the questions remain how this emerging great power would actually rise to its pre-eminence, what the world order would look like as a result of this change, and more important, whether the world, particularly nations around it, have already prepared for this eventuality. Over all, it is worthwhile to understand What China is thinking about its future and whether China is able to shape the international system?

To answer these questions, this paper aims at analysing China's grand strategy to become a global player . A nation's grand strategy can be understood as its overall project with an aim at amassing all kinds of power hard and soft, available to achieve its goal, be it the nation best security or other ambitions. Grand strategy should comprise a set of perceptions, assumptions and actions about how a nation can maintain and enhance its own security in view of its national resources and international environment. A nation would formulate a grand strategy through searching the causal links between the security objectives and all the means available to achieve the goals.[2]

China's grand strategy has been generally influenced by three major factors. First, with a bitter *past* history of national humiliation the Chinese have long suffered, Beijing will make every effort to protect itself from any possible aggression and further to maximise its core interests. Over the last one and a half centuries, the Chinese have lived with a murky memory that the nation had been invaded, its sovereignty encroached and its national pride hurt. Generations of leaders under whatever regimes have strenuously struggled for building a strong nation and thus reducing the possibilities that China could be suppressed again. The Chinese today aspire to make the nation a strong and prosperous great power capable of guarding its national sovereignty and territorial integrity.

Second, as a current major regional player , China has emphatically striven to amass every power to be able to shape the region's order. China's growing economy has made it a strong competitor vis-à-vis the USA in influencing the way regionalism is emerging. Its rising power has offered nations in the region opportunities to prosper but its increasing assertiveness has also prompted region's players worry about its formidable threat. China's rapid ascendancy has also rendered Washington to re-formulate its strategic plan and to reassure its allies in the region of its determination to guarantee regional security.

Third, to be a future global great power, China would endeavour to enhance its capabilities to be a leading power that would be able to challenge the US dominance, set the global agenda and dictate the rules of the game at the world's level. China's global projection would start by reinforcing its leading role in region's security and then expand its influence over global affairs. China's global role has been widely accepted by areas beyond its immediate borders and the thesis of 'China way' or 'Beijing consensus' has also been highly debated. The continuing rise of China will equip it with more leverages to influence the future outlook of the international system.

Over all, the long-term objective of China's grand strategy is to build the nation into a leading great power China's grand strategy with its rising power and increasing assertiveness will alter the security environment and re-shape the balance of power vis-à-vis the USA in Asia and beyond.

China's Grand Strategy: Discourse and Capability Building

China, like any other previous great powers, is driven by its unparalleled growth for its greater international role, not necessarily by a master plan for global prominence. China is vigorously converting its newly-obtained economic power into formidable political and military influence in the region and beyond. Yet, Beijing has attempted to formulate discourse that could justify its global project and set the tone for its grand strategy

Predient Hu Jintao of the PRC outlined China's future relations with the outside world and the global order as a whole at the UN in September 2005. He proposed the notion of 'building a harmonious world', a domestic-policy equivalent, the 'harmonious society' whose formal aim is to apply state power to narrowing the domestic divide between the haves and have-nots and reducing growing social tensions. In a similar vein, 'building a harmonious world' notion was designed as a new route to 'lasting peace and common prosperity' that will allow different civilisations with divergent social systems to co-exist harmoniously and peacefully in an emerging global order where China will play an important role. [3] In contrast to the current US-dominated world, the future international political and economic order is characterised by the 'democratisation' of international relations where China does not seek hegemony or predominance but the US supremacy should be balanced. [4]

However, the 'building a harmonious world' idea is only a symbolic gesture to question, if not yet challenge, the West-dominated world order, but not a substantial agenda that could provide detailed roadmap of achieving that particular goal. It also remains ambiguous about China' role in making the 'harmonious world' a reality. The question as to whether China benignly *aspires* to see a 'harmonious world' to become possible or whether China has the ambition to *make* it true leaves ample room for imagination.

In parallel with the 'harmonious world' notion, a view of how China can compete to become the world's 'number-one power' is another vision of projecting China's future. [5] This idea puts the 'Rise of China' before a rise of world order and espouses that China needs to purse a military rise in order to sustain its economic and political influence around the globe. It claims that China should take advantage of the on-going 'period of strategic opportunity' to keep the current rise at a rapid pace to the extent that China could narrow the gap with the USA. Its ultimate goal is to rival American hegemony and to become the world's number one in economic, political, cultural and military fronts.

On the whole, the 'number one power' thesis of China's strategic goal is not necessarily contradictory to the 'harmonious world' discourse because a friendly international environment where the US dominance remains intact, at least for the time being, and China continues to grow serves the interests of China that offers it best opportunities to compete with the American global status in the future. China has attempted to secure for itself a favourable position globally in order to sustain the momentum in its economic, political and military thrust. Before its grand strategy can fully materialise, Beijing will endeavour to shrink the power gap with Washington and to increase its relative power. Not only can its advance on all fronts help China move up to a global power level, it can also enhance the legitimacy of the Chinese government within.

China's steady advance in military power has been specifically identified as clear reflection of its formidable power China has increased its military budget by double-digit amounts almost every year since 1989. The figures for actual defence spending are usually two to four times larger than the numbers China officially provides. As a result, China's real defence expenditure has virtually quadrupled over the last few decades. China now is the second biggest military spender , next only to the USA. In purely defensive terms, China's military budget increases, happening since the end of the Cold War, when most of countries were reducing their military budgets dramatically, seems to lack any justification as China faces no real external threat.[6] Beijing's explanation for such striking increases in military spending during peaceful times is that China urgently needs comparable military capabilities to match its rising economic power and international status.

China's military modernisation has reinforced its capabilities in all Services, including navy, air force, ground troops, marine and missile forces. The PLA has acquired advanced surface combatants and submarines, precision-strike fighter jets, air-to-air refuelling aircraft, satellites, unmanned aerial vehicles, a variety of ballistic, cruise and tactical missile systems, and an extensive command, control, communications, computers, intelligence,

surveillance and reconnaissance (C4ISR). It is particularly noteworthy that
with better precision guided capability and longer ranges, the PLA missile
forces could pose serious threat to its neighbours and make it costly for the
USA to defend. In addition, China has aspired to be a maritime power
capable of blockading crucial sea lanes of communication (SLOC) in the
western Pacific region. To maximise the dramatic efect of its military build-
up, the PLA successfully tested the destruction of a weather satellite in
space by a ground-based medium-range ballistic missile. Over all, China
has been able to significantly strengthen its capabilities applicable to various
regional contingencies.

China's Geostrategic Posture

With its mounting capabilities and influence, China has cultivated an all-
dimensional strategy in accordance with its geostrategic location towards
almost all areas and countries around it. This is enumerated in the succeeding
paras.

Russia

China's key geostrategic posture has revolved around American supremacy
and aimed at associating with 'like-minded' countries. With the shared
concerns about the US predominance in the post-Cold War era, China has
reinforced its strategic co-operation with Russia established in 1996. Both
have been concerned about the expansion of NA TO, US missile defence
system and American overall unilateralism in a unipolar world. These two
military powers conducted large-scale joint military manoeuvres in 2005 for
the first time in their bilateral relations. Their leading roles in the Shanghai
Co-operation Organisation (SCO) have made the mechanism more suited
to become a platform of military co-operation among member states. Beside,
both China and Russia have island disputes with the Japanese in the region
and Tokyo has recently been locked in tense relations with these strong
neighbours. The future China-Russia strategic ties in East Asia will raise
special concerns of the USA and Japan.

Central Asia

In addition to Russia, China has been also enthusiastic about its relations with the CentralAsia, a strategic choke point between China and the Middle East. China took the initiative in 2001 to ally with Central Asian nations under the framework of the SCO. In addition to China and Russia, the SCO includes four CentralAsian countries of Kazakhstan, Kygyzstan, Tajikistan and Uzbekistan. Obviously, it is Beijing's strategy to extend its influence in a remote area that is strategically important but has been constantly ignored by the outside world. China is particularly enthusiastic about rich energy resources of the region.

With the US increasing military presence in Central Asia after the 9/11, Beijing was highly wary of American influence on its western frontier and intended to counter-balance the US supremacy in the region. [7] The Chinese leadership even went as far as requesting Washington to withdraw its troops and terminate its military bases in Central Asia. In line with its rising influence in the region, China has strengthened the importance of the SCO which has gradually focused on security affairs. Countries around have become increasingly involved in the mechanism and expressed their desires to be part of it.

South Asia

Relations between India and China have become a major concern in regional security, despite steadily improving their ties for the last ten years or so. While China is rising, India has also ascended to the status that would render India a peer competitor of China over the long term. [8] In view of India's competition and its strategic importance, China has attempted to control events in India's geographic vicinity in recent years. China's continuing build-up of its national power is highly dependent upon the enegy supply. Therefore, Beijing is immensely concerned about a security dilemma posed by the US supremacy in the high seas stretching from the Persian Gulf to the Indian Ocean to the South China Sea, a maritime zone where India is in a key strategic position.

China has been pressing ahead its strategy in the Indian Ocean by vigorously securing bases and cultivating close relations with littoral states around India. China has created a pattern of behaviour in the Indian Ocean by forming a 'string of pearls' which are bases and seaports scattered around the area linking the Middle East with coastal ChinaWith its informal strategic alliances with the countries around, China would be able to check India's rise and monitor maritime activities in the region. These relationships have provided China with the foundation of a strategic maritime infrastructure to facilitate its future military access to the Indian Ocean.[9]

Southeast Asia

China has been able to gain a 'short cut' to the Indian Ocean by getting access to the Bay of Bengal with its intimate relations with the Burmese military junta. More than half of China's energy resources come through the Straits of Malacca. In the event of a military conflict, China's economic lifeline would be endangered if the SLOC were blockaded. The short cut offers China alternative routes to bypass the choke point at the Malacca Strait. China has meticulously planned for contingencies, including direct access to the Indian Ocean. As a result, many of the ASEAN member states have been vigilant about China's growing importance of shaping the region's security and they would be very reluctant to see an expansionist and hegemonic China.

Meanwhile, Beijing has made strenuous efforts to soften its image and to develop concrete relations with the ASEAN. China has actively participated in theASEAN Regional Forum (ARF), a platform for countries involved to focus on security issues. China has also signed the 'T reaty of Amity and Co-operation' initiated by theASEAN to promote region's peace. Moreover, China agreed with the position taken by the ASEAN in the 'Southeast Asian Nuclear Weapons Free Zone Treaty' and the 'Declaration on the Conduct of Parties' in the South China Sea. On the whole, China has clearly recogised the vital importance of SoutheastAsia and has attempted to actively involve itself in the regions affairs in order to secure its strategic interests in the area.

South China Sea

Countries around the South China Sea have long struggled for its control, not only because of its rich natural resources but also due to its strategic position between the two oceans. China has become more forceful in claiming the control of as much as 80 per cent of the South China Sea, including sovereignty over islands disputed with some Southeast Asian states like Vietnam, the Philippines and Malaysia. China was infuriated by a joint submission of sovereign claims over the South China Sea made by Malaysia and Vietnam to the UN Commission on the Limits of the Continental Shelf.

China has demonstrated its growing maritime enforcement capabilities in the region, including long-range deployments. Its advanced submarines have steamed through the East China Sea into the Pacific, South of Japan. China has also extended its air power into the South China Sea by introducing its airborne early warning, stealth and night-flying capabilities, and aerial-refuelling, simulated bombing raids programmes etc.

Over all, the South China Sea has become a crucial area for China to demonstrate its ability to project co-ordinated military power . China has even gone as far as, for the first time, grouping the South China Sea into the category of a 'core'national interest, at par withTibet and Taiwan, with the implications that China would use military force to protect its claimed sovereignty over land and sea. [10]

Island Chains

China's maritime ambition encounters serious obstacles in the Pacific Ocean as South Korea, Japan, Taiwan and the Philippines all have security ties with the USA. From Beijing's perspective, China is enclosed by concentric, layered island chains which are taken by the USA   to squeeze China' s strategic space and blockade China from island strongholds. The PLA Navy has been modernising to break through the first island chain from Japan through the Philippines to SoutheastAsia. China may also have the ambition to project its naval power to cross the second island chain running through Guam toAustralia.

Taiwan Strait

Among the parties around the first island chain,   Taiwan is in a strategic position to determine the region's future balance of power. China's naval ambitions to exert influence into areas beyond its nearest waters will rely upon its ability to secure theTaiwan Strait. China will attach lower priorities to other areas, until it is able to amass a local superiority of force over the US military and itsAsian allies in security interests closer to mainland China. Much of China's previous military build-up was geared towards deterring the USA from getting involved in a possible conflict over   Taiwan. As a result, Beijing has increased its capability to prevent the USA and its possible allies from attempting to intervene in a cross-strait contingency.[11]

Taking into account the much superior American forces, the Chinese have developed formidable capabilities of asymmetric warfare that could increase the US vulnerabilities and prevent its intervention in the T aiwan Strait. Among other weapons, China's missiles deployed in its southeast coastal provinces have been perceived by the Taiwan people as the greatest threat. China's strategic missile forces, the Second Artillery Corps of the People's Liberation Army (PLA), has vigorously modernised its theatre ballistic missile forces since the mid-1990s and has vigorously developed a formidable class of indigenous cruise and ballistic missiles with precision strike capabilities. The combination of 300-km range DF-11, 600-km range DF-15 short-range ballistic missiles (SRBMs) and 200 ground launched cruise missiles (GLCM), along with their surveillance and targeting abilities, deployed directly opposite Taiwan, have increased Taiwan's vulnerability under threat of being targetted. [12]

Taiwan is in the most strategic important position, both geographically and politically, in East Asia. Since China may currently be in a position to challenge the US regional primacy and will not engage in serious clashes with countries around, the T aiwan Strait will decide how the two great powers, the USA and China, would accommodate each other's increasing presence in East Asia. The control of Taiwan could enable China to break the international blockade against its maritime security . If Taiwan came under the PLA's complete influence, the PLA Navy (PLAN) could further its maritime defensive perimeter outward and control SLOC as China' s maritime ambition is to reach afar in oceans in its future development.

Yet, the reality is that the first island chain in whichaTwan is crucial is not becoming less defensible as some tend to suggest. With the improved bilateral relations across the Taiwan Strait, Taiwan is more secure, not less. Beijing has been perfectly aware that any military confrontation occurring in the Taiwan Strait would evolve into a major conflict of the great powers and thus, sabotage its hope of a global power status.

Korean Peninsula

China has also tried to strengthen its strategic position in northeast Asia by seeking balancing policy in the region. On the one hand, Beijing has helped the North Korean regime develop its economy and save it from collapsing. On the other hand, China has also precluded it from making further trouble that would endanger China's relations with the USA. Beijing has leveraged the six-party talks by pinning Pyongyang down to the peace negotiations and impeding anyone from taking extreme measures. The *Cheonan* incident in March 2010 may have indicated that China would continue its support for the North Korean regime despite the US and its allies' frustration, but it also clearly showed that Beijing would still be in the key position to influence the future security in the Korean Peninsula.

China's 'Charm Offensive': Soft Power

Beijing is perfectly aware that hard power alone cannot achieve its goal of great power status. After its advocacy of 'peaceful rise' created a counter-effect that the same might sound aggressive, China proposed a new idea of 'peaceful development', emphasising the importance of using soft power to dispel the image of an emerging giant. Beijing has acknowledged that outright balancing against the USA would immediately provoke America's fierce response. But the use of soft power, for instance engaging in bilateral and multilateral diplomacy, could reduce the US suspicion and enhance China's overall power. Beijing's programmes of foreign aid and international trade have vigorously invested abroad, particularly in developing economies, billions of dollars in some strategic industries, including oil production, mining, transportation, electricity production and transmission, telecommunications, and other infrastructure. These no-strings-attached programmes have rendered the recipient countries to willingly co-operate with China on key international affairs. Many developing economies have also advocated the 'China model' that inspires them to follow

In addition to concrete assistance, China has also focused on cultural dimension and set up many Confucius Institutes around the world in order not only to promote Chinese civilisation, but also to cultivate a benign image of China. Its recent efforts to promote the Chinese language and culture have significantly increased the resonance of Chinese culture abroad. It looks that China's soft power is in rise with its increase in cultural influence beyond its borders.[13]

Also, with its active participation and leading role in multilateral institutions, China could seize the opportunities to ease the international constraints under the current unipolar system. [14] Beijing has actively participated in UN peace-keeping missions and hosted international negotiations over regional conflicts, such as the six-party talks on the Korean Peninsula nuclear problem, as a way to establish its image as a responsible stakeholder in the region and beyond.

Conclusion: Future of China's Grand Strategy

Despite all the discourse and real actions that it has adopted to assert its global status, it is still too early to tell whether China's long-term strategic objective is to make itself an equal partner with the USA or 'first among equals'. Nor is it clear, if Beijing will be content with the status quo for the foreseeable future should its relative power continue to rise. [15] Yet, it is perfectly evident that *currently* the Chinese have few incentives and capabilities to challenge the USA in the global arena as long as Washington enjoys much superior advantages. Meanwhile, Beijing has claimed that China should be assuming more responsibilities in East Asia, this is happening at a time when the USA is also shifting its attention back to the Western Pacific.

In light of its relative weakness vis-à-vis Washington, what Beijing could hope most for the time being is to achieve parity with Washington by internally accelerating its development and amassing its overall national power and externally engaging in diplomatic alliance globally. Meanwhile, China has to maintain a healthy relationship with the USA in order to prevent any misunderstanding or errant behaviour from compromising its global ambition. Therefore, China's strategic logic follows the premise that a stable international environment is essential for China's continuing ascendancy in economic and military terms without provoking a hostile US response. [16] Therefore, a continuing US presence in Asia may still be in Beijing's interests.

However, in the long run, the bilateral relationship between the two giants may not necessarily look promising if their ties turn sour, particularly at a time when the Chinese ambition is perceived as threatening. It is therefore worthwhile to understand how the Chinese nationalistic aspirations internally would increase the possibility of China's assertive approach externally. The notion of 'a harmonious world' where China is leading renders Chinese people to dream of China being a global 'champion'. China's fifth-generation leadership assuming office after 2012 may have to answer more populist demands from the people. The government then may have to take more assertive approach towards the outside world, and the US in particular. It, therefore, remains to be seen whether China will see the USA as the chief competitor for world's dominant power. It will be in the interest of all parties around to prevent Beijing from provoking a hyper-nationalist backlash when China is rising to its global prominence.

From Washington's perspective, the rationale for American presence in Asia is to deter the rise of hegemonic forces that would confront the US predominance.[17] A rising Chinese military with its assertive approach will conflict with the US strategic interests and will certainly meet American resistance. As to the countries around China that are increasingly suspicious of Beijing's mounting power to threaten their security, they would look into the possibility of creating counter-balancing policy vis-à-vis China by forming alliance partnership with the distant USA. [18] America's interests in Asia may be secured only when those economically vibrant democracies in the region remain the USA allies and are free from the control of other great powers.[19] The US will continue improving their capabilities and reducing their vulnerabilities. That is why the USA is actively increasing its presence at a time when China's challenge is imminent.

However, a possible containment policy taken by the USA and its allies will be a risky and a counterproductive option for America's China policy. A hostile containment strategy will not only be difficult to develop because

China's neighbouring nations will not necessarily join forces with the USA, if they have to take sides, but could also easily cause China' s backlash against the USA. Unfortunately , many in China have perceived that Washington is now taking an active containment policy towards China from the Korean Peninsula all the way to India by taking measures like conducting joint military exercises and constructing an Anti-Ballistic Missile (ABM) network. Some even suggest that a conflict with the Americans may be inevitable.[20]

Therefore, the best scenario for region's security would be a healthy relationship between the two great powers. There is no doubt that China is continuing to rise to its regional and global prominence to the degree that the gap between the USA and China would be reduced.Yet, the question remains whether the two great powers will see each other as potential threat and strategic adversary in the future. If such a scenario is emerging, East Asia would become the most dangerous flashpoint where countries would have to take sides and a regional military confrontation between the two camps would become a distinct possibility.Another scenario could be that the two big powers continue to work together to create a favourable environment where China continues to integrate itself into the international system and the US presence remains the cornerstone of Asia's security. The overall responsibility of maintaining the region's peace not only depends upon China's benevolence but also on the USA and its allies to make concerted efforts in helping shape China's grand strategy in favour of a stable global order

Endnotes

1. Barry Posen, *The Sources of Military Doctrine: France, Britain, and Germany between the World Wars* (Ithaca, NY: Cornell University Press, 1984), p. 13.

2. Avery Goldstein, *Rising to the Challenge: China's Grand Strategy and International Security* (Stanford, CA: Stanford University Press, 2005), p. 19.

3. For a comprehensive review of debates ov er China's visions of global order , see William A. Callahan, *China: The Pessoptimist Nation* (Oxford: Oxford University Press, 2010).

4. Zheng B ijian, "China's 'Peaceful Rise' to Great -Power Status," *Foreign Affairs*, Vol. 84, No. 5 (S eptember/October 2005), p . 24.

5. For instance, Liu Mingfu, *The China Dream: The Great Power Thinking and Strategic Positioning of China in the Post-American Age* (*Zhongguo meng: hou meiguo shidai de daguo siwei zhanlue dingwei*) (Beijing: Zhongguo youyi chuban gongsi, 2010).

6. June T eufel Dreyer, "China's Power and Wil l: The PRC's Military Strength and Grand Strategy," *Orbis*, Vol. 51, No. 4 (F all 2007), p. 648.

7. Chien-peng Chung, "The Shanghai Co-operation Organisation: China's Changing Influence in Centr al Asia," *China Quarterly*, Vol. 180 (December 2004), p . 995.

8. David Walgreen, "China in the Indian Ocean Region: Lessons in PRC Grand Strategy," *Comparative Strategy*, Vol. 25, No. 1 (January 2006), p. 59.

9. James Holmes, "China's Energy Consumption and Opportuni ties for U.S.-China Cooperation," Testimony before the U. S.-China Economic and S ecurity Review Commission, 14 June 2007 , see <ht tp://www.uscc.gov/hearings/ 2007hearings/written_testimonies/07_06_14_15wrts/ 07_06_14_holmes_statement.php >.

10. Michael Richar dson, "Beijing Projects P ower in South China Sea, " *The Japan Times*, 9 May 2010, see < http://search.japantimes.co.jp/cgi-bin/ eo20100509mr.html>.

11. Barry R. Posen, "Command of the Commons: The Military Foundation of U.S. Hegemony," *International Securit y*, Vol. 28, No. 1 (Summer 2003), p. 22.

12. Martin Andrew, "China's Conventional Cruise and Ballistic Missile Force Modernization and Deployment," *China Brief*, Vol. 10, Issue 1 (January 2010), pp. 5-7.

13. Sheng Ding and Robert A. Saunders, "Talking up China: An Analysis of China's Rising Cultural Power and Global Pr omotion of the Chinese Language, " *East Asia*, Vol. 23, No. 2 (Summer 2006), pp . 3-33.

14. Avery Goldstein, *Rising to the Challenge: China's Grand Strategy and*

International Security (Stanford, CA: Stanford University Press, 2005), p. 127.

15. Robert s. R oss, "Assessing the China Thr eat," *The National Inter est*, No. 81 (Fall 2005), p. 87.

16. Yuan-kang Wang, "China's Grand Strategy and U.S. Primacy: Is China Balancing American P ower," The B rookings I nstitution, July 2006, see < ht tp:// www.brookings.edu/papers/2006/07china_wang.aspx >.

17. Joseph S . Nye, "The Case for Deep Engagement, " *Foreign Affairs*, Vol. 74, No. 4 (July/August 1995), p. 91.

18. The constitution of counter-balancing coalition is in accordance with Realist theory of balance of power . See Wi lliam C. W ohlforth, "The Stabi lity of a Unipolar World," *International Security*, Vol. 24, No. 1 (Summer 1999), pp . 5-41.

19. Daniel Blumenthal, "China' s Grand Strategy ," *American Enterprise I nstitute for Public Policy Research* , 29 April 2010, see < http://www.aei.org/article/ 101988 >.

20. For instance, Colonel Dai Xu in the Chinese Air Force speaks on China's military Str ategy, *Chinascope*, January/February2010, see <http:// www.britannica.com/bps/additionalcontent/18/49760899/Dai-Xu-on-Chinas-Military-Strategy# >.

Session V – Fifth Paper

Professor Richard Rigby

Most of the things that I would normally say on the subject, have been said in my presentation yesterday. Later, when I was asked, if I could make few more observations I agreed to do so.

Firstly, it is really true that things look different, depending on where you are looking at them from. We just heard a European view today During the last one and a half day we have seen how India looks at China; that is invaluable and of course that view is also to be accepted in its context. From Australia's point of view, when we look at China, it is true to say that we principally look at China's foreign relationships i.e. China and the World. First of all, we look at China and the USA (which is not surprising) because the USA is our principal ally (a guarantor of our security) and China is our principal trading partner. The relationship between China and the USA, more than anything else, set our overall strategic environment. So, by and large when things go well between China and the USA, we are pretty happy; and when they are not going well, we feel a bit uneasy In the context of China and the USA, of course, we look very much at Taiwan; and we derive considerable comfort from the improvement in the cross-strait relationship with the advent of the Kuomintang (KMT) regime under President Ma. We hope that sort of situation continues to hold.

We then look at China and Japan – another very important country and a strong friend of Australia. It is still a very major economic partner. We look at China's role on the Korean peninsula and we look at China' s role with countries of ASEAN and South East Asia. It is only then, (and I am speaking in generalities) of course, there are exceptions, but in general, it would only be then that we would turn to China and South Asia – specifically China and India. In that context, we have to get used to thinking a lot more about 'China-India' and 'India-China'. That is partly , and very much a reflection of India's own growing importance and India's growing importance to Australia. The fact is that in many areas we do share a broad strategic congruity.

Let us now talk about alliances. People were earlier talking about, whether China does not like to do alliances and India does not do alliances either. But, certainly in terms of common interests and common values, there is a whole broad range of strategic areas where we feel very comfortable with India. Therefore, we need to talk carefully about India's relationships with China; specially when we think about the way China is operating in the world. That is why I am here. I am sure, the High Commissioner, my old boss, who is here this afternoon too will keep Australia upto the mark in that regard.

Now a few remarks on China' s strategic intent, i.e. how Australia looks at China?

Firstly, I would place 'regime survival'as the topmost priority of China. I would completely endorse what Ashley Tellis said about the primacy of the domestic realities and challenges. It is already on the way to meeting these challenges.

The general view that I take about China is that their strategy is to become dominant in the region first, and thereafter move to their doctrinal high global role. They want to prevent T aiwan's independence and over time, move towards reunification. Somebody asked, whether there was a timetable? I don't believe that there is a timetable at the moment. But, if China began to feel that we were returning to the situation we saw in the last few years of Chiang Ching- kuo' s presidency, when we saw T aiwan moving further away, then things might start to look diferent again.

They want to develop a BlueWater Navy to operate specifically in the Indian Ocean, as well as the neighbouring seas.

Strategic Nuclear weapons are part of the force structure which they see is necessary to realise this intent (of global role). The Nuclear arsenal reflects the importance Beijing gives to Strategic Forces, as the umbrella under which its formal interests to advance in and beyond the Asia-Pacific would remain protected. This would, as well, suit China's own aspiration, to become a strong power in the region.

China, in this sense is very sensitive about Taiwan because it does not want any power to build-up around it to threaten the Chinese mainland. China will never again want to be in a position where they can be pushed around by anybody as they were, in an utterly unfortunate situation about one and a half century ago.

Now, in all of this the USA is the principal strategic adversary It is not to say that China wants to go to war against the USA or the USA with China. Given that the USA is principal strategic adversary, that is where I beg to differ slightly with suggestions made by Professor Park today China's capabilities are clearly oriented to meet surface requirements, as long as the Taiwanese issue exists as a potential cause for conflict between China and the USA. However much that danger is reduced, (I personally pray and doubt that it will happen) but, as long as that possibility exists, Chinese planners will see the need to plan for the possible conflict with the USA. Therefore, they will give it everything they possibly can. Of course, remove Taiwan from the equation and China still has all those capabilities.   The question raised by Professor Park is absolutely opposite. Those capabilities combined with the Chinese behaviour in recent times, which the Chair has set out very well, would certainly discomfort many others and provide ample grounds for continuing security dilemmas within the region, which we all have to think about very seriously

Session 5: Discussion

Issue Raised

The way Sino-Indian relationship is going, although nobody wants it, it could lead to a conflict. In that case if the countries were forced to choose, how many of them will support us? We had hardly any success in this regard in 1962 and the China of today is very different!

Responses

(a) The fact is, it is going to take time before people would have the freedom to decide whom to support, given the economic inter-dependence that exists today. A large number of countries in region are dependent on China economically. It will be a few years before they will be able to disengage. Whether the Chinese would wait that long, before doing something, is to be seen.

(b) Perhaps, we should depend on our own capability rather than go looking for support.

(c) If you do not develop necessary capabilities, you may find yourself in a rather awkward position. Pursuance of excessive 'non-alignment' might give other people fewer incentives to support you when the chips are down. There is always a tight balancing act between protecting your autonomy and protecting it so strongly that nobody has any incentive to support you when things get difficult.

(d) It is not an 'either ' 'or' situation; but on balance, if you look at Indian perceptions and Indian attitudes, it will be more in favour of 'independence of policy' rather than alignment.

Issue Raised

It is observed that almost all the nations connected with China are enthralled by China's progressive military and economic power. That being so, what are the affected nations' efforts to counter that? At best, what appears is that a checkmating effort is going on for doing 'this and that'. Is there any collective or individual action being taken (by India), to induce diplomatically or otherwise through world organisations, to try and bring China onto a more acceptable democratic line?

Responses

(a) This question cannot be addressed in definitive terms, because what is being seen is that there is already a certain lose kind of coalition which is forming, in which the USA itself is playing a very important part in trying to (if not contain China) but to nudge China in a sort of direction that you are talking about, where China is a responsible stake holder in the international system or it is on a responsible path. Ultimately however it depends upon, what China wants to do; whether it wishes to be part and parcel of an existing system, which has been put in place by the USA or whether, as it would appear, it also wishes to be on the side of the table which is writing the rules. China certainly wishes to be on the side writing the rules.

(b) Taiwan may be a good example of 'dealing with China'in the past couple of years. In the last six decades   Taiwan has encountered a very difficult and hostile relationship with China actually. In the last two years, whatTaiwan has been doing is to actually encourage China; not only economically , as most of you have been aware. Besides economic cooperation, Taiwan has actually signed fourteen formal agreements with China. This year the Chinese tourists are going to be Number one, in terms of numbers of tourists going to Taiwan – more than one million. When the Chinese go back (fromTaiwan) to China, many of them ask the same question: Why the Chinese, living in different parts of the world, actually enjoy such a high degree of democracy and human rights, and why those in China cannot? I do not have the time to elaborate on how much they influence each other . Firstly, we have to reduce tension. Secondly we have to institutionalise the bilateral relations and thirdly, we are actually thinking how, as a small country Taiwan can actually shape, what China should look like in the future.

(c) Economic interdependence certainly should have a moderating influence in terms of any potential tension between the two countries, but it is no guarantee that tensions will not arise as has been the historical experience. So one should not take it for granted that a strong interdependence will be able to obviate tensions between countries. The USA-China relations, the manner in which these have developed is a very good example of that.

Issue Raised

If we are to think about China making a transition from being 'shaped to shaping', one wonders what the shaping agenda for China is, beyond what is called narrow tangibles? The list of narrow tangibles is pretty wide. China's advancing territorial interests, prevailing on Taiwan and blunting human rights criticism is a big agenda. But the striking thing about China's growing comprehensive power is (it seems to be continuing) to tell us 'to be advancing the narrow tangibles agenda'; and when China does have an opportunity in G-20 or International Financial Institutions (IFIs) or other forums to present a shaping agenda. What is the underlying big idea behind the shaping agenda?

Response

The objective of the shaping agenda is not to advance certain collective goals. The objective of the shaping agenda is to simply make it easier for China to achieve whatever its immediate security interests are. There may come a point when the shaping agenda focuses on larger issues of collective goals. But for the moment even the collective goals that China seeks to promote are in fact oriented to advancing its narrow security interests. Whereas in the past, say 10 years ago, the Chinese were content to let others provide the environment within which they made their choices; today China wants to go out and shape that environment so that it is not entirely dependent on the choices of others.   A very good example is the new investments being made for protection in the sea lines of communication (SLOC). Ten years ago, the Chinese would have been quite comfortable with the US Navy providing the public goods and not worrying about it. Today, there is clearly a discomfort with relying entirely on the US Navy, even if you can't quite get rid of them. So, they are still in that early phase of a transition but it is oriented, very much to securing what I would think are their immediate security interests.

Issue Raised

To what extent is the Chinese posturing, or assertiveness, driven by the PLA? Is it much more now than before or much more than the foreign office or any other organ of the State?

Response

First, the PLA starting from the very first day of its establishment, actually belongs to the Party. So, the Party chief has every authority over the PLA. Second, in recent years, the outside world has been aware that the Party in its own ways, has been increasing its power. It seems that China's foreign policy to some extent also depends upon the shaping of their military posture. Foreign policy and military posture are two parallel lines. However, in the formulation of the foreign policy the Ministry of ForeignAffairs as also the President of China, still have a great say and legitimacy. In future, if ever, there is any military confrontation, for example betweenTaiwan and China and also involving the USA, the PLA may wield some influence in shaping the foreign policy. So, as long as the environment is friendly and peaceful, particularly during peace time i.e. most of the time, the Chairman of the CCP, who is also the Chairman of the Central Military Commission will control the PLA to a large extent.

Issue Raised

Yesterday, a panelist had alluded to the shift in the PLA   strategy from 'calculative' to an 'assertive' strategy, which would take some time for it to actually take shape. If that be so, we could face increased strategic coercion by China and there is a need for us to develop a comprehensive nuanced approach to tackle such coercion. Conflict is likely to happen only if there is a miscalculation by either side. Under these circumstances, what would be the nuanced approach to tackle such coercion, till such time time we have bridged the gap in the comprehensive national power?

Response

There is a very simple nuanced strategy it is called 'speak softly' and 'carry a big stick'.

Issues Raised

(a) Will China's rise result in global economic hegemony inspite of its limitations in natural resources; like iron ore, oil, and other strategic materials?

(b) China's stance over Arunachal Pradesh, Tibet, Dalai Lama, stapled visas to J&K people, denial of visas to an Indian Army Commander, its disputes with neighbours over islands in the South China Sea – all these could gravitate the democratic countries like India and Japan against China, which is a totalitarian state. Will this affect re-alignment of forces in future?

Responses

(a) China is already the second lagest economy in the world today It will do every possible thing to maintain their course of economic progress.

(b) One should refrain from making prediction on what is going to happen tomorrow because, we still do not have a very clear pictorial mosaic regarding China's internal stability. China's actions reflect very much a functional interpretational behaviour . We do not know how stable China really is. The most dangerous situation would be, if the present power elite i.e. the Communist Party's top leadership, felt that the internal situation was getting out of control, they could resort to a very aggressive foreign policy politically or even militarily Otherwise, if you look at the Tibetan or the Xinjiang question, nobody seriously thinks that a couple of millions of 'waverers' could take away 1.6 million sq kms from China.

(c) The reaction to unrest in those areas is quite frankly hysterical because the present leadership is very much scared that the protracted unrest in these areas could function as a catalyst to trigger major process towards de-stabilisation in China i.e. among the Han Chinese population. We must look at this 'complex of problems'the Chinese leadership is faced with. It is difficult to answer questions like use of uprightness right now. We should not look at border issues, and 'this or that'. Let us focus more on the internal dimensions and look at its foreign behaviour as a function of the internal situationAsking for 'real stability of China' would be the most interesting question.

(d) These are some very wise words. W e should be looking at the 'Internal Dynamics in China'to work out, what Chinas 'grand strategy' would be.

Issues Raised

(a) It was mentioned that China is not taking any drastic steps till it builds-up its CNP to a 'deferential' which can preclude its use to meet its national interests. What is the running risk in allowing its adversaries to build up their CNPso that the differential reduces? China's growth towards increasing urbanisation is proceeding at a fast pace. Compared to its 'GoWest policy, what is the contradiction in that particular aspect?

(b) China is displaying its CNP through assertive behaviour and increasing its influence in the countries of SouthAsia. What could be the Chinese motivation behind these actions?

Responses

(a) The strategy of 'deferring resolution' is always a gamble. But it is a reasonable gamble if you assume that your growth rates will remain superior to the growth rates of the other partyIf that assumption fails, then of course you have lost the opportunity to resolve something, when you could have done so, on your terms. Chinese leadership, for various reasons has assumed that they would be able to sustain growth rates that are better than those of their neighbours.

(b) In the case of China versus Japan, that is a reasonable judgement; because one cannot imagine Japan (a mature economy) being able to sustain the kind of growth rates that China is maintaining already (even later when those growth rates get depressed). With respect to India, one cannot be sure of the calculus, because if one looks at Chinese economic performance over the next two or three decades, there may be a sharp downturn in economic performance. It is hardly convincing that the current strategies that they are talking, of 'Going West' etc, will allow them to sustain those growth rates.

(c) The biggest concern prevailing currently is whether China can, as a result of its birth control policies of the last 50 years, sustain its labour force growth at the level that is required to maintain double digit economic growth consistently. It has become very clear that if you look at Chinese 'innovational' performance, it has simply not kept pace with what would be required if you substitute 'labour for 'technology' in order to sustain growth. So, it is a gamble.

(d) On the 'urbanisation' issue, there is tension only in principle and not in practice because the population ratios in the western areas are so small that China can still pursue an urbanisation strategy while pursuing a 'Go West strategy', at the same time. It is quite remarkable of what China has in mind with respect to urbanisation. China hopes to by about 2025, really have 70 per cent of its population in urban centres.

This is going to be of course in the eastern half of the country. However, they will do what they need to do in the west; because 1.6 million people out of a billion do not really count for much.

(e) Chinese intentions in developing relation with Myanmar, Bangladesh, Sri Lanka, Pakistan, Nepal etc have obviously been going on for a while very steadily. The object is to keep us restricted within South Asia, in fact within the sub-continent; and also keep us under pressure through these countries. But, there is a lot of concern in China of late about the situation in Pakistan. They are to all intent and purpose drawing 'back up plans' in case their strategic investment particularly in the western half of Pakistan is threatened. The second aspect is their increasing influence in Nepal – things can change. They are looking primarily at the rail-link as the game changer. But the situation there can change. It is not that the Government in Nepal will be with them all the time. Similarly, there is a variable in Myanmar also. The Chinese cannot rest assured that their policies would continue to hold for the next 5-10 years. We have to keep a watch on the Chinese efforts to progress into these areas and see what we can do about them to safeguard our interests.

Session 5: Chairman's Concluding Remarks

Shri Shyam Saran, IFS (Retd)

First of all, I would like to thank all our very distinguished panelists for having given us an extremely comprehensive view of China's capabilities as well as its vision of how it sees its own emergence in the next couple of decades. There are, of course, many uncertainties.

I would like to give my own perspective on this particular subject. Firstly, I would like to point out that what you see as China's projection of power, frankly speaking is not unusual. One of the impressions I have is that lot of people here seem to consider this somehow as unusual that China is asserting power or that China is projecting power. Of course that is going to happen if a country is going to increase its capabilities as China has – both economic capabilities as well as military capabilities. This is something we should expect. This is what I would expect India to do if its own economic and military capabilities rise. So, I don't think, we should put this into category of unusual behaviour on the part of China. It is rather normal behaviour on the part of any emerging power.

Secondly, I would say, if there is a certain Chinese characteristic to this emergence, it is a very unique Chinese capability of using short term opportunities to put in place long term assets. I think China is much better at this than perhaps many other established powers and emerging powers like India. I think what you see happening in Asia-Pacific, my perception is that (this is an argument we had with the USA before) there is a transformation taking place in this region. And, if the USA has receded its presence, even if it is going to come back at a certain point of time as it is trying to do today the terrain in the meantime would have changed. Because China would have put in place, during that particular period, long term assets which are now part of the ground reality. Changing that ground reality is going to be far more complicated, far more difficult than if the USA had not in fact taken its eyes off the ball. So, this is a quality of China as a strategy which is perhaps somewhat to my mind a unique capability

The third point I would like to make is and connected with the second is, China's perception that even if the USA is going to be a pre-eminent power or pre-dominant power , it is in relative terms in secular decline. Therefore, China in a sense has the opportunity to stake a claim to, in fact change the ground reality while the going is good. I believe that is a wrong perception. If there is one power which has the capability of bouncing back from the crisis, which has capabilities in terms of technological excellence, in terms of creative entrepreneurship and sheer brain power – that is the United States of America. So any calculation that the USA is no longer a power to contend with is a wrong perception. If, there is going to be a miscalculation on part of China in the future, I believe that is going to be the miscalculation.

Fourthly and lastly, coming closer home to India, Mr Jaydev is quite right, in saying that, what China does with Pakistan or what it does in our neighbourhood, is actually 'low cost high game strategy'. It involves lower risks, because you are not confronting India directly in fact you are telling India, 'we would like to have a very close and a friendly relationship with you' but at the same time you are able to keep India 'boxed in' by what you do with Pakistan or what you may do tomorrow with Nepal or what you would perhaps do with Sri Lanka.Again, not unusual behaviour at all!

What is the challenge for India? If you are going to create space for China, China will occupy that space. So our challenge is that how do we ensure that you do not create the space that China can occupyThe question which was raised about our own infrastructure development, I agree that over a period of time, we did allow a certain complacency to develop with respect to our own capabilities on our side of the border , specially with respect to border infrastructure. I can only say that over the last few years, better late than never, a tremendous amount of ef fort is being put in that direction. I myself, at the instance of the Prime Minister , did a border infrastructure survey right from the eastern sector down to JammuA number of very important recommendations came out of that particular survey , including not just road building but a lot of other aspects of the border infrastructure. In our own way, perhaps, not as expeditiously as we would expect the Chinese to do with the kind of system they have. But I would say that particular plan of developing our own capabilities on our side of the border is something which is being put in place. I hope it will be put in place sooner rather than later.

Thank you very much for your attention. This has been a very productive session, I am sure, for all of us and let us give a hand to all our panelists who did such a great job.

Valedictory Address

Shri Kanwal Sibal, IFS (Retd), FormerForeign Secretary, India

Thank you very much for giving me the honour to make the V aledictory Address. The subject 'China' s Quest for Global Dominance: Reality or Myth' is very pertinent, topical and very much on our minds. It is something which is under discussion in many countries and many forums: As I heard you say General, you have already discussed China' s grand strategy, its economic future, the development of its military capabilities and strategic posture; which means you have covered every possible aspect of China' s Rise. Since you have very distinguished panelists, I am sure everything that is needed to be said has been said. Now what is it that I can say   , which would be new and which would provide some fresh insight? I am very doubtful that I will be able to accomplish that task, nevertheless, I will attempt to give you my own thinking on the subject under discussion.

I am sure you have done this, but let me ask the question : How do you define global dominance? Does this mean that China is going to supplant the United States of America (USA)? We are all agreed that the one country that dominates the world is the USA. So, are we persuaded or are we convinced that China's goal is to dominate the globe? Which, therefore, would mean that China intends to supplant the USA.

The other is the G-2 concept which implies that China does not seek to singly dominate the globe but wants to do it or hopes to do it alongwith the USA. So, you would have two super powers on the same model that existed even before, in Cold War – but now with China supplanting the Soviet Union.

The third possible scenario could be that China would become a strong pole in a multi-polar world, which means it is not a G-2 situation but it is the kind of scenario that many talk about. It is that the future global international order would revolve around several poles with the USA, European Union (EU), Russia, China, Japan and India being cited as those poles.

Now, since the subject is 'Chinas Quest for Global Dominance,'let us for a moment examine, whether it can really supplant the USA? We have of course to ask the question: What is the time frame that we are talking about? If the assumption is for next 5 to 10 years or 15 years, in which it can supplant the USA, I think this is an extremely unrealistic scenario. I do not believe that Chinese, if they are pragmatic, would believe in this illusion or for that matter, even for the next 20 to 40 years that they can really supplant the USA. Therefore, the manner in which the subject matter of this seminar has been put as, 'China's Quest for Global Dominance', seems to me a bit rhetorical. Will China be able to get over its per capita handicap? It is all fine, when we say Chinas economy has overtaken Japans and will overtake that of USA in next 15 to 20 years and whatever the scholars say in absolute size the answer is 'Yes', but in per capita terms it will be far far below with that of the USA or for that matter major European powers. So, let us not get confused by absolute figures, because the strength of economy and hence the strength of China as a power will be linked to the growth of its per capita income to the levels of the West. Then if you begin to think of that, what are the kind of resources that China would need to be able to reach those levels? It would be mind boggling, where will those resources come from? Can those resources be achieved in a peaceful environment? Will China need to assert itself militarily in order to grab those resourcesWill it really be able to do so? These are the questions that arise? Therefore, linked to this is a question of, 'Development of Chinas Military Capability'. But, China cannot supplant the USA unless it builds a military capability which is superior to that of the USA.

Now, there are many who say that, all said and done, China is assertive and China is causing fear But, if you look closely at Chinas conduct, there is a degree of rationality in it. They are not building-up their military capability too rapidly or too fast. They are relatively moderate in so far as that is concerned because their aim is not to compete with the USA but to have enough power to deter the USA. Now, that will not give them the capacity to supplant the USA, but it will give them the capacity to deter the USA. So, there is a big difference in this. But supposing for a moment that they begin the uphill task of building-up their military capabilities to that level. It cannot come about overnight. It will be a slow grinding process. The world will be watching. What will the world do? If it becomes clear that, China is out to dominate the globe, what will the other countries do, led by the USA. Would not the strategies of those countries be put in place, well in time in various ways, to prevent or even disrupt the growth of China to that level of dominance. Then again this question of global dominance is predicative on the rapid decline of the USA. We just heard Shyam Saran say that, "It will be a misconceived notion that the USA is going to decline and progressively become weaker and weaker and therefore would continue to cede space to China and in fact the USA has the capacity to bounce back". Therefore, we have to make a very careful assessment and not a wishful assessment. Part of the reason why we say that USA will not decline is because we do not want the USA to decline in the context of China' s rise. But, a much more serious scholarly analysis can be made, as to what is the slope of America's decline, if you look ahead. I do not think that there is going to be that kind of rapid decline of the USA in the foreseeable future that will leave space for China to become increasingly more dominant.

This is also to presuppose the withdrawal of the USA from Asia. But I do not think the USA is thinking of withdrawing from Asia. On the contrary, even though as was said earlier, once they have ceded space and China has occupied it, it might be more difficult to reoccupy it. Nevertheless, the trend is in that direction, and even during President Obamas' visit here, if you look at what he said about deepening the relationships in East   Asia: of strengthening alliances; of recognising that India has role to play in that area and of higher engagement, one does not see any sign of the USA withdrawing from the Asia-Pacific region. And, even if constrained by economic circumstances or other complusions, assuming that the USA cannot maintain that level of presence, what time frame will the USA withdraw from Asia?

Now, there is a very important 'joker in the pack'.   Assuming for a moment that signs are clear that the USA is withdrawing from Asia and is a declining power, and China is out to dominate the globe, what will Japan do?

I would ideally hope and wish that Japan goes nuclear . At one go they neutralise China. Just as China has used Pakistan to strategically neutralise India, I think China can be strategically countered and neutralised by a nuclear Japan. Of course, that will require a huge change of mindset in Japan. But, there are these options available. There is a current of thinking in Japan which is not against Japan going nuclear

Then, when we talk about supplanting of the USA, are we thinking of the Euro-Atlantic area also? Does China have any interest or capacity to dominate Euro-Atlantic area also? OK, one can imagine they may wish to dominate Asia or part of Asia-Pacific but do they have at all any capacity, now or in the future in any scenario, to dominate the Euro-Atlantic area? This will pre-suppose the disappearance of NATO. Are we thinking of that as a real possibility? Of course if this sort of thing begins to happen, then it would begin to worry everyone, then the USA could theoretically play the Russian card against China as they played the Chinese card against the Soviet Union. That can of course complicate China' s quest for China' s global dominance.

Now in terms of G-2, if that is the scenario, are we thinking of a division of responsibility whereby China is ceded dominance over the Asia-Pacific region and the USA keeps its control over Euro-Atlantic region, I do not think this is at all a bargain that would appeal to the USA because the US already dominates the Euro-Atlantic region. There is no Chinese threat there. So why should they agree to make this kind of a division to give up their stabilising role or whatever role they have in Asia-Pacific region. So, G-2 can simply mean that in the Asia-Pacific region, the USA and China will find a *modus operandi* where they avoid the possibility of a clash or confrontation, but with the USA remaining physically present in this area, however, it accommodates China to the extent that China feels reassured that the USA's aim is not to de-stabilise it. In other words, if it is a question of not doing their exercises in the Yellow Sea or some concessions of that nature, may be the USA could make them. But anything beyond that to my mind, is an unrealistic scenario.

When you talk about the G-2, then we have to think about Europe' s reaction. Why should Europe accept the division of global order between the USA and China? Who will persuade Europe that this is alright? Especially in a scenario where the USAwould be actually a declining power for them even to agree to G-2, would the USA be able to persuade Europe that they should become a second or a third rate player? I do not think so.And, will they be able to persuade Russia? Russia, because of the recent of global financial crises has suffered a setback, but it has begun to bounce back and its growth rates have already become positive. It is a huge military power.It has enormous physical resources. It is a permanent member of the Security Council. No decisions of a defenceful nature about the world and its hotspots can be taken without Russia's agreement. Russia, while it is conscious of the fact that China has become very strong, certainly psychologically and otherwise, it has not yet conceded that it should defer to China. In fact, until recently it was Russia that was taking the lead to bring China within certain configurations of power which Russia itself was supposed to lead. The initiative to have the Russia-India-China dialogue came from Russia. The initiative to have the BRIC configuration came from Russia.

In the SCO, Russia is not ceding space to China even though China has enormously more economic power. But Russia is doing it in a manner where the security part remains within its purview. With its economic size and resources, China obviously is more present and Russia is trying to bounce back and get involved even in economic profits. So, it is not easy to persuade Russia that the world could be or should be divided between the USA and China.

There is, of course, India and our view Would we accept a division of the world amongst the USA and China? Who will persuade India that we must yield to this scenario? Even if our capacity to resist it may be relatively limited; but, we do have the capacity to resist it. Now I am not talking about the USA's security interests in the Asia-Pacific region because if the USA has extended itself to Japan andTaiwan etc., it is with a purpose in view It is in the defence of the 'Homeland of the USA   ' that, it must absolutely dominate the seas. It must absolutely dominate the Pacific-Ocean so that no power can emerge in the Pacific Ocean which can threaten the west coast of the USA. Therefore, they are not going to withdraw , because withdrawal would mean inviting a security and strategic threat closer to their borders; and, of course, there is this whole issue of Taiwan.

Let me conclude this part by saying that the Cold war paradigm will not work. In the Cold War the USA and the Soviet Union had some sort of a division of responsibilities but it was as part of a two power controlled *'confrontation'*. But when we talk of G-2 we are not talking over controlled two power confrontation but we are talking about controlled two power *'cooperation'*. So, it is a very different context.

Now the third scenario, China a strong pole in a multi-polar world. First of all, we have been bending around this vocabulary of a 'pole', while I don't know what it means here. Pole should ideally mean a pole around which a constellation of countries revolve and their foreign policies and economic policies are linked to or dominated by this pole. Ideally from the Indian point of view, we could be a pole in the SAARC area and if our energy relations with Gulf becomes so intensive in the years ahead, may be, we could influence a little the direction of these countries policies. But we are not the only players there. The US is there and now China is there in a big way. Similarly South EastAsia, theoretically I will include Myanmar in that, could also be an area which could defer to a rising Indian power; but, again they have strong competition there with China and the USA.

So, if you talk about China, if it is going to be a pole, which are the countries that are going to revolve around China and defer to China in a cooperative manner? The concept of the pole is cooperative, not a confrontationist or a relationship that is full of tensions. So, which are these countries: Vietnam, Indonesia, Philippines, Japan,Taiwan? I can't see which will be the countries that are going to be circling around the Chinese pole. Now, if by calling it 'strong pole'simply means that China will have a greater say in the management of global affairs, yes, of course. Certainly, China already has an increasing say in financial and economic matters and as member of the UN Security Council, although, it has not been very proactive. Recently, it has become more assertive about its positions. It has an increasingly important role in the management of global affairs.

If you look at the USA, the reason why USA is in fact the strongest pole in the world, it is because it provides security it provides technology it provides markets, it is the operations of its multi-national companies which has networked the global economy in the interaction of the economic interests of the USA. It is a country that sets the pace for modernisation. Its cultural influence is tremendous. Look at the attraction that the world has in terms of educational opportunities in the USA. In fact what you see around the world increasingly is a deep attachment to the globalised needs in various countries to the USA. Can China achieve that stature in global affairs? I doubt it very much. I think China lacks for the time being all these attributes that the USA has and I cannot see in the next 10-20-30 years being able to develop those attributes which would make it that kind of a pole.

Will Taiwan, Japan, ASEAN etc. be willing to come under Chinese protection? Is it a conceivable scenario? And, if they do, against whom? What will be the threat they perceive for countering which they need China' protection, the USA? As it is, if you look at India or the way ASEAN has configured its own relationships within that region, they have tried to avoid and successfully so, intra-regional disputes. It is a very consensual organisation. They have insulated themselves from tensions as much as possible. They have developed this ASEAN Regional Forum (ARF), where they have very successfully and artfully made rest of the competing countries agree that all of them would cooperate within the ASEAN and leave ASEAN free to develop itself without tensions. This is a remarkable sense of diplomacy. So why should they come under China's protection, as I said, against which threat? Will they for example look to China to arbitrate their disputes? I can't see that. In fact they have huge disputes with China over the Paracel islands, over the Sprately islands, about China declaring that the South China Sea is its core interest. In fact there are problems that are coming up on the horizon which will demand much closer relationship between the ASEAN and the USA; and India may also be drawn into this progressively. Yes, what they can certainly do is to be far more cautious in provoking China, conscious of China's strength and capacities, that they may do purely as a pragmatic exercise.

Then, if you look at China's quest for global dominance, in whichever the scenarios that I have mentioned, we have to look at China's economic policies and what they portend in terms of China' s future role? I am sure this subject has been discussed whether it is a model of export led growth, close internal market, its mercantilist tendencies. The whole issue of financial imbalances etc. will allow them to play that kind of role, unless there is major and fundamental change in how they manage their economy and how the economy relates to the rest of the world. Can China for example at all emulate the USA? Because the USA market is absolutely central to global economic and financial stability Ultimately, money keeps flowing into USA but at the end of it, there is this confidence that the American economy, a fourteen trillion Dollars economy which is contributing so much to running the global economy can collapse, it simply cannot. There is of course, the great advantage that the Dollar has, as the international reserve currency , although, the Euro has made a dent into it, nevertheless, key international commodity trade etc is done in Dollars. Can the Yuan ever think of becoming that kind of an international reserve currency to supplant the Dollar? Because that is what will cause, if not supplant, at least to take away a very major chunk of the US reserve currency for it to then be able to have that kind of global dominance in whichever category But, if the currency has to require that kind of status, it will mean complete transformation of the working of the Chinese economy. You will need transparency you will need openness, you will need the play of market forces and of course it means limiting State control. Because, the exchange rate of the US Dollar or the management of the exchange rate is not in the hands of the US Government. It is far more a product of a federal reserve and market forces in the Wall Street.

Then, there is a lar ger question of China' s vulnerabilities, because China's road has been spectacular China's dependence on the global market as a result has increased enormously. So, how will China balance its quest for dominance? With their dependence for their modernisation, and future growth to be able to reach that stage, where they can dominate; their dependence on the global market and in particular the US market, there is a huge vulnerability. It is fine that the USA is dependent on China, but so is China dependent on USA.

They have also geographically extended themselves enormously in search for raw materials – Africa, Latin America and God knows where. This makes them vulnerable, because they need these resources to fuel their future growth in the quest for dominance. The lines of communication can be cut because the Chinese Navy is never going to be strong enough to be able to prevent that possibility So, that is their vulnerability In addition to that of course is the question of poverty still in China; the under development, the disparities etc and, of course, their political system, and inherent contradictions between their open economy their close political system and to what extent this dichotomy can continue to work in China's favour? The intolerance of dissidence within the country is a huge political vulnerability for China. Look at the way they are reacting to the grant of a the Nobel Peace Prize to one of the Chinese dissidents – going on knocking at the doors of various foreign governments not to attend the function – that is the level that they have to go down to. Despite everything, they do not have that kind of self-confidence. Tibet and Xinjuang, I would not mention.And, then of course the issue of intellectual property rights and China's increasing reputation as a serial violator of intellectual property rights. How this is going to impact on the future economic activities with China? Investment in China, transfer of technology and things like that are becoming an issue already.

India's concerns have been mentioned. So I will not spell them out except to say that we all know what they are.We have this border problem with China and the problem of China building-up Pakistan since years as a strategic counter-weight to India. India has rightly said, they keep themselves in the background and they avoid open confrontation with India and yet they effectively neutralise India and in fact strategically emasculate India by their nuclear and missile cooperation with Pakistan. I think the Prime Minister was quite right when he said recently "China is using India's vulnerabilities in Kashmir and with Pakistan to keep India in a state of low level equilibrium". Our dilemma is that China looms much lar ger on India's mind than *vice versa*. We have no instrument to contain China. But, if we team up with others to do so, assuming that others would be ready to do so, it will entail loss of independence or judgmental policy China has no such constraint. It dominates Pakistan and it can use Pakistan to constrain us without loss of independence or judgmental policy. But, unfortunately we do not have that option. We have of course, in this part of our dilemma, the economic pull of China. Now, here is a huge economy growing at such spectacular speed, do we ignore it or do we leverage some part of that growth in our favour? Pragmatic decisions have to be taken. So we are continually being caught between engagement and mistrust. And we have not been able to find a way out of this.

In essence, our politics, our strategic thinking and our business is pulling us in different directions. We are very concerned about the cyber -attacks and warfare etc. and the inroads China is making into our power sector at certain levels and then you have Reliance going in signing deals worth 10 billion dollars with Shanghai Electric Corporation.

So, I will conclude by saying that the subject matter of today's seminar 'China's Quest for Global Dominance: Reality or Myth?', I would say that it is neither a reality nor a myth.

China, with its huge population, has a performing economic model for the time being. It has a single mindedness in terms of pursuit of power and there is, looming behind all this, a shadow of Nationalism that is emerging which will give China motivation to continue to seek to become more and more important in the management of her global affairs. But, there is a big 'but' that this success which they are hoping to achieve has to come through cooperation and not confrontation.

Vote of Thanks

Lieutenant General PK Singh, PVSM, AVSM (Retd)

Ladies and Gentlemen, all that remains for me to do is to thank Ambassador Sibal, the Chairpersons, the Participants and the Speakers at our seminar I am indeed grateful to them for having come from all over the world, to be here. I am especially grateful to the Chief of Naval Staff for finding so much time to attend today's proceedings.

I must also thank each one of you, specially the participants who have stayed on till the end. I would like to mention that next year in November we will have the third round of discussions on China. We will be sending communication about it to all of you in good time.

Notes